C Ref.

CONCISE DICTIONARY OF GREEK LITERATURE

Concise Dictionary of

GREEK LITERATURE

James Mantinband Ph.D.

Peter Owen • London

PETER OWEN LIMITED
50 Old Brompton Road London SW7
★
First British Commonwealth edition 1963

Printed in the U S A
Bound in Great Britain

etc., when they have been felt to be significant. Articles are primarily on authors, but also on works, categories, mythological figures, and other subjects. The criterion throughout has been usefulness and ease of reference, and to this end, Latin titles are given when they are the familiar ones, and the Latinized spelling has been used almost always (e.g. Aeschylus and Ajax, not Aischylos and Aias). The only exception occurs in the transliteration of unfamiliar titles from the Greek. Cross-indexing has been used in cases where a name might conceivably appear under either of two headings, as in the case of some of the Byzantine authors.

The most useful reference works are: the *Oxford Classical Dictionary,* Rose's *Handbook of Greek Literature,* and Wright's *History of Later Greek Literature,* in English; in German, the monumental Schmid-Stählin *Geschichte der Griechischen Literatur* (to A.D. 530), and for the Byzantine period, Krumbacher's *Geschichte der Byzantinischen Literatur* (527-1453; in French, Croiset's *Histoire de la littérature grecque* and Puech's *Histoire de la littérature grecque chrétienne jusqu'à la fin du IVe siècle.* For general information, Pauly-Wissowa: Real-Encyclopädie is indispensable. For concise bibliography, Nairn's *Classical Handlist* will be found most useful. Dates are A.D. unless B.C. is specified. For the Byzantine period, Runciman's and Diehl's books on *Byzantine Civilization and Byzantium, Greatness and Decline* provide useful summaries.

Preface

Anyone attempting to compile a Dictionary of Greek Literature must first answer two questions: what is Greek? and what is Literature? I have tried to interpret both of these in the broadest possible sense. Included, therefore, in this volume are not only classical authors and works, but also those of the Hellenistic, Roman and Byzantine periods. Thus Greek Literature is considered as an entity from the time of Homer to the fall of Constantinople in 1453. Four main periods are to be noted: the Classical (from the beginnings to the death of Alexander), the Hellenistic or Alexandrian (until ca. 150 B.C.), the Greco-Roman (to the death of Justinian), and the Byzantine (to the Fall of Constantinople). Jewish and Christian works and authors are also included, if important, but to a lesser extent than the classical ones.

Naturally, some selection was necessary to keep this volume within practical limits. It is obviously impossible to include all the Byzantine exegetical, homiletic, apologetic, polemic and hagiographical writers, or all the Alexandrian commentators (e.g. Schmid-Stählin's index lists about 8000, and Krumbacher's lists nearly 6000 authors); it is, however, hoped that no important authors or works from any period have been omitted from the more than 2700 entries in this dictionary.

As to the second question, there are included works on science, mathematics, music, medicine, philology, theology,

A

Abaris

Legendary servant of Apollo, believed to be a Hyperborean (q.v.), living at the time of Croesus. To him was ascribed a poem on the Hyperboreans.

Ablabius

Bishop of Nicaea in the 5th Century. Pupil of Troilus of Side. Belonged to the later Sophistic.

Abradatas

Husband of Pantheia in a romantic episode of the *Cyropaedia* of Xenophon (q.v.).

Abro

Three people of this name are to be distinguished:
1) An Athenian author who wrote a work on Greek festivals (lost).
2) A Grammarian of Rhodes in the time of Augustus.
3) An extremely dissolute Argive. "The life of Abro" became a proverbial expression.

Abureius

An Arabian sophist of the 4th century, mentioned by Libanius.

Abydenus

Pupil of Berosus (q.v.), fl. 268 B.C. Wrote a history of the Chaldeans, Babylonians and Assyrians, partially preserved by Eusebius.

Acacius

Three people of this name are to be distinguished:
1) Bishop of Caesarea, disciple of Eusebius.
2) Also of Caesarea, a sophist. Possibly author of a comedy, *Okypous.*
3) Bishop of Beroea (d. 432). A bitter opponent of St. John Chrysostom.

Academy

A park in Athens, the site of Plato's school, the oldest in Europe. Founded in 385 B.C. it survived until it was closed by the emperor Justinian in A.D. 529.

Acastus

Myth. Son of Pelias. He took part in the Calydonian boar hunt and the Argonauts' expedition. His wife loved Peleus, and when rejected by him she falsely accused him (cf. Joseph and Potiphar's wife, Bellerophon and Hippolytus stories).

Acathistus

A hymn still used in the Greek Orthodox Church. A song of thanks to the Virgin Mary, by an unknown author, for the threefold rescue of Constantinople from the Avars (626, 677, 717).

Acesander

Historian, of unknown date, who wrote on Cyrene.

Acestes

Myth. A Trojan prince, exiled from Troy, who founded Egesta or Segesta in Sicily.

Achaeans

Properly, the inhabitants of Southeastern Thessaly, and the north coast of the Peloponnesus, but in Homer, a general term for the Greek followers of Achilles and Agamemnon at Troy. In Hittite and Egyptian texts the term is also used of the Greeks in general.

Achaeus (1)

Eponym (q.v.) of Achaea. A very dim mythological figure, variously called the son of Poseidon, Zeus, Xuthus, and Haemon.

Achaeus (2) of Eretria

Athenian tragedian, born ca. 484 B.C. Wrote tragedies and satyr-plays. Highly esteemed for the latter, which were thought second only to those of Aeschylus. His style was described as lucid, but sometimes enigmatic.

Acharnians, the

Comedy by Aristophanes, produced in 425 B.C. In this earliest surviving Greek comedy, the hero Dicaeopolis, disgusted with the war and the politicians, makes a separate truce for himself and his family. The chorus of Acharian charcoal-burners attack him for this. A host of comic characters, anxious to get in on the ground floor, so to speak, invade the scene. The play is notable for its satire of Euripides and his use of rags, and its mock tragic style.

Achatius

Bishop in Asia Minor, middle of the third century. Wrote on *Acts of the Martyrs.*

Acheron

A river in Thesprotia (Epirus), which ran through gorges and disappeared in some places; hence it was supposed to lead to Hades.

Achilleis

According to some theories on the composition of the Iliad (see Grote, Wolf, Homeric Question), a poem dealing with the Wrath of Achilles was the kernel or nucleus of the epic. This was supposed to have been equivalent to the following books of the Iliad: I, VIII, XI-XXII. This theory, popular in the nineteenth century, has gone somewhat out of fashion today. H. J. Rose has a good discussion of the whole problem in his *Handbook of Greek Literature,* and so does C. M. Bowra in the *Oxford Classical Dictionary.*

Achilles

The hero of Homer's Iliad (q.v.), a mighty warrior, proud, sensitive, impulsive, capable of tremendous rage and brutality, but also of kindness and compassion. The whole plot of the Iliad revolves around his wrath and its consequences. He is primarily a tragic figure, aware that he is soon to die. The story of his invulnerability does *not* appear in Homer, or indeed until the *Achilleid* of Statius.

Achilles Tatius (1)

Alexandrian novelist, author of *Leucippe and Clitophon,* ca. 300 A.D. The story is a romantic one, sometimes almost a parody of earlier romantic novels. It is full of miraculous escapes and erotic episodes. The style is lively and descriptive. His identification with Achilles Tatius (2) seems unlikely.

Achilles Tatius (2)

Third century (?) author of a Greek commentary on Aratus, the only extant part of his work on spheres. Sometimes identified with the author of *Leucippe and Clitophon.*

Acilius, Gaius

An early Roman historian who wrote in Greek. When the three Greek philosophers (Critolaus, Diogenes, and Carneades) came to Rome as spokesmen for their respective schools, Acilius was their interpreter.

Acominatus, Michael

Elder brother of the historian Nicetas (q.v.) Born in Phrygia ca. 1140. Wrote history, polemics, homiletics, panegyrics, and others speeches; letters, and poetry. His style was formed on classical models, such as Isocrates, and shows this influence in the use of sonorous phrases, word-sequences, etc. Pupil of Eustathius (q.v. 2).

Acominatus, Nicetas

Born in Phrygia in the middle of the 12th century. Byzantine historian and polemicist. Wrote a history of the years 1180-1206 in 21 books. Also wrote a work on the statues destroyed by the Latins in 1204; panegyric speeches, and poetry. Brother of Michael Acominatus. His chief theological work is the *Thesaurus Orthodoxias,* containing polemics against Jews, pagans, Saracens, Armenians, Latins, etc.; discussions of the 44 heresies, the Iconoclastic and other controversies, etc. It is a continuation of the Panoplia of Zigabenus (q.v.)

Acropolites, George

Byzantine author, 1217-1282. Chancellor in 1244, General in the war against Michael of Epirus in 1257. Wrote a chronicle covering the time from the destruction of Constantinople by the Crusaders in 1203 until the restoration in 1261. Like many Byzantine authors, he was a versatile writer, producing poetical, rhetorical, and theological, as well as historical works.

Acrostics

A popular form in Latin and Greek works. Used in the Sibylline oracles. Found in the Palatine Anthology (q.v.). The acrostic often gives the author or the title of the work.

Actaeon

In mythology, a hunter who, because he happened to see the goddess Artemis bathing, was changed by her into a stag and torn to pieces by his own hounds. According to other versions of the story, he boasted of being a better hunter than Artemis.

Actium, Battle of

14 lines from an epic poem on the Battle of Actium exist, on a British Museum Papyrus. Author and date unknown.

Acts of the Apostles

Second volume of Luke's book on the beginnings of Christianity. Late first century. Shows the widening of the circle of Christianity into the western provinces, from Asia to Europe, and finally into Rome. See Luke, New Testament.

Acts of the Martyrs

Any of several accounts of the early Christian martyrs. The three oldest are the *Depositio Martyrum,* the *Syrian Martyrology,* and the *Carthaginian Martyrology.* All three are used in the *Martyrologium Hieronymianum.* The first official martyrology was compiled under Sylvester I. See Justin Martyr. Other examples: *Acts of the Martyrs of Lyon, Scili, Acts of Apollonius, Martyrdom of Pionius,* and numerous others.

Acts of Paul, John, Peter

See Pseudepigraphica, Apocrypha N.T.

Acts of Pilate

See Nicodemus, Gospel of.

Acusilaus

An Argive who lived before the Persian Wars. Wrote, or compiled *Genealogiai,* translating and correcting Hesiod.

Acyndinus, Gregory

Byzantine scholar and theologian, who translated St. Thomas Aquinas into Greek, in the first half of the fourteenth century. Little is known about his life.

Adaeus of Mytilene

Third century (?) author of a work on composition in architecture and painting. Nothing is known about him.

Adam, Book of

A Greek work telling of the story from Genesis, and continuing it after the expulsion from the Garden of Eden. It goes back to Jewish legends, but shows Christian handling (There is also a Latin *Vita Adae et Evae*).

Adamantius

Jewish physician and rhetor, 2nd cent. A.D.

Addaeus

Macedonian poet of the 4th century B.C. Wrote an epitaph for Alexander the Great, and an epigram on an ox.

Admetus

Mythological king of Pherae in Thessaly. Husband of Alcestis (q.v.).

Adonis

In mythology, a beautiful youth, loved by Aphrodite. Killed by a wild boar (or by Ares and Hephaestus). Appears to have been a fertility and vegetation deity. His cult existed in several places, and was chiefly popular with women, who worshipped him with mourning and pageants.

Adonizusae

(Women at the Festival of Adonis) Poem by Theocritus (q.v.)

Adrastus

In mythology, the son of Talaus, king of Argos. Leader of the Seven Against Thebes.

Aeacus

In mythology, the son of Zeus and Aegina, father of Peleus, and grandfather of both Achilles and Ajax. Known for his piety and righteousness, he became a judge of the dead. According to one legend, the population of his island had been decimated by a plague, and he prayed Zeus for help.

The god then changed a swarm of ants into men, hence the name Myrmidons.

Aëdon

In mythology, the daughter of Pandareos, who envied Niobe (q.v.) for her many children. She planned to kill one of them at night, but by mistake she killed her own son Itylus instead. In her grief she was changed into a nightingale.

Aegeus

In mythology, the father of Theseus. (Apparently Aegeus was identified with Poseidon of Aegae, thus Theseus is sometimes called the son of Poseidon.) He gave refuge to Medea on her flight from Corinth, and married her, but drove her out when she tried to poison Theseus (q.v.). According to the most prevalent story, he leaped into the sea which was named after him, because he thought Theseus was dead.

Aegimius

1) A physician from Elis who wrote a work about the pulse.

2) Title of a lost poem ascribed to Cercops of Miletus, an epic poet of the 6th century B.C.

Aegis

A goatskin breastplate, worn by Zeus and Athena. It causes a thunderstorm when shaken, but is also used to protect friends and frighten enemies, in the *Iliad.* The most plausible theory is that the aegis was originally a stormcloud, but was regarded as a goatskin because of the confusion of the words aix (goat) and kataigis (hurricane). (See Hanfmann in OCD)

Aegisthus

In mythology, the only surviving son of Thyestes (q.v.), although another version of the myth makes him the offspring of an incestuous marriage between Thyestes and his daughter. The story of his intrigue with Clytemnestra (q.v.) and the murder of Agamemnon (q.v.), and of the return of Orestes (q.v.) who slew Aegisthus and Clytemnestra, is told in extant plays by all three of the tragedians, as well as in the *Odyssey*. Aeschylus represents him as a pusillanimous weakling, hiding behind the skirts of Clytemnestra. In Euripides, however, he is a courteous person who dies, ironically, because of an act of hospitality.

Aelian (Claudius Aelianus) (1)

Taught rhetoric at Rome around 200 A.D. The extant works include *De Natura Animalium,* a collection of moral tales and anecdotes dealing with the animal world; the *Poikile Historia,* a similar collection which deals with people; and the *Epistolai Agroikikai,* consisting of exercises in style, in the form of letters. There are also fragments of works on divine justice and providence. All Aelian's ideas have a thoroughgoing Stoic viewpoint, and he is especially bitter against the Epicureans. He was known for the simplicity and purity of his style. To be distinguished from Aelian (2).

Aelian (2)

Almost certainly not the same as (1). Author of a *Tactica* dealing chiefly with the Macedonian phalanx. Aelian lived in the early part of the second century, probably in Trajan's reign.

Aelius Aristides

See Aristides.

Aelius Dionysius of Halicarnassus

Not to be confused with the lexicographer or the historian (see Dionysius for these). Author of a textbook on music.

Aelius Promotus

A physician from Alexandria in the middle of the second century. A portion of his book on cures *(Dynameron)* survives.

Aello

See Harpies.

Aeneas (1)

Vergil's hero appears in the *Iliad,* where he is also known for his piety. He fights with Achilles, and is saved from death by Poseidon, who prophesies that he and his descendants will rule over the Trojans.

Aeneas (2) of Gaza

A sixth century sophist, pupil of the Neoplatonist Hierocles. We have over 25 letters by him and a dialogue *Theophrastus* which shows a knowledge of Plato (*Gorgias*) but not of Aristotle.

Aeneas (3) Tacticus

Fourth century B.C. author of several works on tactics, of which one, dealing with the defense of besieged cities, has survived. It is interesting for the study of the Hellenistic *Koine* (q.v.), and as an indication of the political and social conditions in Greece of the fourth century.

Aenesidemus of Knossos

A Sceptic of the first century B.C. His works (all lost) include the *Tropoi tes epoches* (a work against the reliability of the senses), *Kata Sophias, Prote Eisagoge,* and others. Diogenes Laertius gives many details of his life.

Aeolic

One of the main Achaean dialects (see Dialects). The epic dialect is largely a mixture of Ionic (q.v.) and Aeolic. The lyric poetry of Alcaeus and Sappho is in the Aeolic (Lesbian) dialect.

Aeolus

In mythology, the ruler of the winds. In Homer he is represented as a mortal. He gives the winds to Odysseus tied in a bag to prevent them from blowing. In later poetry (Vergil) he is a minor god.

Aeschines (1)

One of the Ten Attic Orators (q.v.). Ca. 390-after 330 B.C. Most of our knowledge of Aeschines is colored by the hatred of Demosthenes, his enemy, who accused him of tergiversation and corruption, as well as of misleading the public. After his retirement he became a professional sophist in Asia Minor. His speeches: *Against Timarchus, On the Embassy, Against Ctesiphon.* Actually, he was a successful and forceful orator, and probably suffers unduly from the invidious, if inevitable, comparison with the far greater figure of Demosthenes (q.v.). His style and vocabulary are simple and effective. The twelve letters attributed to Aeschines are forgeries.

Aeschines (2) Socraticus

A disciple of Socrates, who was present at the latter's trial and death. A teacher of rhetoric, he wrote speeches, as well as a series of highly esteemed Socratic dialogues (*Miltiades, Callias, Aspasia, Alcibiades,* and others).

Aeschylus

525/4-456 B.C. The first of the three great Athenian tragedians. He fought at Marathon, and his first victory on the stage was in 484. His extant plays (see under the individual titles) are *Suppliants, Persians, Seven Against Thebes, Prometheus Bound, and the Oresteia* trilogy (*Agamemnon, Choephori, Eumenides*). Aeschylus spent some time in Sicily and died there. The legend of his death is as follows: an eagle, carrying a tortoise in its talons, mistook the bald head of Aeschylus for a rock, and dropped the tortoise on it to crack the shell. There is an epitaph which may be by the poet himself, mentioning Marathon, but not the tragedies. Pausanias thought that Aeschylus had written it. Lost plays include *Laius* and *Oedipus,* which formed the first part of the trilogy ending with the *Seven Against Thebes; Prometheus Unbound* and *Pr. the Fire-Bearer* (ending the Prometheus trilogy), and nearly 80 others (for the complete list, see the Oxford Classical Dictionary or Schmid-Stählin).

Aeschylus is chiefly known for his expression of a lofty and purified theology, for his magniloquent diction, for his exciting stage-effects (e.g. the crimson carpet in the *Agamemnon,* the Furies in the *Eumenides,* etc.), and his interest in profound moral problems (crime and punishment, Hybris and Nemesis, etc.). His plots are usually simple and straightforward, and often disregard the so-called "unities." Aeschylus, more than any other single figure, is probably responsible for the invention of the drama as we know it, the dramatic dialogue, decorative costumes, stage-effects and spectacle, etc. His plays abound in rich and magnificent descriptions (battles, storms, volcanoes, and even lists of geographical place-names), and in newly-coined compound words, for which he was ridiculed by Aristophanes. He wrote about ninety plays, and won the first prize thirteen times.

Aesculapius

See Asclepius.

Aesop

Reputed author of the body of beast-fables, in which animals point out morals for people (e.g. the *Fox and the Grapes*). Said to have been a slave in Samos in the sixth century B.C. The earliest extant collection is that of Babrius (q.v.). "Aesop's Fables" are mentioned by Plato and by Aristophanes.

Aesop, Life of

Appeared in a Byzantine introduction to Aesop's Fables, and said to be by Planudes (q.v.). A popular work in Byzantine times.

Aethiopica

See Heliodorus (4).

Aethopis

One of the lost poems in the Epic Cycle (q.v.). Among other events, it told of the death of Achilles.

Aethra

In mythology, the mother of Theseus (q.v.). Since both Aegeus and Poseidon were said to be Theseus' father, ingenious explanations had to be invented. Rose in OCD gives a good summary.

Aetia

The longest and most famous work of Callimachus (q.v.), containing 3000-4000 lines. The framework, as described in the prologue, shows Callimachus transported to Helicon in a dream, and asking the Muses about history, ritual, mythology, etc. Probably a collection of etiological legends and myths. How much continuity there was between the various elegies or *Aetia* is not known.

Aetiological myth

See Etiological Myth.

Aëtius (1)

An eclectic of the first or second century A.D., whose *Xunagoge peri Areskonton* summarized the opinions of the Greeks on natural philosophy. These have been preserved in the *Epitome* (pseudo-Plutarch) and in the *Eclogae* of Stobaeus, and are valuable sources for the ideas of philosophers whose works are lost.

Aëtius (2)

A physician of the sixth century A.D. who wrote a work on diagnosis and pathology.

Aëtius (3) of Antiocheis

A heresiarch who renewed the Arian heresy. Called the "atheist."

Africanus

See Julius Africanus.

After-life

At various periods there were different ideas on the after-life, and often contradictory concepts existed side by side. Following are some of them: (1) The dead continued to live in the tomb. (2) The dead lived in the realm of Hades, a gloomy underground place first described in Homer (Od. 11), where good and evil go alike. (3) The Isles of the Blessed, an Eleusinian concept, at the ends of the earth, or Elysium, appears in Hesiod and Homer. (4) The Eleusinian Mysteries incorporated the system of rewards and punishments with the idea of the immortality and transmigration of the soul (Orphics and Pythagoreans held these beliefs). Plato, influenced by the above, worked some of the "Orphic" beliefs into his philosophical system of the Theory of Ideas (See *Vision of Er*). Aristotle virtually denied the survival of the soul.

Against Apion

A work in defense of the Jews by Josephus (q.v.). Apion was an Anti-Semitic Alexandrian scholar.

Agamemnon

(Myth.) Son of Atreus, brother of Menelaus. In the *Iliad* he is represented as the commander-in-chief of the Greek forces, a harsh and somewhat overbearing man whose quarrel with Achilles (q.v.) is the episode around which the whole plot revolves. His sacrifice of his daughter Iphigenia appeared in the *Cypria* (See Epic Cycle), and is mentioned by the tragedians. In Aeschylus, Agamemnon is a more tragic figure, who is guilty of hybris at the very moment when he is disclaiming it. His death is described in the *Agamemnon,* the first play in the *Oresteia* (q.v.) trilogy, as well as in the *Odyssey* (passim) and the *Electra* plays of Sophocles and Euripides. His guilt varies as that of Clytemnestra increases or decreases. His children include Orestes, Electra, Iphigenia, and Chrysothemis (Homer, however, mentions Laodice and Iphianassa; presumably, they are Electra and Iphigenia).

Agapetus

Sixth Century deacon of Hagia Sophia, who wrote a *Mirror for Princes* in 72 chapters, consisting of advice and injunctions, dedicated to the young Justinian, on the moral, religious, and political duties of a monarch.

Agatharchides of Cnidos

Greek grammarian and Peripatetic who was guardian to a young Ptolemy of Egypt, ca. 116 B.C. He wrote the following works: *On Asia, On Europe, On the Red Sea,* on troglodytes, and historical epitomes, dealing with various wonders. Excerpts survive, concerning elephant-hunts, the name of the Red Sea, gold-mining, etc.

Agathemerus

Of unknown date, probably under the Roman Empire. Wrote a geographical work (*Geographias Hypotyposis*).

Agathias, surnamed *Scholasticus* (A.D. 536-82)

Lawyer, poet, and historian of Byzantium. Best known for compiling the *Circle* of epigrams on which the existing *Anthology* (q.v.) is based. It contains about 100 epigrams by him, but they are of little merit. His history, *The Reign of Justinian,* is a sequel to that of Procopius, and covers the years 552-8, including the campaigns of Narses against the Goths, Vandals, Franks, and Persians. The *Daphniaka* are erotic myths.

Agathinus, Claudius

Founder of the Pneumatic school of medicine. Wrote works on the pulse, on fevers, etc.

Agathocles of Cyzicus

Ionian historian, of uncertain date, who wrote a history of his country. Fragments survive in Müller (F.G.H.).

Agathon of Athens

Tragic poet (ca. 450-ca. 400). Plato's *Symposium* was a feast celebrating his victory. Noted for writing a tragedy (*Antheus*) not taken from legend or mythology, but entirely of his own invention. He was criticized by Aristotle and parodied by Aristophanes, but the scarcity of the fragments makes it very difficult to come to any valid conclusion as to his literary merit.

Agave, or Agaue

(Myth.) Mother of Pentheus. In a Bacchanalian frenzy, she tears her son to pieces, believing him to be a lion. See *Bacchae* (Euripides).

Agenor

In mythology, king of Tyre, father of Europa.

Agias (or Hagias)

Reputed author of the *Nostoi* (Returns). See Epic Cycle.

Agon

In Old Comedy, the dramatic debate that forms the kernel of the play. Examples: the debate between Euripides and Aeschylus in the *Frogs;* the one between Just and Unjust Discourse in the *Clouds* (qq.v.).

Agon Homeri et Hesiodi

An account, in hexameters, of a debate, or competition, between Homer and Hesiod. Hesiod asks Homer questions, which the latter answers correctly. Then Hesiod recites nonsense verses, which Homer completes in a manner which makes sense of them. Each poet recites his best passage and then, though the judges select Homer as the winner, Hesiod gets the prize, because he encouraged peace, while Homer wrote about war. The work apparently dates from the time of Hadrian (second century A.D.), in its present form, but it was known at least as early as the time of Aristophanes, who quotes from it. Part of it seems to derive from the *Mouseion* of Alcidamas (q.v.).

Agrippa the Sceptic

Of unknown date. Wrote five *Tropoi tes epoches* (grounds of doubt).

Aiantides

An obscure Alexandrian poet, sometimes mentioned as one of the Pleiad (q.v.).

Aias

See Ajax.

Aidos

Personification of the sense of shame that prevented people from wrongdoing.

Ainoi

Fables by Archilochus (q.v.).

Aischrion

Writer of iambics and choliambics, unknown date.

Aither (Aether)

Personification of the upper stratum of air.

Ajax

The familiar Latinized form of Aias. Two Homeric heroes bore this name: (1) Son of Telamon, the "Greater" Ajax. Called "bulwark of the Achaeans." The *Little Iliad* tells the story of his madness and suicide (Cf. Sophocles' *Ajax*) after the Judgment of the Arms. According to some legends, he was invulnerable. Homer portrays him as strong, brave, but slow of speech (cf. Shakespeare's "beef-witted" Ajax). (2) Son of Oileus, the "Lesser" Ajax. Drowned by

Poseidon for blasphemy. The totally different natures of the two men is the best argument against supposing that they were originally one.

Ajax

The earliest surviving play of Sophocles tells the story of the madness and suicide of Ajax (1), and the subsequent argument over his burial. The play falls into two parts, marring its dramatic unity, according to some critics. However, when we remember the tremendous importance of the burial rite to the Greeks, we see that the second half of the play is not anti-climactic, but integral to the drama (cf. *Antigone*).

Alastor

In mythology, the brother of Nestor, killed by Heracles. The story contains elements of incest and cannibalism. The word *alastor* comes to mean an avenging power and even the criminal upon whom this power is visited. Thus Orestes uses the word of himself (N.B. He is *both* an avenging power and a criminal).

Albinus (1) Postumius

An early Roman historian who wrote in Greek.

Albinus (2)

Teacher of Galen (q.v.) ca 150 A.D. Wrote a *Prologue to Plato* and a text on Platonic philosophy, with an admixture of Peripatetic and Stoic elements.

Alcaeus (1)

B. ca 620 B.C. Lyric poet of Mytilene in Lesbos. His fragments deal with politics, seafaring (one famous poem was imitated by Horace in his "Ship of State" ode), some are from drinking-songs, love songs, hymns to the gods, etc. He used a variety of meters, and had a simple, vivid, direct style. Alcaeus wrote in the Aeolic dialect, and invented the Alcaic strophe (one of Horace's favorite meters).

Alcaeus (2), 4th Century B.C.

Called by Suidas a writer of Old Comedy, but the titles seem rather to indicate Middle Comedy (e.g. *Pasiphae*). The existing fragments, which come from eight plays, are mostly examples of mythological burlesque.

Alcaeus (3) fl. ca. 200 B.C.

Author of about 20 epigrams in the *Anthology,* including political lampoons (like those of Catullus) against Philip V.

Alcestis

In mythology, the wife of King Admetus, who gallantly gives up her life for her husband by special arrangement with the Fates. But, either because of the intercession of Heracles, who wrestled with Hades or Thanatos (Death), or for some other reason, she did not die. The most familiar treatment of the legend is the *Alcestis* of Euripides, which contains comic elements not unlike those in *Much Ado About Nothing,* and which is the basis for Gluck's opera of the same name.

Alcestis

Play by Euripides. (438 B.C.) Despite tragic elements (see above article) the play has comic overtones. The selfishness of Admetus is nicely opposed to the heroism of Alcestis. The scene between the king and his aged father, who refuses to die for his son, is an excellent one. At the end Heracles, who has successfully wrestled with Death and succeeded in winning Alcestis back to life, comes in with a veiled figure (Alcestis, of course; cf. *Much Ado*), and he persuades the bereft Admetus to look after the girl. The play was the fourth in a tetralogy (i.e. in place of the satyr-play), and is sometimes classified as a tragi-comedy.

Alchemy

Most of the early Greek texts are pseudonymous and include the *School of Democritus,* the *School of Mary the Jewess,* and the *School of Zosimus,* beginning ca. 100 A.D.

and running until the 5th century. All deal with the common interest in changing baser metals into gold and silver, a belief in the four elements and the fifth (quintessence) which can change the other four, etc. Other texts include those of "Moses," "Ostanes," "Cleopatra," "Comarius," "Hermes," "Agathodaemon," et al.

Alcibiades

Of the two Platonic dialogues of this name, the second is certainly spurious, the first may be also.

Alcidamas

Rhetor of the 4th century B.C., Pupil of the sophist Gorgias (q.v.) Extant under his name are the following: *Peri ton tous graptous logous graphonton* or *peri sophiston;* and the spurious *Odysseus kata Palamedous prosodias.* An important lost work was the *Mouseion.*

Alcides

The patronymic for Heracles (q.v.).

Alcimenes

An early comic poet. Only his name is known.

Alcinous

In the *Odyssey,* the king of the Phaeacians, who hospitably receives Odysseus, and sent him to Ithaca on one of his own ships.

Alciphron

2nd cent. A.D. sophist of Athens, who wrote letters, in imitation of Lucian, which reflect the daily life of the people.

Alcmaeon of Croton

Pupil of Pythagoras who wrote a book on nature (*peri physeos*). A physician and scientist, he is said to have been the first to perform an operation on the eye.

Alcman (fl. 654-611 B.C.)

Lyric poet who lived in Sparta but probably came from Asia Minor. Wrote lyrical poems, mostly choral odes which were sung by choirs of maidens (*Parthenion*). Alcman is said to have been the inventor of love-poetry. He wrote with great charm and simplicity in varied meters.

Alcmeon (Alcmaeon)

In mythology, the son of Amphiaraus (q.v.). Like Orestes, he avenged his father's death by killing his mother Eriphyle, after which he was pursued by the Erinyes. Afterwards he became the leader of the Epigonoi. He is, incidentally, the subject of A. E. Housman's delightful *Fragment of a Greek Tragedy*.

Alcmena (Alcmene)

In mythology, the mother of Heracles (q.v.).

Alecto

One of the Furies or Erinyes.

***Alethes Historia* (True History)**

See Lucian.

Alexander (1)

See Paris.

Alexander (2) the Great

See Arrian, Plutarch, *Ephemerides*, Callisthenes, Eumenes, etc.

Alexander (3) the Aetolian

Tragic poet, fl. ca. 280 B.C. A member of the Pleiad (q.v.). His works included *Astragalistai* (The Dice Players), two elegies: *Apollo* and *The Muses;* and two epyllia: *Halieus* (the Fisherman) and *Crica (Circa?)* and other works include *Phaenomena* (cf. Aratus), epigrams, Ionic Poems, etc.

Alexander (4) "Polyhistor"

Fl. 80 B.C. Wrote "works without number" (according to Suidas) including literary criticism, history, geography, descriptions of Delphi, Rome, the Jews, wonder-stories, etc. His output was vast but undistinguished.

Alexander (5) Second cent. A.D.

Rhetorical writer who wrote a *Techne* comparing the rival schools of Apollodorus and Theodorus, also a *Peri Schematon* which influenced later writers.

Alexander (6) of Abonuteichos

Author of a new cult of Aesculapius, he gave oracles, etc. Described by Lucian in a bitter account (*Alexander* or the *False Prophet*).

Alexander (7) of Aphrodisias

Peripatetic philosopher who flourished ca 220 A.D. One of the best commentators on Aristotle (*An. Pr., Topica, Metaphysics,* etc.), he also wrote a work *On the Soul* and other works (*peri eimarmenes, peri pyreton,* etc.) have come down under his name. Most of them are probably spurious.

Alexander (8) of Tralles

Byzantine physician (525-605) who wrote a medical work *Therapeutika* in 12 books, which was influential on the medicine of the Middle Ages.

Alexander Romance

Late story of the deeds of Alexander the Great, attributed to Callisthenes (See Callisthenes, Pseudo-Callisthenes). Very influential in the Middle Ages.

Alexandra

See Lycophron.

Alexandria

Egyptian city founded by Alexander the Great, which

became the greatest center of learning and culture during the Hellenistic period. The Library of Alexandria, founded by Ptolemy I, contained over half a million volumes.

Alexandrian Erotic Fragment

See *Erotic Fragment.*

Alexandrian Poetry

During the centuries following the death of Alexander the Great, Alexandria was the cultural center of the Greek (Hellenistic) world. Pastoral poetry, epyllia, epigrams, didactic and elegiac poetry flourished during this period, as did learning of all sorts: astronomy, mathematics, geography, philology, etc. See Callimachus, Apollonius of Rhodes, Herodas, Antimachus, Meleager, Aratus, Eratosthenes, Theocritus, Moschus, Nicander, Bion, Euphorion, Lycophron. It was the age of the savant and scholar-poet.

Alexias

See Anna Comnena.

Alexipharmaka

Work on poisons and antidodes by Nicander (q.v.).

Alexis (ca 372-270 B.C.)

Middle Comedy poet. He is said to have written 245 plays, some of which belong to the New, rather than Middle, Comedy. Wrote mythological burlesques, comedy of manners, love stories, etc. His fame was great, and, judging from the fragments we have, not undeserved.

Allegory

Occurs as early as Homer and Hesiod. See also Metrodorus of Lampsacus, Theagenes. Allegorical interpretations of Homer were common. Philosophers (e.g. Plato—Allegory of the Cave) were fond of using allegory, especially the Stoics (e.g. Chrysippus) and the Neoplatonists (e.g. Porphyry).

Almagest

The system of astronomy of Claudius Ptolemaeus (Ptolemy), known by its Arabic title (*Megale Syntaxis* became *Al-Majisti* and finally *Almagest.* See Ptolemy.

Alpheus of Mytilene

A lyric poet of the time of Augustus.

Alypius

Third or fourth century A.D. author of an *Eisagoge Musike,* one of the best sources of our knowledge of Greek music.

Amarantus of Alexandria

First-second century A.D. author of a commentary on Theocritus, and of a work *Peri Skenes* giving historical accounts of stage performances and possibly biographies of actors as well.

Amatores

A pseudo-Platonic work.

Amazons

In mythology, a fierce race of female warriors, who figure in many of the Cyclic myths. Their queen Penthesilea was killed by Achilles. Hercules (and also Theseus) campaigned against the Amazons to get the girdle of the queen. According to a fanciful etymology they were supposed to cut off the girls' right breasts (a+mazos) to prevent interference in archery.

Ambo

A long *ekphrasis* or description of the pulpit of Santa Sophia by Paulus Silentarius (q.v.).

Ambrosia and Nectar

The food and drink (usually, but sometimes reversed) of the gods. Pindar, Homer, and others mention their conferring immortality on anyone who partakes of them. Athena gives Penelope an ambrosial wash in the *Odyssey,* to make her more beautiful (younger?).

Ameipsias

Comic playwright of Athens, contemporary with Aristophanes. His *Konnos* in 423 B.C. was above Aristophanes' *Clouds,* and his *Komastai* (Revellers) defeated Aristophanes' *Birds.* But both of these plays are of doubtful attribution and may well have been by Phrynichus (q.v.2). Aristophanes called Ameipsias vulgar and banal.

Amelesagoras

Wrote a series of wonder-tales, and possibly a fourth-century *Atthis,* though this is doubtful.

Amelius, Gentilianus

See Gentilianus.

Amerias

Macedonian, of unknown date, who compiled *Ethnikai Glossai* and a *Rhizotomikon* (botanical work).

Ammianus Marcellinus

Syrian Greek of the 4th century A.D. Wrote a valuable history (in Latin).

Ammonius (1)

Pupil of Aristarchus in the second century B.C. Wrote a commentary on Homer, on Plato's borrowing from Homer, and commentaries on Pindar and Aristophanes.

Ammonius (2) Saccas

Third cent. A.D. of Alexandria. Born a Christian, he reverted to paganism. He was the teacher of Origen (1) and Origen (2), Longinus and Plotinus, and one of the founders of Neoplatonism, although he wrote nothing himself. His nickname was *Theodidaktos* (Taught by God).

Ammonius

At least ten other authors of this name are to be distinguished:

3) The teacher of Plutarch, an Egyptian Academic.

4) Son of the above who wrote a commentary on Homer. (not the same as Am. 1).

5) A Christian author, contemporary of Origen (not the same as Ammonius Saccas).

6) An epic poet.

7) A monk and writer of exegetical works.

8) A grammarian who wrote a lexicon of synonyms.

9) An atthidographer.

10) A Neoplatonic, pupil of Proclus.

11) A Peripatetic philosopher.

12) A Presbyter of Alexandria.

See Krumbacher, Schmid-Stählin.

Amoebean Verse

A feature of pastoral poetry, which consists of couplets or stanzas recited or sung alternately by two characters (Theocritus, Vergil and Horace all furnish examples). Frequently represents singing contests.

Amometus

Wrote a travel book about the Uttara-Khru people north of the Himalayas, ca 300 B.C.

Amphiarai Exelasis

A poem of the Epic Cycle (q.v.)

Amphiaraus

In mythology, a soothsayer who took part in the expedition of the Seven Against Thebes, after being compelled by his wife who had been bribed with a necklace (see Adrastus, Eriphyle & Alcmeon). His son Alcmeon avenged his death.

Amphilochus

In mythology, brother of Alcmeon (q.v.), his comrade

in the expedition of the Epigonoi, and in the slaying of their mother Eriphyle. A soothsayer who took part in the Trojan War, but not in Homer. Killed by Apollo in Soli.

Amphilochius (1)

Christian theological writer, born ca. 340 A.D. in Cappadocia, a cousin of the great Gregory of Nazianzus. Most of his writings are lost; there survive seven sermons, a polemic writing, an iambic poem to Seleucus, and a letter.

(2) There is another writer of the same name, an Athenian who wrote on agriculture.

Amphion and Zethus

In mythology, the sons of Zeus and Antiope. The former was given a lyre by Hermes and became a great musician. He built the walls of Thebes by drawing the stones with the magical music of his lyre. Niobe was his wife.

Amphis

Middle Comedy author. Wrote a *Gynaikokratia* (Government by Women) and a *Dithyrambos* which dealt with musical innovations.

Amphitryon

In mythology, son of Alcaeus, husband of Alcmena (q.v.).

Anabasis

An account by Xenophon (q.v.1) of the attempt by Cyrus the Younger to defeat his brother Artaxerxes. At the battle of Cunaxa Cyrus was defeated and killed, and Xenophon became the leader of the ten thousand Greek mercenaries in their effort to reach "civilization."

Other works with this title were written by Arrian and Sophaenetus (qq.v.).

Anabole

In Homer, the striking of the lyre when the poet began to sing. Later, a solo in the dithyramb.

Anacharsis

A Hellenized Scythian ca. 600 B.C. who was killed when he tried to introduce orgiastic worship of the "Mother of the gods." He was called one of the Seven Sages, and proverbs attributed to him occur frequently.

Anacreon

Lyric poet of Teos, born ca. 570 B.C. His poems include monodic hymns to Artemis, Eros and Dionysus, love-songs and drinking-songs. He also wrote elegiac poems of commemoration, dedication, and epitaphs. His meters are simple, his style lively, witty, and imaginative. He is supposed to have died from choking on a grape-stone at an advanced age.

Anacreontic

Type of verse named after Anacreon (vid. supr.). Usually brief songs dealing with the joys of love, wine, and the like.

Anagnorismos* or *Anagnorisis

Aristotle's terms for the sudden discovery of a relationship, at a critical moment in a tragedy. The maximum effect occurs when this is combined with a *peripeteia* or dramatic reversal, as in the *Oedipus* of Sophocles.

Anagnostes, Constantine

Byzantine poet. prob. 13th cent. Author of a poem of thanks in 92 verses to the Secretary Constantine. One of the first to use vulgar as well as literary language, acc. to Krumbacher.

Anagnostes, John

Byzantine author of a work describing the Turks' conquest of Thessalonica in 1430 A.D.

Anaischyntographoi

(lit. "shameless writers")

Popular writers on erotic and pornographic subjects in Alexandrian times.

Analogy and Anomaly

A keen struggle raged between two opposing schools of Alexandrian grammarians. The analogists held that verbs and nouns could be classified into orderly declensions and conjugations according to similarity, while the anomalists were more interested in the many irregularities and differences. The basic question was whether language was a natural growth or an arbitrary convention. Such grammarians as Aristophanes of Byzantium, Aristarchus and Dionysius Thrax (qq.v.) were analogists, and Chrysippus the Stoic was an anomalist (he wrote four books *peri anomalias*). Julius Caesar wrote a (lost) work *De Analogia.*

Ananius

A minor writer of iambic verse, contemporary with Hipponax (q.v.)—i.e. 6th cent. B.C. using the same meters. We have one fragment in which he discusses the merits of various kinds of fish.

Anastasius, Patriarch of Antioch

Only Latin translations of this important writer are extant. Important for his works on the Trinity. Much honored and quoted by later Byzantine authors, e.g. John of Damascus, Maximus Confessor. He opposed the policy of Justinian.

Anastasius

There are several other writers of this name, as follows:
2) Anastasius Sinaites, a 7th century monk. His chief work was a guide (*Odegos*) to his brothers on the successful combating of the Monophysite heresy.
3) Writer of church poetry; 4) Hagiographer; 5) A Librarian, 6) A Hymnographer.

See Krumbacher.

Anatolius

Christian author on philosophy, mathematics, astronomy, and rhetoric. There are several other writers of the same name. For complete list, see Schmid-Stählin and Krumbacher.

Anatomy

Alcmaeon of Croton (q.v.) performed dissections. See Hippocrates, Diocles, Aristotle, Galen, Erisistratus, etc.

Anaxagoras (ca. 500-428 B.C.) of Clazomenae

One of the foremost Pre-Socratics. Teacher of Pericles. He held that matter is infinitely divisible into particles of the same matter (*homoeomeries*)—a rejection of atomism. The prime mover of the universe is *nous* (mind). Due to conflicting testimony, it is difficult to reconstruct his philosophic and cosmological system. See Porteous in OCD for full discussion, including bibliography.

Anaxandrides

Middle Comedy poet of the 4th century B.C. He wrote 65 comedies, of which 42 titles survive, and won 10 victories. Several of the plays were mythological burlesques.

Anaxarchus of Abdera

Sceptic, follower of Democritus, teacher of Pyrrhon. His nickname was *Eudaimonikos,* because he held that happiness was the *summum bonum.* Was known in antiquity as a flatterer of Alexander the Great, whom he accompanied on the Asiatic campaigns, and by whom he was highly esteemed.

Anaxilas

Middle Comedy poet of the 4th century B.C. He wrote mythological burlesques (e.g. *Circe*), comedies of daily life (e.g. *Agroikos, Auletes*), parodies of Plato. One of the fragments deals with the new music of the time.

Anaximander

Ionian Pre-Socratic philosopher. Born in Miletus in 610 B.C. Ca. 546, he wrote the first treatise in Greek prose. He was probably the first to picture the whole universe as under a single law. He revolutionized astronomy by regarding the earth as spherical. He introduced the gnomon, and drew the first map of the earth.

Anaximenes (1) of Miletus fl. 546 B.C.
Pupil of Anaximander. Held that the universe is governed by a physical, rather than moral, law. All things come from air. When rarefied this becomes fire, when condensed, wind, cloud, water, earth, stone.

Anaximenes (2) of Lampsacus ca. 380-320 B.C.
Historian and rhetor, teacher of Alexander the Great. The *Rhetorica ad Alexandrum* formerly attributed to Aristotle is probably his work. Fgts. survive of other works: the *Hellenica, Philippica, History of Alexander.*

Anaxippus
New Comedy poet. Four comedies are attributed to him.

Ancoratus* or *Ankyratus
Treatise on Christian doctrine by Epiphanius (q.v.).

Andocides (ca. 440-390)
One of the Ten Attic Orators. His speeches include *De Reditu* (on the Return), *On the Mysteries, On Peace.* The speech *Against Alcibiades* is a forgery. Despite a looseness of style and an overfondness for long parentheses, he had a good narrative style. He took an active part in public life. The speech *De Mysteriis* is a successful defense he made when he was accused in 399 B.C. of illegally taking part in the Mysteries. Apparently he died in exile.

Andreas (1) d. 217 B.C.
Alexandrian physician. Wrote works on snake-bites *(peri Dakteon), Narthex* (a pharmacopia describing various plants and roots), and a work on superstitious beliefs. Only fragments.

Andreas (2) ca. 650-720 Called Hierosolymites
Archbishop of Crete. Wrote sermons on Feasts, Mary

and the Saints, and the *Megas Kanon* (Great Canon) his chief work, in 250 strophes, consisting of lyrics of varying meters, all strung together into one work.

Andreopulus

See Syntipas.

Andromache

In mythology, the wife of Hector. The Euripides play *Andromache* deals with events after the Fall of Troy. Andromache is the slave of Achilles' son Neoptolemus and the mother of his child. Neoptolemus has married Hermione, daughter of Helen and of Menelaus, who wishes to kill Andromache and her child. Hermione concurs in the plot, but Andromache is saved by the timely arrival of the aged Peleus. The play is chiefly interesting for the contrasting feminine psychologies, though the plot is weak and melodramatic.

Andromachus

Three authors of this name are to be mentioned:

1) A physician, from Crete.
2) A. the Younger, a pharmacologist.
3) A rhetor from Neapolis in Syria.

Andromeda

In mythology, a maiden chained to a rock as prey for a sea monster. She was rescued by Perseus (q.v.) who then turned her wicked uncle Phineus to stone by showing him the head of Medusa (q.v.) A lost play of Euripides was entitled *Andromeda.*

Andron of Halicarnassus

A writer on genealogies of families and cities, and possibly author of an *Atthis.*

Andronicus Camaterus

See Camaterus.

Andronicus (1) of Hermupolis

Writer of epic, drama, dithyramb, etc. in the 4th cent. A.D.

Andronicus (2) of Rhodes

Peripatetic philosopher of the first century B.C. who arranged the works of Aristotle and Theophrastus in about 40 B.C.

Androsthenes of Thasos

Sailed with Nearchus (q.v.) and wrote an account of the voyage, together with his exploration of the Persian Gulf.

Androtion 4th cent. B.C.

Pupil of Isocrates; accused of an illegal proposal by Demosthenes. Wrote an *Atthis* which was an important source for Aristotle.

Anecdota Graeca

Several collections. For complete listing, see Liddell & Scott Greek Lexicon, vol. I.

Anima, de

Work by Aristotle on the mind (soul).

Ankyratus

See *Ancoratus,* Epiphanius.

Anna Comnena

B. 1083. Byzantine Empress and historian. She wrote a history *Alexias,* imitating the style of Thucydides and Polybius. It was a history of her father Alexius Comnenus (1069-1118), and a continuation of her husband's history (see Bryennius). A true humanist, she endeavored to adopt the literary, instead of the spoken, Greek language. The greatest of women historians.

Anniceris of Cyrene

3rd cent. B.C. Philosopher of the Cyrenaic (q.v.) school.

Anomaly
See Analogy.

Anonymus
For complete listing (*Argentinensis, Epic on Diocletian,* etc.) of works too numerous to be recorded here, see Liddell and Scott, vol. I, or index in Schmid-Stählin.

Anonymus Antattacista
Opponent of Phrynichus the Atticist. See *Lexica Segueriana.*

Anonymus Iamblichi
Wrote a philosophical work in which is found the *Protreptikon* of Iamblichus (q.v.).

Anonymus Seguerianus
(3rd cent. A.D.) author of a *techne tou politikou logou* referring to the work of Alexander (q.v.5). The work throws some light on rhetorical teaching.

Antaeus
In mythology, a giant, son of Earth and Poseidon, who compelled all passers-by to wrestle with him. Heracles defeated him by lifting him off the ground, as he became stronger from contact with his mother the Earth.

Antagoras of Rhodes
Alexandrian poet of the 3rd cent. B.C. who wrote a *Thebais,* epigrams, and a *Hymn to Love.*

Ante-Nicene Fathers
See Irenaeus, Hippolytus (2), Clement, Origen. The term simply means "before the Council of Nicaea (325)" and includes, therefore, the Apostolic Fathers (q.v.) and all the early Apologists.

Anthea and Abrocomes
See Xenophon (2).

Anthology

The name means "bouquet" and was first used for a collection of poems in the Byzantine period. The Palatine Anthology is the greatest collection of Greek epigrams, but many others were made by individual poets or on individual subjects. The first large collection was the *Garland* of Meleager (q.v.) ca. 90 B.C. Philippus of Thessalonica (q.v. 2) in about 40 A.D. added to the collection the epigrammatists since Meleager. In ca. 570 A.D. The Byzantine poet Agathias (q.v.) compiled his *Circle* of epigrams, including many from the previous *Garlands* and adding many contemporary ones, arranging them according to subject. In the tenth century, Cephalas (q.v.) made the present Anthology by rearranging all the previous collections (i.e. those of Meleager, Philippus, and Agathias). In the 14th cent. the collection was re-edited by Planudes (q.v.). Highet calls it "a mine of jewels choked with masses of lumber." (OCD)

Antidorus of Cyme

The first to refer to himself as "grammatikos." He wrote, ca. 300 B.C. a work on Homer and Hesiod, and a treatise on style (?).

Antigenes

Dithyrambic poet of the 5th cent. B.C. One poem of his survives in the Palatine Anthology (13.28). It is a dedicatory poem for tripods.

Antigone

In mythology, the daughter of Oedipus (q.v.) and subject of one of the finest plays of Sophocles. Forbidden by edict of her uncle Creon to bury her brother Polynices (qq.v.) who has died attacking the city of Thebes, she defies the edict by throwing dust on the corpse. When she returns to replace the dust and pour libation she is caught, thus bringing about her own death as well as the deaths of Haemon and Eurydice (the son and wife of Creon). Tiresias (q.v.) warns Creon that he is committing a double offense against the gods by leaving a dead body unburied, and putting a living person (i.e. Antigone) in an underground cavern. He sets out to right these wrongs, but it is too late. Antigone has hanged herself. Haemon kills himself over her body, and Eurydice takes her own life. In some ways it seems that Creon, not Antigone is the tragic hero of the play (otherwise, why is Eurydice introduced, and why are Haemon's and Eurydice's bodies brought on stage, but *not* that of Antigone herself?). The character of Antigone has been variously interpreted: as a harsh person with a "martyr-complex" who suffers because of *hybris,* or as a noble and heroic maiden who defies the laws of the State only to obey a higher, divine law, and whose suffering is wholly undeserved. In the *Oedipus at Colonus* (q.v.) which precedes the action of the *Antigone,* although it was written many years later, Antigone is the prop and support of her aged, blind father, and begs her brother Polynices to give up the attempt on Thebes, but in vain. Euripides treats the myth somewhat differently, but his play is lost.

Antigonus of Carystus

fl. 240 B.C. Bronze-worker and writer. Wrote works on the history of art, on style, on the lives of the philosophers, etc. He is supposed to have had a good, flowing style, but the collection of anecdotes which survives has little merit. Diogenes Laertius and Athenaeus preserve fragments.

Antimachus (1) of Teos

Eighth cent. B.C. (?) Reputed author of the *Epigoni* in the Epic Cycle (q.v.).

Antimachus (2) of Colophon

Born in the middle of the fifth cent. B.C. We know of five works by A. An epic, the *Thebais,* and other poems called *Lyde, Deltoi, Artemis,* and *Iachine* (?) Antimachus was the founder of Narrative Elegy. Plato was very fond of his verse, but Callimachus thought it "stodgy and involved." The fragments seem to justify the latter verdict. His chief importance is that, 100 years before the Alexandrian scholar-poets, he made an edition of Homer.

Antiochus (1) of Syracuse

Greek logographer of the 5th cent. B.C. who wrote a history of Sicily and of Italy. His style, according to Strabo, was simple and old-fashioned.

Antiochus (2) of Ascalon (born ca. 125 B.C.)

Founder of the Fifth Academy, frequently quoted by Cicero, who attended his lectures in Athens. His doctrine was eclectic, combining Academic, Peripatetic, and Stoic elements.

Antiochus (3) of Athens

Wrote a popular work on astrological lore. Date unknown, but not later than 300 A.D.

Antiochus (4)

A seventh-century ascetic. Wrote, ca. 620 a *Pandektes tes Hagias Graphes* (Holy Encyclopedia) dealing with monastic ethics and dogma.

Antiochus

Several other writers of this name are to be mentioned:
(5) A. of Aegae, a sophist.
(6) A. of Alexandria, who wrote on Middle Comedy poets.
(7) A poet and epigrammatist of the 4th cent. A.D.
(8) A tragic poet.
See Schmid-Stählin.

Antiope

In mythology, the daughter of the river Asopus. Euripides wrote a tragedy (lost) about her.

Antipater (1) of Tarsus, 2nd cent. B.C.

Stoic, successor of Diogenes of Babylon as head of the school at Athens; teacher of Panaetius. Among his many works, the following are known by title: *peri Theon, peri Mantikes* (On the gods, on Divination). He committed suicide at an advanced age.

Antipater (2) of Sidon, fl. 130 B.C.

Greek epigrammatist. The Greek Anthology has about 75 of his poems. Mostly rhetorical and epideictic, they are of little value, with occasional exceptions.

Antipater (3) of Tyre

Philosopher of the first century B.C., who introduced Cato to the Stoic philosophy. Wrote on marriage, on the soul, on the cosmos, on Being, etc.

Antipater (4) of Thessalonica

The Greek anthology contains about 80 of his poems, the last dating about 15 A.D. His poems are described as "graceful, witty, and unimportant—his attitude to life and art closely resembles Ovid's." (Highet in OCD)

Antiphanes (1)

(ca. 388-ca. 311 B.C.) Middle Comedy poet (possibly two poets). Many of the titles indicate mythological burlesques, some deal with daily life, one compares Tragedy and Comedy, and some of the fgts. are tragic parodies. Over 300 fgts. survive.

Antiphanes (2) of Berge

A writer of *Apista* (incredible tales), of unknown date, but probably before Alexander's time. A sort of ancient Munchausen. From him comes the verb *bergaizein* (to tell tall stories).

Antiphilus of Byzantium (1st cent. B.C.-1st cent. A.D.)

Author of epigrams, about 50 of which are in the Greek

Anthology. Some are rhetorical paradoxes or describe strange accidents. He specialized in epigrams with a surprise or pointed ending, and thus points the way for Martial.

Antiphon (1) (ca. 480-411 B.C.)

One of the Ten Attic Orators. An aristocrat, he never (or hardly ever) appeared in court himself, but wrote speeches for others, which gained him a great reputation. Works: The *Tetralogies* consist of (1) the opening speech of the prosecution, (2) the reply for the defense, (3) the answer by the prosecution, and (3) the defendant's conclusion. There are three of these Tetralogies, and all deal with homicide. Also we have *The Murder of Herodes* (unlike the *Tetralogies,* which are rhetorical exercises, this deals with a real case), *On the Choreutes,* and the speech *Against a Stepmother.* His style, though sometimes crude, is vigorous and precise, with periodic sentences and carefully balanced antitheses. Antiphon was condemned and executed for his share in the revolt against the Four Hundred in 411 B.C.

Antiphon (2)

A sophist of the 5th cent. B.C., sometimes confused with Antiphon (1) the Orator. He wrote on truth, politics, concord, and the interpretation of dreams.

Antiphon (3)

A tragic poet, put to death by the Elder Dionysus of Syracuse.

***Antiquitates Romanae* (Rhomaike Archaiologia)**

See Dionysius of Halicarnassus.

Antisthenes (1) (ca. 455-ca. 360 B.C.)

Follower of Socrates and founder of the Cynic sect. He also influenced the Stoics. According to his philosophy, happiness is based on virtue, which comes from knowledge, and therefore can be taught. Antisthenes wrote several dialogues

(*Heracles, Aspasia, Cyrus, Protrepticus, etc.*) interpretations of Homer, and orations.

Antisthenes (2) of Rhodes 2nd cent. B.C.
Wrote a work entitled *Diadochai philosophon,* and a history of Rhodes down to his own time, used by Polybius.

Antoninus Liberalis
A mythographer of the 2nd cent. A.D. (?) wrote a collection of *Transformations (Metamorphoseon synagoge)* based on Hellenistic sources.

Antonius Diogenes
Wrote, ca. 100 A.D. a fantasy in 24 books entitled *Ta hyper Thoulen apista* (The Marvels beyond Thule).

Antyllus
Physician of the Pneumatic School-2nd cent. A.D. Wrote on dietetics, therapeutics, and surgery (*Cheirourgoumena).* Only fragments survive.

Anubion
Date unknown (prob. 1st cent.) Author of a didactic poem on astrology.

Anyte of Tegea
Poetess fl. ca. 300 B.C. There are 20 epigrams by her (The so-called "Red Lilies" of Anyte), of great charm, in the Greek Anthology, mostly mock epitaphs for animals, some are nature-poems.

Aphrodite
Goddess of love and beauty. Her birth from the sea is supposed to account for her name (*aphros* = foam). In poetry she is usually a symbol of passion and romantic love, and as the generative force of Nature (cf. Lucretius).

Aphrodite, Hymn to
See *Homeric Hymns.*

Aphthonius of Antiocheia

Athenian rhetor and teacher. Wrote a *Progymnasmata* to the *Techne* of Hermogenes. Date unknown, prob. 4th cent. A.D.

Apion "Pleistonikes" (i.e. "Victor in many contests")

Son of Posidonius, successor to Theon as head of the school of Alexandria. At Rome under Tiberius and Claudius. He wrote on Egypt, and compiled an alphabetically arranged Homeric glossary based on Aristarchus.

Apocalypse, Apocalyptic Literature

From Gr. *apokalyptein,* to uncover or reveal. All such writings had in common the view that the present evil age would come to a close, the world be purified by fire, and the righteous would take their place in a new and purified world. They (i.e. these writings) usually arise in times of oppression by nonbelievers, tyrants, etc. and are a typically Christian, or late Hebraic phenomenon. Examples are the canonical *Daniel* and *Revelation,* but many others were produced: *Book of Jubilees, Shepherd of Hermas, Assumption of Moses, Apocalypse of Peter, Ascension of Isaiah. Ezra IV,* etc. Regularly they purport to have been written by the great men of the Old Testament, to whom angels revealed the things to come. The essential difference between them and the Prophets is that the latter arose in times of prosperity, as a warning, the former in times of oppression, as a means of inspiring hope.

Apocalypse of Abraham

A Christian re-working of Jewish legend. Tells of revelations received by Abraham. See also *Testament of Abraham.*

Apocalypse of Moses

See Book of Jubilees.

Apocalypse of St. John

The earliest Christian apocalyptic literature. Also known as *Revelation.* See Apocalyptic lit.

Apocrypha, N.T.

The books included in the New Testament are only a selection of a much larger literature. Some of these other works are included in the Apostolic Fathers. Others, known as *Apocrypha,* probably never had any valid title to acceptance. Mostly they appear to be deliberate fabrications, in imitation of the canonical N.T. writings (Gospels, e.g. *Gospel of the Hebrews, of Peter, of the Infancy;* Epistles, e.g. *Epistle of Paul to the Laodiceans;* Acts, e.g. *Acts of Paul and Tela, Acts of John, of Thomas,* etc.; Revelations, e.g. *Apocalypse of Peter).* See also *Shepherd of Hermas, Epistle of Barnabas, Ezra, Sibylline Books,* pseudepigrapha.

Apocrypha, Old Testament

Books found in the Septuagint (q.v.) but not in the Hebrew Bible. They are as follows: *Esdras* I and II, *Tobit, Additions to Esther, Wisdom of Solomon, Wisdom of Jesus the son of Sirach, Baruch,* with the *Epistle of Jeremiah, Song of the Three Children, History of Susannah, Bel and the Dragon, Prayer of Manasses, Maccabees* I and II. There is some difference in terminology; Catholics call these "deuterocanonical" and reserve the name Apocrypha for other works which the Protestants call Pseudepigrapha. See apocalyptic lit, Pseudepigrapha, Judith.

Apollinarius

Three people of this name are to be distinguished.

(1) A. of Hierapolis, an Apologist.

(2) A writer of epigrams.

(3) Bishop of Laodicea who wrote 150 hexameter versions of the Psalms.

Apollo

God of prophecy, healing (also plagues), and music. Not a sun-god until he becomes identified with Helius (q.v.). It is perhaps significant that Apollo is the only important Greek god with no Roman counterpart. His oracle at Delphi was the most important of the Greek oracles, and was proverbial for its ambiguity.

Apollo, Hymn to

See Homeric Hymns.

Apollodorus (1) of Gela

New Comedy poet, contemporary of Menander. Not the same as Ap. (2) of Carystus.

Apollodorus (2) of Carystus

Also a New Comedy poet. Wrote 47 plays and won 5 victories. His *Hecyra* was the original of Terence's play of the same name, and his *Epidikazomenos* of Terence's *Phormio.*

Apollodorus (3) of Alexandria

Scientist and physician of the third cent. B.C. His chief work (On Poisonous Creatures) was the source for all later pharmacologists. Also wrote a work about lethal poisons.

Apollodorus (4) of Pergamum ca. 104-22 B.C.

Rhetor and teacher of the Emperor Augustus. To Apollodorus, rhetoric was a science (*episteme*) with fixed rules; to his opponent (Theodorus) it was an art (*techne*) with freer methods. Cf. Analogy and Anomaly.

Apollodorus (5) of Athens (middle of second cent. B.C.)

Pupil of Aristarchus, and a man of great and varied learning. Works: *Chronology* (from the Fall of Troy to his own day) in comic trimeters; Mythology (*Bibliotheke,* a study of heroic mythology. There is an extant work of this name, but not Apollodorus'); *On the Gods, on Geography,* and works of etymology, commentaries, etc.

Apollodorus (6)

Stoic philosopher who wrote on ethics and physics and logic. There are several other writers of this name, including a poet, a tragedian, a commentator on Euripides, an actor, an Epicurean, and a historian. Complete list in Schmid-Stählin.

Apollonides

Four writers of this name are to be mentioned:
(1) A. of Nicaea—early 1st cent. A.D. Wrote on proverbs, on false history, and on Demosthenes.
(2) A. of Smyrna, an epigrammatist.
(3) A historian.
(4) A Stoic philosopher.

Apollonius (1) of Rhodes

Epic poet of the third cent. B.C. His *Argonautica,* telling of Jason's quest of the Golden Fleece, his love for Medea, etc. is extant. It is in imitation of Homeric style. The part dealing with Medea and her love for Jason is very moving and influenced Vergil. Apollonius also wrote epigrams, poems on the founding of cities, and works on Hesiod, Archilochus, etc. He was a great enemy of Callimachus (q.v.).

Apollonius (2) of Perga fl. 225 B.C.

Mathematician. Wrote a work on conics, of which four books survive in Greek, and three in Arabic. Ap. gave names to the hyperbola, parabola and ellipse. Also wrote on *Tangencies, Plane Loci, Determinate section, Ratios,* a *General Treatise,* on the *Cylindrical Helix,* the *Burning Mirror,* and *Unordered Irrationals.*

Apollonius (3)

Author of a 2nd cent. B.C. compilation of Marvels. See Paradoxographers.

Apollonius (4) of Citium

Alexandrian physician of about 50 B.C. A commentary on Hippocrates survives. Other works are lost.

Apollonius (5) Dyscolus

Alexandrian grammarian. Wrote 29 books, mostly on syntax. Four survive: on the *Pronoun, Conjunction, Adverb,* and *Syntax*. Although his own syntax was far from perfect, he had an enormous influence on later grammarians.

Apollonius

Also, mention should be made of the following:

(6) Apollonius Mys, Physician of the 1st cent. B.C.

(7) Ap. Sophista, who compiled a Homeric Lexicon, ca. 100 A.D.

(8) Ap. of Tyana, a Neopythagorean sage and wandering ascetic (See Philostratus 2).

(9) Ap. of Tyre, hero of an anonymous Latin Romance. Greek original is lost.

(10) A grammarian.

Also, a Neo-Sophist, a tragedian, a physician, a writer on mechanics, a rhetor, an astrologist, a Stoic, and many others. For complete list, see index of Schmid-Stählin.

Apollophanes (1)

Athenian writer of comedy, ca. 400 B.C. One title: *Kretes.*

Apollophanes (2)

Stoic philosopher, disciple of Zeno of Citium.

Apologists

Defenders of early Christianity against attacks. See

Quadratus, Aristides, Preaching of Peter, Justin Martyr, Athenagoras, Theophilus, Origen, etc.

Apology

A formal speech of defense in a law court. The most famous is Plato's *Apology of Socrates,* an extremely moving document in which the aged Socrates first answers the formal charges (physical and metaphysical speculation, sophistry, atheism, and corrupting the youth) and convincingly refutes each of them in short order, then enters into the real *Apology* for his own way of life, his unceasing search for truth and virtue in answer to the oracle, his way of questioning others to find out whether they possess virtue, etc. Convicted by a small margin, he then well-nigh forces the jury to condemn him to death, by ironically suggesting that his punishment should be public maintenance in the Prytaneum for the rest of his life. In the last section, he speaks of death, which is either a state of complete nothingness, or a journey of the soul to another world. In either case, Socrates says it is a good thing. The speech is marked by great earnestness and sincerity, not untinged with irony.

Apology of Socrates

Xenophon (q.v.) also wrote a work of this title, designed to show why Socrates did not defend himself at this trial. It is very inferior to Plato's work.

Apology for the Christians

See Justin Martyr.

Apomnemoneumata

See Xenophon's *Memorabilia.*

Apostolic Fathers

See Clement (of Rome), Polycarp, Barnabas, Hermas, Ignatius.

Apostolius

Made a collection of proverbs in the 15th century. See Paroemiographers.

Appendix Planudea

The additions made by Planudes to the Anthology (qq.v.).

Appian of Alexandria

Historian, Second cent. A.D. His work *Romaica* treats of the various Roman conquests: (Basilike, Italike, Saunitike, Keltike, Sikelike, Iberike, Annibaike, Libyke, Makedonike and Illyrike, Hellenike and Ionie, Syriake, Mithridateios, Emphylion, Aigyptiakon, Hekatontaetia, Dakike, Arabios.) It goes down to the Empire under Trajan. Appian was an honest admirer of Roman imperialism and wrote in a simple *koine.*

Apsines of Gadara

Athenian rhetor, ca. 190-250 A.D. His *techne* has survived. Other works are lost.

Aquila

Translated the Bible. See *Hexapla.*

Arabius Scholasticus

A Byzantine lawyer in Justinian's time. Wrote a fine epigram on his villa by the Bosporus.

Araros

Son of Aristophanes, who also wrote plays, beginning ca. 375 B.C.

Aratus (1) of Soli (ca. 315-240 B.C.)

Didactic poet. Most famous work: the *Phaenomena* (a versification of a prose treatise by Eudoxus, on astronomy). A. also wrote epigrams, elegies, and other scientific works (e.g. *Iatrika),* hymns, Paegnia, and a collection *ta kata lepton* (from which the Catalepton attributed to Vergil took its name).

Aratus (2) 271-213 B.C.
Statesman of Sicyon. Wrote *Hypomnematismoi* (memoirs).

Arbitration
See *Epitrepontes* (Menander).

Arcadius of Antiocheia
Grammarian of the late Empire who wrote an *Onomatikon* or table of noun inflexions. An extant epitome from Herodian is falsely ascribed to him.

Arcesilaus ca 315-240 B.C.
Philosopher and founder of the Middle Academy.

Archedicus
A New Comedy playwright.

Archelais
Poetess, author of elegiacs. Prob. 1st century B.C.

Archelaus (1)
Philosopher of the 5th cent. B.C. Pupil of Anaxagoras, and perhaps the teacher of Socrates.

Archelaus (2)
From the Egyptian Chersonese. Writer of epigrams *(Idiophue)* on marvels (see Paradoxographers).

Archestratus of Gela
Contemporary of Aristotle. Wrote a work entitled *Hedypatheia* on good things to eat, which may have been the source for a similar book by the Roman Ennius. Two other writers of this name should be mentioned:
1) A lyric poet.
2) A tragedian.

Archias

There seem to have been five poets of this name, (all writers of epigrams) as follows:

1) Cicero's contemporary, whom he defended in the *Pro Archia.* Two epigrams in the Anthology are attributed to him.

2) Epigrammatist from Byzantium.

3) Epigrammatist from Mytilene.

4) Epigrammatist from Macedonia.

5) Epigrammatist called *Neoteros.*

Archigenes

Greek physician at Rome, ca. 100 A.D. He influenced Galen, and wrote many medical works, all of which are lost.

Archilochus of Paros (ca. 700 B.C. (?)

Iambic & Elegiac poet, perhaps the inventor of elegy. We have considerable remains of his work: epigrams, trimeters, diatribes, fables, poems on war, eclipses, drinking, etc. He has a lively and personal style. The best-known poem explains his throwing away his shield to save his life.

Archimedes Ca. 287-212 B.C.

The greatest mathematician of ancient times. Invented the water-screw and other machines, established the theory of the lever, invented the science of hydrostatics, dealing with the ways bodies behave in liquid, according to their shape and specific gravity, and made many important contributions to mathematics. His extant works include: *On the Sphere and Cylinder, Measurement of a Circle,* the *Sand-Reckoner, On Conoids and Spheroids, On Spirals, Plane Equilibrium, On Floating Bodies, Quadrature of a Parabola, the Method.* Lost works include a work on levers, on mirrors, etc. The most famous story about him tells how he ran through the streets of Syracuse shouting "Eureka" (I have found it) after discovering how to find the proportions of gold and silver in the crown of Hieron. He is supposed to have said: "Give me a place to stand on and I will move the earth." He was killed when the Romans sacked Syracuse in 212.

Archimelus

Court poet of Hieron II of Syracuse. Wrote epigrams.

Archippus ca 400 B.C.

Comic playwright. His best-known play is the *Ichthyes* (Fishes) in which fish declare war on men. Other titles: *Herakles Gamon, Ploutos* (?) He was known for his imitations of other playwrights and was famous (or infamous) for his puns.

Archytas of Tarentum 4th cent. B.C.

Said to be the founder of mechanics. He solved the problem of doubling the cube. A Pythagorean in philosophy, he was visited by Plato and enjoyed a great reputation. Fragments of his mathematical works remain.

Archytas

There were two other writers of this name: (1) A Neoplatonic philosopher; (2) Archytas of Amphissa, an epic poet.

Arctinus

Epic poet of the 8th cent. B.C. (?). Wrote the *Iliu Persis* (Sack of Troy) and the *Aethiopis,* two of the poems that come between the *Iliad* and the *Odyssey* in the Epic Cycle (q.v.). He may also have been the author of the *Titanomachia.*

Areius (or Arius)

Four writers of this name are to be mentioned:

(1) Philosopher, author of a *Lexicon Platonicum,* teacher of Augustus (A. Didymus) See Arius.

(2) A Physician.

(3) A "Homeric poet."

(4) Presbyter of Alexandria (d. 336 A.D.).

Areopagiticus

A political speech by Isocrates (q.v.).

Ares

Greek god of war and personification of the warlike spirit. Unlike Mars, his Roman counterpart, Ares was not a very popular god, and had no moral functions. In the *Iliad,* he is on the Trojan side. Homer relates the amusing story of the affair between Ares and Aphrodite in Book viii of the *Odyssey.*

Aretaeus of Cappadocia

Medical author, ca. 150-200. He wrote on the causes and symptoms of disease, on cures, surgery, etc.

Aretalogus

A professional teller of tall tales. The word *Aretalogy* is sometimes used for a collection of such tales.

Arethas b ca. 860 A.D.

Archbishop of Caesarea, scholar and theologian. Pupil of Photius. Wrote exegetical works, speeches, commentaries on Plato, Lucian, and Eusebius. He was responsible for MSS. of Euclid, Aristides, and especially, the famous MS. of Plato brought to England from Patmos by Clarke.

Argentarius, Marcus

A Greco-Roman poet. His poetry dealt with love, humor, satire, and was Horatian in tone. Probably identical with a rhetor of the same name.

Argonautica

See Apollonius of Rhodes. The story deals with Jason's quest for the Golden Fleece, his love for Medea, etc. The Argo is called the first ship and those who sailed in it (including all the great heroes and persons of the time) were called Argonauts.

Argives

Literally, inhabitants of Argos; in Homer the term is used of the Greek forces, who are also called Achaeans and Danaans.

Argos

(1) A city in the Peloponnesus, the domain of Agamemnon.
(2) In Mythology, a monster sent by Hera to watch Io, and slain by Hermes.
(3) An Argonaut, and builder of the ship Argo.
(4) The old dog of Odysseus, who lives just long enough to recognize his returning master, and then dies.

Ariadne

In mythology, daughter of King Minos of Crete. She rescued Theseus (q.v.) by giving him a thread with which he escaped from the labyrinth after killing the Minotaur. He took her with him when he fled, but abandoned her on Naxos.

Arimaspeans

A legendary people of the North. They had one eye, and fought with griffins who guarded a hoard of gold. See Aristeas.

Arion

Wrote dithyrambs ca. 625 B.C. and is thus one of the ancestors of tragedy. Said to be the first to give names to his poems. Nothing of his work survives. The most famous story about him is that he was thrown overboard from a ship and carried ashore by a dolphin (Herodotus).

Aristaenetus

Epistolographer of the 5th cent. A.D. We possess two books of erotic letters, consisting of love-tales, encomia of female beauty, etc. The motifs come from Alexandrian elegy and New Comedy.

Aristaeus of Croton

Son-in-law and disciple of Pythagoras. Wrote a work on harmony.

Aristaeus (2) Mathematician of the 3rd cent. B. C. Wrote on conics.

Aristagoras (1)

A comic playwright. Wrote a Mammakythos (The Booby).

Aristagoras (2)

A historian who wrote on Oriental countries.

Aristagoras (3)

Made a map of the earth.

Aristander

Alexander the Great's interpreter of dreams.

Aristarchus (1) of Samos ca. 310-230 B.C.

Mathematician and astronomer. His chief claim to fame is as the author of the Heliocentric Theory (i.e. that the earth moves around the sun). His only extant work is a treatise on the sizes and distances of the sun and moon. He is said to have invented an improved sun-dial.

Aristarchus (2) of Samothrace ca. 215-145 B.C.

Head of the library of Alexandria. His writings include critical recensions of Homer, Hesiod, Archilochus, Pindar, etc. He sought to remove corrupt and interpolated lines from the text. Other works include commentaries on the epic, lyric, tragic and comic poets and on Herodotus; and several critical treatises. He was equally renowned as a grammarian, etymologist, textual, and literary critic.

Aristarchus (3) of Tegea

Contemporary of Euripides, said to have written 70 tragedies and won two victories. Titles include *Tantalus, Achilles, Asclepius.*

Aristeas (1)

Supposed author of a poem on the Arimaspeans (q.v.).

Aristeas (2)

Jewish Historian. Wrote *Peri Ioudaion* (On the Jews).

Aristeas, Letter of

A letter giving an account of the translation of the Septuagint (q.v.).

Aristias

5th century (B.C.) playwright who competed against Aeschylus. Titles include: *Perseus, Tantalus, Antaeus,* satyr-plays.

Aristides (1) of Miletus

Wrote or compiled ca. 100 B.C. the (lost) *Milesiaka,* and is credited with several other works as well. The *Milesiaka* were erotic, obscene tales. A Latin translation was very popular in Rome.

Aristides (2) Aelius

Famous sophist, exponent of the New Sophistic (d. 189 A.D.) 55 ceremonial speeches survive, in good clear Attic style, full of rhetorical devices, long periods, etc. The *technai* ascribed to him are spurious. The *Panathenaikos* (a eulogy of Athens), the *Sacred Discourses,* and the *Peri Rhetorikes* are some of the most celebrated of his orations.

Aristides (3) Quintilianus

Author (3rd or 4th cent. A.D.) of an extant work on music (*Peri Mousikes*). Seems to have been a Neoplatonist.

Aristides (4)

An early Christian Apologist, author of a work *Peri Theosebeias.*

Aristides (5)

An epic poet of the third century B.C.

Aristippus (1) of Cyrene

Companion of Socrates. Has been called the founder of the Cyrenaic school (q.v.) but this is probably a confusion with Aristippus (2) grandson of (1), who taught that pleasure is the chief good (Hedonism).

Aristobulus (1)

An Alexander-historian. It is said that Alexander the Great was so disgusted by A's flattery that he threw his book overboard.

Aristobulus (2)

Alexandrian Jew of the 2nd cent. B.C. who wrote a commentary on the Pentateuch and an exegesis of the Law of Moses.

Aristocles (1) of Pergamum

Sophist and rhetor of the 2nd cent. A.D. Wrote a *Techne Rhetorike* and letters.

Aristocles (2) of Messana

2nd cent. A.D. Peripatetic philosopher. Wrote on philosophy, on Homer and Plato, on Ethics, etc.

Aristocles (3)

A paradoxographer (q.v.) of uncertain date.

Aristodemus

The following are to be distinguished:

(1) Historian, who wrote a (lost) history of Greece.

(2) Alexandrian grammarian who wrote on Pindar, homonyms, etc.

(3) Ar. of Nysa, grammarian, teacher of Strabo.

(4) Made excerpts from Herodian.

Aristomenes

Athenian comic playwright, contemporary of Aristophanes. Titles include: *Hylophoroi* (or *Koleophoroi*), *Admetus, Dionysius Asketes.*

Ariston

The following are to be distinguished:

(1) Stoic philosopher, pupil of Zeno.

(2) Son of Sophocles, also a tragedian, and father of Sophocles the Younger.

(3) A Peripatetic ca. 200 B.C. Made a collection of *Anecdotes* and *Characters*.

(4) Another Peripatetic philosopher. (from Kos)

(5) Another Peripatetic philosopher. (from Pergamum)

(6) A physician.

(7) A famous flute-player.

(8) A writer of epics and satyr-plays.

See Schmid-Stählin.

Aristonicus

Alexandrian grammarian who wrote commentaries on Hesiod and Pindar, and was occupied with critical recensions of Homer. Dates from the Age of Augustus.

Aristonous

A Corinthian citharode of the 3rd cent. B.C.

Aristonymus (1)

A comic playwright, contemporary of Aristophanes.

Aristonymus (2)

A historian.

Aristophanes of Athens (1) ca 450-ca 385 B.C.

The greatest of ancient comic playwrights; only writer of Old Comedy whose works have survived (See individual titles: *Acharnians, Knights, Clouds, Wasps, Peace, Birds, Lysistrata, Thesmophoriazusae, Frogs, Ecclesiazusae, Plutus*). A political conservative, A. is exceedingly free with personal lampoons on great figures of the day (e.g. Cleon, Euripides, Socrates). His comedies usually begin with a so-called "Happy Idea" (In the *Birds,* the building of the Utopia,

Nephelococcygia, in the Frogs, the descent of Dionysus to Hades to bring back a poet, etc.). The rest of the play is a development of this idea, in an almost Gilbert-and-Sullivan kind of topsy-turvydom. The plays of Aristophanes are noted for their wit, fantasy, obscenity, personal abuse, slap-stick, satire, and beautiful lyrics. The poet Heine compared Aristophanes to a tree with nightingales singing in the upper branches, and monkeys chattering below. For sheer comic invention and brilliance he is probably without rival. It it sometimes difficult fully to appreciate the numerous topical references, and it is especially hard to translate the many delightful puns. In addition, Aristophanes has had his detractors among prudes of all times, with the result that the most popular plays are not necessarily the best. But the dirt in Aristophanes is nearly always good clean dirt, with nothing shameful or furtive about it. As for influence in posterity, there has been virtually none. Modern comedy stems from the New Comedy, not the Old, and eventually may go back to some of the plays of Euripides. Aristophanes was a completely unique phenomenon. For titles of lost plays, see Rose or OCD.

Aristophanes (2) of Byzantium ca. 257-180 B.C.

Succeeded Eratosthenes as head of the Library at Alexandria. A versatile and profound scholar, famous for his scientific, linguistic, textual and literary researches. Made editions of the *Iliad* and *Odyssey,* Hesiod, Alcaeus, and Anacreon, as well as the first complete editions of the odes of Pindar, and of the plays of Euripides. His classification of the best writers is the basis of the Alexandrian canon. His *Lexeis* or *Glossai* was probably a series of special articles classified either by dialect or by subject. Also, he wrote books of proverbs, a grammatical treatise, and a work on animals.

Aristophanes (3) of Thebes

Historian who wrote a history of Thebes.

Aristophontes

A novelist or writer of romances. Little is known beside the name.

Aristos of Salamis

A writer of Alexander-history.

Aristotle (384-322 B.C.)

Born in Stagira, son of Nicomachus. Went to Plato's school and remained for 20 years, leaving to found his own school. Tutor of Alexander the Great, on whose death he left Athens. He died a year later. His early popular works are all lost, and only his course-outlines or lecture notes survive. These were not intended for publication, but perhaps as outlines for pupils who missed the lectures. List of works: Genuine: *Prior Analytics, Posterior An. Topics, Sophistici Elenchi, Physics, De Caelo, De Generatione et Corruptione, Meteorologica, De Anima, Parva Naturalia (De Sensu et Sensibiliis, De Memoria, De Somno, De Somniis, De Divinatione per Somnum, De Longitudine et Brevitate Vitae, De Vita et Morte, De Respiratione), Historia Animalium, De Partibus Animalium, De Incessu Animalium, De Generatione Anim. Metaphysics, Nicomachean Ethics, Politics, Rhetoric, Poetics.* Probably genuine: *De Interpretatione, De Motu Animalium, Eudemian Ethics.* Doubtful: *Categories, Magna Moralia.* For list of lost and spurious works, see Schmid-Stählin or OCD. See also *Constitution of Athens.*

Aristotle's chief characteristics are: his love of classification, his orderliness of mind, and his great common sense. He took all knowledge for his province, and he not only assembled and classified existing knowledge, but made significant additions (e.g. in the fields of logic, which he may be said to have invented; literary criticism; zoology, etc.). Although he was much influenced by his master Plato, he rejected certain cardinal points of the latter's philosophy (e.g. the Theory of Ideas). He was a firm advocate of the

Golden Mean, in politics, drama, ethics, etc. He observed, collected, and classified, whether the subject was biology, politics, or literature. His political and even ethical thought is always arranged and classified in a scientific way as if it were biology. The vocabulary of logic and philosophy is Aristotelian: the distinctions between universal and particular, premise and conclusion, subject and attribute, matter and form, potentiality and actuality—he introduced these antitheses by name. It is somewhat ironic that this man, who represented the sum total of human knowledge of his day, should have been, albeit unwittingly, responsible for the retardation of knowledge centuries later. For the Middle Ages, Aristotle was "The Philosopher." For Dante, he was the "Master of those who know." (See under separate headings of his works for fuller discussion.)

Aristoxenus b. 375-360 B.C.

Peripatetic philosopher, pupil of Aristotle, musical theorist. He wrote on the *Principles and Elements of Harmonics,* on instruments, listening, on the *Elements of Rhythm, On Music, On Melody,* on flutes, tragic poets, lives of philosophers, Pythagorean maxims, and other subjects. In his love of classifying into categories, he is a worthy pupil of Aristotle. His chief importance is in the field of music.

Aristoxenus

Two others of this name are to be distinguished:

(1) A. of Selinus, a comic playwright.

(2) A physician.

Arius

Presbyter of Alexandria (256-336). Exponent of the famous "Arian Hersy" on the nature of Jesus. Condemned by the Council of Nicaea in 325. Wrote poetry and letters.

Arius Didymus

1st cent. B.C. Teacher of Augustus. Wrote a *Consolatio*

to Livia on the death of Drusus, and a doxographical work on Stoic and Peripatetic ethics.

Arrangement of Words, on

Title of a work by Dionysius of Halicarnassus (q.v.) Dealing with prose style, rhythm, structure, etc., it is of special importance because it preserves some beautiful portions of Sappho and Simonides.

Arrian (1) (Flavius Arrianus) of Bithynia, 2nd cent. A.D.

Pupil of Epictetus (q.v.) Works: *Discourses* and *Manual, Periplus* (Voyage around) the Black Sea, *Indike, Anabasis of Alexander, Cynegeticus, Alanike* (on tactics), history of the Diadochi. His style is simple and unadorned, for which he has been condemned by purists. His *Anabasis* is one of our best sources for the history of Alexander the Great, and the *Discourses* and *Manual (Enchiridion)* are important for the picture and teachings of the great Stoic teacher Epictetus.

Arrian

Mention should be made of the following:

Arrian (2) Wrote an epic poem on Alexander, and translated Vergil's Georgics into Greek.

Arrian (3) the Younger, a historian of the latter part of the 3rd cent.

Arrian (4) who wrote a work against astrology.

Arrius Antoninus

Grandfather of the emperor Antoninus Pius, who wrote Greek epigrams which reminded Pliny of Callimachus and Herodas.

Artapanus

A Jewish historian who lived in Egypt. Fragments of his history survive, dealing with Joseph, Abraham, and Moses (e.g. Abraham teaching Astronomy to the Egyptian Pharaoh,

Moses as the originator of Philosophy, art, hieroglyphics, and animal worship!)

Artemidorus (1)

A grammarian from Tarsus, in the 2nd-1st cent. B.C., who collected and edited the works of the Bucolic Poets.

Artemidorus (2)

Geographer from Ephesus, fl. ca. 100 B.C. who sailed around the Mediterranean, wrote books on geography, and calculated the length and width of the world.

Artemidorus (3)

Wrote a book on the interpretation of dreams, which is extant, also on divination and palmistry.

Other writers of the same name include:

(4) A writer of erotic elegies.

(5) An editor of the works of Hippocrates.

(6) An astrologer.

Artemis

Greek goddess of the forest and the chase; twin sister of Apollo. A virgin goddess, helper of women in childbirth. In mythology she often appears as a spiteful and vindictive goddess (cf. Actaeon, Iphigenia, etc.). She was frequently identified with Hecate and Selene.

Artemon

The following should be distinguished.

(1) 2nd cent. B.C. Edited the works of Aristotle.

(2) 2nd or 1st cent. B.C. of Cassandreia. Bibliographer. Possibly identical with (1).

(3) Wrote a commentary on Pindar. Sometimes identified with (2).

(4) 1st cent. A.D. Wrote a book on dreams that come true.

(5) Wrote a work on *Famous Deeds of Women.*

Ascension of Isaiah

See Apocalyptic Literature.

Asclepiades (1)

Student of Isocrates (4th cent. B.C.). Wrote a book on the myths of Greek Tragedy.

Asclepiades (2) fl 270 B.C.

Alexandrian epigrammatist. Ca 40 poems in the Anthology are his. Probably the first to introduce some of the common symbols (Eros the archer) into love-poetry. His poetry shows great imagination and tenderness. Influenced Callimachus and Horace. Also called Sicelidas.

Asclepiades (3) of Prusa (died ca 40 B.C.)

A physician and writer on medicine. Influential on later writers. Fragments survive.

Asclepiades (4) of Myrleia

Philologist and historian of the 1st cent. B.C. Wrote a history of Bithynia, and a history of scholarship, also on Homer, Theocritus, orthography, Pindar, Thucydides, etc.

Asclepiades (5) of Athens

Tragic poet of the 2nd century.

Asclepiades (6) of Mendes

Grammarian and historian in the time of Augustus. Wrote a work entitled *Theologoumena,* and probably also an *Aigyptiaka.*

The following should be distinguished:

(7) An Alexander-historian.

(8) A historian of Cyprus.

(9) A grammarian, from Nicaea.

(10) A pharmacologist.

Asclepiodotus

The following should be distinguished:

(1) A writer on tactics, 1st cent. B.C.

(2) Neoplatonic physician.

(3) Physician of the 5th cent. A.D.

Asclepius (Aesculapius)

God of medicine. In the *Iliad* he is a mortal, but in Hesiod and Pindar he is the son of Apollo. His cult was a popular one, including the ritual of incubation, and mingled faith healing and miracles with good therapeutic procedures (e.g. diet, baths, exercise). Hygeia (health) was his daughter.

Asianism

An emotional and flowery type of rhetoric (q.v.).

Asius of Samos

7th or 6th cent. B.C. Wrote genealogies, satirical hexameters, and elegiacs.

Aspasius

The following should be distinguished:

(1) A peripatetic who wrote on Aristotle's works.
(2) Wrote a commentary on Aeschines.
(3) of Byblus, Sophist.
(4) of Tyre, Sophist.

Aspis or, the Shield of Heracles

See Hesiod.

Assumption of Moses

See Apocalyptic Lit.

Asterius of Amaseia

Bishop of the 4th cent. A.D. Wrote speeches and sermons.

Astrology

After the death of Alexander, astrology became important. There was a huge mass of astrological literature, and some of the reputable astronomers (Hipparchus and Ptolemy) believed in it. See Schmid-Stählin and OCD for a complete listing.

Astronomia

A lost epic on the star-myths, ascribed to Hesiod.

Astronomy

See Thales, Anaximander, Pythagoras, Meton, Eudoxus, Aristarchus (1), Hipparchus, Eratosthenes, Theon (2) Posidonius, and especially Ptolemy. Aristarchus was the first to suggest a heliocentric theory. The most important names are Hipparchus and Ptolemy. The former was the first to make systematic use of trigonometry, improved the existing instruments, and discovered the Procession of the Equinoxes; the latter's great work, the *Syntaxis,* gave definite form to that of Hipparchus, dealt fully with the epicycle and eccentric hypotheses and formulated a theory about the motions of the planets. See Heath in OCD for a good discussion of the subject.

Astyanassa

Maidservant of Helen; legendary originator of pornographic literature (see anaischyntographoi).

Astyanax

In mythology, the son of Hector and Andromache. After the Fall of Troy he was thrown from the walls and killed by the Greeks, to prevent him from becoming another Hector. (See *Trojan Women*).

Astydamas

There were two Fourth Cent. poets of this name, father and son, and it is difficult to tell which is which. One of them, probably the son, wrote plays entitled *Hector, Alcmeon, Achilles, Athamas,* and *Antigone,* and was highly regarded. Only a few lines are preserved from the two.

Atalanta

In mythology, an extremely swift-footed maiden who would marry no one who could not outrun her. She was defeated in a footrace by Hippomenes (or Melanion) who got three golden apples from Aphrodite and threw them during the race. She was delayed by stopping to pick up the apples and so lost the race. Possibly identifiable with Artemis.

Ataraxia

State of calmness, freedom from emotional disturbance. Chief goal of the Epicureans.

Ate

Personification of moral blindness. Daughter of Zeus. The result of *Hybris,* punished by Nemesis. Hesiod makes her the daughter of Strife and sister of Lawlessness.

Athamas

In mythology, the son of Aeolus, and father of Phrixus and Helle. The former was brought by a golden-fleeced ram to Colchis; the latter fell off into the Hellespont, which was named after her. See Rose for fuller details (Handbook of Gk. Myth. or OCD).

Athanasius (1) 295-373

Bishop and patriarch of Alexandria. Was involved in the Arian heresy (on the nature of Christ) as its chief opponent. Most of his writings deal with this controversy: three books *Against the Arians,* two *Against the Pagans,* also a *Life of St. Anthony.* Many other works ascribed to him (two dialogues against the Macedonians, and the dialogues *On the Trinity*) are spurious.

Athanasius (2) of Alexandria

A Neoplatonist, who wrote commentaries on Aristides and Hermogenes.

Athena

Goddess of warfare, crafts, wisdom, and especially the goddess of Athens. Probably originally theriomorphic, as suggested by her epithet *glaukopis* (which may mean bright-eyed or owl-faced). She is always associated with owls. She was born, without a mother, from the head of Zeus. Even in Homer, she is a personification of wisdom, and regularly battles for her favorites (e.g. Achilles and Odysseus). Among the myths about her is the contest between her and Poseidon for the territory of Athens.

Athenaeus (1)

Fl. A.D. 200. Wrote the *Deipnosophistai* (Doctors at Dinner, or Experts on Dining, which is not quite the same). In 15 books, this work is a fascinating repository of all sorts of miscellaneous information: literature, law, philosophy, medicine, anecdotes, etc. Most important for the excerpts quoted from a large number of authors whose works are otherwise lost.

Athenaeus (2)

Author of an extant work on siege machinery (*peri Mechanematon*).

Athenaeus (3)

Physician in Rome under the Emperor Claudius (ca. 50 A.D.) Founder of the school of Pneumatists.

Athenaeus

Two others of the same name should be mentioned:

(4) A rhetor.

(5) A. of Seleucia, a Peripatetic philosopher.

Athenagoras of Athens

Christian philosopher and apologist of the 2nd cent. Wrote an *Appeal on Behalf of the Christians,* and a work *On the Resurrection.*

Athenaion Politeia

See *Constitution of Athens.*

Athenian Constitution

See Old Oligarch. *Constitution of Athens.*

Athens

The cultural center of Greece and of the world not only in the Fifth Century, or Age of Pericles, which produced such towering and varied men of genius as Aeschylus, Sophocles, Euripides, Thucydides, Socrates, Aristophanes, the Sophists, the architects and sculptors (e.g. Phidias, etc.); but also in the Fourth Century, when philosophy and rhetoric became the chief forms of literary activity (e.g. Plato, Aristotle, Demosthenes, Isocrates, etc.), and indeed until Justinian closed the schools there in the sixth cent. A.D. During the Roman period, Athens was the "University town" (the Academy, Lyceum and Stoa were located there), where young Romans were sent to school, and Athens generally maintained this position of intellectual supremacy during the whole of antiquity, though Alexandria and Rome eventually superseded her.

Atlantis

A mythological island near the Straits of Gibraltar. There have been many attempts to identify this island, which, however, is completely fictitious. The first example of a philosophical Utopia. Plato's *Critias* deals with its constitution.

Atlas

In mythology, the giant who held up the heavens. He was identified with the Atlas Mountains in N.W. Africa.

Atossa

Queen of Persia, who was supposed to have invented the art of letter-writing.

Atreus

In mythology, the son of Pelops. When his brother Thyestes seduced Aerope, his wife, Atreus served Thyestes' children to him at a banquet. This gave rise to the Curse on the House of Atreus, and the doom of Agamemnon, etc. treated by the tragedians (see *Oresteia, Electra, etc.*)

Atropos

One of the three Fates (q.v.).

Attaliates, Michael

Byzantine lawyer, statesman and author of the 11th cent. Wrote a compendium of law, a History of the years 1034-1079, and a Statute for the almshouse and cloister founded by him. Especially interesting is the list of books in the library of the cloister.

Atthis

A type of literature dealing with the history of Attica, containing information on chronology, mythology, cults, topography. Hellanicus' history was not really an *Atthis.* See Cleidemus, Androtion. Other atthidographers include Demon, Philochorus, Phanodemus, Aelanthius, Amelesagoras (?), and Ister.

Attic

The dialect of Attica. See Dialects.

Attic Orators

The ten chief orators of Athens: Antiphon, Andocides, Lysias, Isocrates, Isaeus, Lycurgus, Aeschines, Demosthenes, Hyperides, and Dinarchus. The origin of this "canon" is not known. See under the individual names.

Attica

The promontory or peninsula in Eastern Central Greece, consisting of Athens and the surrounding territory. It was said to have been fused into a single Athenian state by Theseus (q.v.). This fusion is called the *synoikismos.*

Atticism

Properly speaking, "Attic" in style. The term usually refers to the reversion to a simpler style than the over-florid "Asianism" (q.v.), and a doing away with much of the false and unnecessary ornamentation that had become characteristic of that style.

Atticus, Herodes

See Herodes Atticus.

Attis

See Cybele.

Auctor peri Hypsous

See "Longinus."

Aurelius, Marcus (121-180 A.D.)

Roman emperor 161-180. His *Meditations* were not meant for publication, but were a kind of private diary of Stoic reflections and admonitions to himself.

Autarkeia

"Self-sufficiency," the goal of the Cynics (q.v.).

Autocrates

Athenian writer of Old Comedy. Suidas said he wrote tragedies too.

Autolycus of Pitane

Astronomer and mathematician, fl. ca. 300 B.C. His is the earliest mathematical book that has come down to us (*On the Moving Sphere*). He also wrote *On Risings and Settings*. He criticized Eudoxus' theory of concentric spheres.

Automedon

3rd cent. B.C. (?) writer of epigrams.

Axiochus

A pseudoplatonic work of the 1st cent. B.C.

Axionicus

A writer of Middle Comedy. Wrote a play entitled *Phileuripides* (The Euripides-lover).

Axiopistus

A Hellenistic poet, recognized in antiquity to be the author of some verses falsely attributed to Epicharmus.

B

Babrius, Valerius (?)

Probably 2nd cent. Composed *Mythiamboi Aisopeioi* (Choliambic versions of "Aesop's" fables, plus some original ones). The collection, in simple everyday Greek, enjoyed great popularity.

Babylonica

See Iamblichus.

Bacchae, the

Possibly the last, and certainly the greatest of Euripides' plays. Pentheus, the king of Thebes, refuses to accept the cult of Dionysus, in spite of the warnings of Cadmus and Tiresias. He imprisons the young Lydian Stranger (who may not be the god himself) and cuts off a lock of his hair. In his lack of *sophrosyne* and his moral blindness and self-righteousness he is the true tragic or Aristotelian hero. The god's vengeance is swift and terrible. Pentheus is hypnotized into putting on woman's dress and going into the mountains to watch the rites of the worshippers of Dionysus (who are led by his own mother, Agave). They in turn are hypnotized into believing that Pentheus is a lion, and they tear him to pieces. The scene in which Agave enters, bearing her son's head, and gradually comes to the realization of what she has done, is probably unrivalled for sheer horror. The chorus of Maenads give the play its name, and they emphasize the rapturous aspects of the Dionysiac religion, as the fate of Pentheus and Agave shows its destructive force. The play is not, as some have thought, an "attack" on religion, any more than it is a "defence" of it. It merely points out that this ecstatic form of worship has beneficent and ruinous aspects, without any moral judgment. Unfortunately, there is a large lacuna at the end of the play, and so we do not know whether the Dionysus who appears at the end is the same as the "Lydian Stranger." Many people think he is, and the present editor is of their number.

Baccheius

There were two writers of this name:

(1) A physician.

(2) Baccheius Geron, who wrote an *Introduction to Music,* ca. 300 A.D.

Bacchus

See Dionysus.

Bacchylides

Lyric poet of the 5th cent. B.C., nephew of the poet Simonides. We have remains of 14 epinician odes and dithyrambs. He also wrote hymns, paeans, hyporchemata, maiden-songs, etc. He has always suffered by comparison to Pindar, although his poems, considered by themselves, contain many portions of real beauty and clarity.

Bacis

Either one person or (more probably) a generic term for a class of inspired prophets.

Balsamon, Theodore

Byzantine jurist and Patriarch of Antioch under Manuel I. He was responsible for the compilation of canon law, *Exegesis Canonum* ca. 1175.

Barbucalus, Joannes

Epigrammatist of the middle of the 6th cent. A.D.

Bardas, Caesar

Byzantine scholar who reëstablished the University of Constantinople in the 9th cent. He was regent for his nephew Michael III ("The Drunkard").

Bardesanes

A Syrian Gnostic (q.v.).

Barlaam and Josaphet

Great Byzantine novel, of Indian origin, fusing Buddhist and Christian theology. One of the most popular works of the Middle Ages. Attributed to John of Damascus.

Barnabas, Epistle of

Originated in Alexandria ca. 130 A.D. Once included in the New Testament. Anti-Jewish in sentiment (i.e. doing away with the obligations of the Mosaic Law).

Baruch Book(s) of

Four different pseudepigraphical works were attributed to this figure. They date from the 1st and 2nd centuries A.D. See Apocrypha, O. T. Baruch was the companion of Jeremiah.

Basil (330-379) the Great

Theologian and defender of the Church against the Arian heresy. It was he, more than any other single person, who gave Eastern orthodoxy its permanent form. Wrote treatises *On the Holy Ghost,* Sermons *on the Creation, the Judgment of God, on Faith,* letters, etc. Other works, e.g. sermons on the Psalms, may not be genuine.

Basil I, Byzantine Emperor 867-86

Had the Roman law translated into Greek. First published the *Procheiros Nomos,* then a revised handbook, the *Epanagoge,* which was completed by his son Leo VI in the form of the *Basilica.* Basil also wrote two books of exhortations to his son, on humility, almsgiving, education, courage, chastity, etc.

Basilica

The Chief book of Byzantine state law. Compiled from Justinian's *Codex* and *Novella.* Begun under Basil I, finished under his son Leo VI.

Bassarica

A Dionysiac epic written in the Roman period. Some fragments remain.

Baths of Pallas

Title of a work by Callimachus (q.v.) on the devotées of Athena.

Baton (1) of Sinope

Historian who wrote on Attic history, and on Ion of Chios.

Baton (2)

A New Comedy poet.

Batrachoi

See *Frogs* (Aristophanes).

Batrachomyomachia

(*The Battle of the Frogs and Mice)* Title of an extant parody of Homer written ca. 500 B.C. but with some much later interpolations. Attributed to one Pigres (q.v.). The war breaks out because a frog has drowned a mouse. The gods at first remain neutral, but Zeus finally sends a host of crabs to defeat the mice. Mouse-heroes are called Tyrophagus, Leichopinax, and Psicharpax (Cheese-eater, Plate-licker, Crumb-Snatcher), and the frog-champions have such names as Borborocoites and Physignathus (Mud-wallower and Cheek-puffer).

Battle of the Cats and Mice

Hexameter poem by Prodromus (q.v.).

Baucis

See Philemon, Erinna.

Beccus, John

Byzantine polemicist of the 13th cent. First he wrote against the Latins, but then, the politics of Michael Paleologus caused him to veer around and he wrote on the Union of the Eastern and Western Churches. This he did by reconciling the teachings of the old Greek Fathers (e.g. Athanasius, the Cappadocians, Chrysostomus, Cyril of Alexandria, et al.) with the Latin dogma.

Bed of Procrustes

See Procrustes.

Belisarius-Romance

Three versions exist. Belisarius, the great general of Justinian, is probably the most romantic figure since Alexander the Great. His life is a story of victories and conquests (Vandals, Italy, Persia), but eventually B. fell into disfavor with Justinian and the hero's downfall resulted. The three versions are all in verse, the first, in 556 unrhymed 15-syllable ("political") lines; the second, by the Rhodian poet Emannuel Georgillas Limenites, in 840 lines, mostly unrhymed; the third, in 997 rhymed political verses.

Bellerophon (Bellerophontes)

In mythology. First mentioned in the Iliad, where he is called Bellerophontes. One story about him concerns Stheneboea (or Anteia), the wife of king Proetus, who tried to tempt him, and upon his refusal, told the king that B. had tried to seduce her. (Cf. Hippolytus, Acastus, etc.) B. was then sent to Lycia with a letter asking for his execution. First he had to fight the Chimaera and the Amazons. Later he accomplished various tasks with the aid of the winged horse Pegasus.

Belthandrus and Chrysantza

A Byzantine verse-romance in 1348 "political" verses, dating from the 12th or 13th cent. The usual romantic story of wanderings, escapes, miracles, and happy ending. (Krumbacher)

Bemarchius of Caesarea (4th cent.)

Wrote a history of Constantine in ten books.

Berenice

Subject of a mock-epic by Callimachus, the *Lock of Berenice,* similar in subject and tone to Pope's *Rape of the Lock.* We know it from the translation of Catullus (#66).

Berosus (or Berossus)

Priest of Bel who wrote a history of Babylon in three books. The first concerns mythology rather than history (it covers a period of 432,000 years and ends with the Flood); the work ends with the death of Alexander.

Besantinus

See Figure-Poems.

Bessarion, Johannes

Byzantine scholar of the 15th cent. (ca. 1395-1472). Translated the Greek philosophers into Latin, and is chiefly responsible for the West's knowledge of Plato and Aristotle. Also wrote works on theology, on Union with the Latins, exegetical works, etc. His collection of books became the nucleus of the library of St. Mark's in Venice.

Bestiaries

Animal stories were a popular form in Byzantine literature. Cf. *Physiologus, Diegesis Paidiophrastos ton Tetrapodon Zoon* (Children's Animal Stories), *Pulologos* (Stories about birds), *Poricologos* (about fruits), etc. Many of them were written in Vulgar Greek.

Bias of Priene

One of the Seven Sages. Fl. ca. 550 B.C.

Bible

See Septuagint, New Testament, *Koine,* Gospels, etc. The Septuagint is the Greek translation of the Hebrew Scriptures (39) books, and the early Christians added their own writings (Gospels, Epistles, Acts) beginning as early as 50 A.D.

Bibliotheca

See Photius, Diodorus Siculus, Apollodorus (5).

Biography

Prior to the existence of biography as a genre, Isocrates and Xenophon had written biographical works (*Evagoras* and *Memorabilia*). Ion of Chios and Stesimbrotus wrote on contemporary figures. The works of Plato give biographical data about Socrates. Theophrastus and Aristoxenus, Duris, Idomeneus, Neanthes, Chamaeleon, Antigonus of Carystus, and others (qq.v.) all wrote biographies of one kind or another. Later practitioners include Plutarch, Polybius, Philostratus, and Diogenes Laertius. Numerous Byzantine historians and chroniclers also provide examples (e.g. Symeon Metaphrastes, Leontius, Theodore Studites, et al.). See under the individual names.

Bion (1) (or Euaion?)

Son of Aeschylus (?) who wrote tragedies.

Bion (2) the Borysthenite (ca 325-ca 255 B.C.)

Studied in the Academy and Peripatos, also influenced by the Cynic school, but followed no one particular school of philosophy. His writings are said to have influenced Roman satire, and were eclectic.

Bion (3) Fl. ca 100 B.C.

Bucolic poet. 17 fragments are preserved. Some are erotic, some pastoral. He has been credited with the *Lament for Adonis,* a poem in 98 hexameters.

Biottus (2nd cent. B.C.)

Comic poet. His play *Poietes* was produced in 168-7 B.C. No fragments.

Birds, the

One of the most delightful comedies of Aristophanes (q.v.). Produced in 414 B.C. Plot is as follows: Two Athenians, Peithetaerus and Euelpides, who are disgusted with the corruption and litigation in Athens, found a new city midway between earth and heaven, called Nephelococcygia (Cloudcuckooland), which blocks the sacrificial fumes from reaching the gods and causes them to capitulate. The chorus of birds have some beautiful lyrics, and there are some very funny comic characters (Tereus, the Hoopoe, formerly a man, now a bird), Meton the astronomer, and a host of nuisances (oracle-monger, parricide, informer, dithyrambic poet, etc.) who all try to get in on the ground floor, so to speak, and are driven off. The embassy from Zeus consists of Hercules, Poseidon, and a non-Greek-speaking foreign god, Triballos. The play thus contains the usual elements of farce, satire, slapstick, obscenity, topical humor, and lovely poetry.

Biton (3rd-2nd cent. B.C.)

Author of an extant work on siege-machinery, and a (lost) work on optics.

Blaesus (2nd or 1st cent B.C. ?)

Wrote works called *Spoudogeloia* which may have been something like the Manippean Satires.

Blastares, Matthew

Byzantine monk, wrote a *Syntagma Canonum* in 1335.

Blemmydes, Nicephorus (ca. 1197-1272)

Tutor of the prince, later a monk in the cloister of Ephesus which he built. His autobiography or memoirs are extremely valuable for the picture they give us of contemporary politics and church happenings. Also wrote a *Mirror for Princes* and poetry, as well as a handbook of logic and physics, and various works dealing with philosophy, theology, geography, rhetoric, etc.

Boeotia

Although this district was supposedly famous for producing stupid, slow, uncreative people ("Boeotian pig" was a familiar epithet), it produced, among others, Pindar and Hesiod, two poets of the first rank.

Boethus of Sidon

There were two philosophers of this name, from the same city. (1) The first was a pupil of Diogenes of Babylon in the 2nd cent. B.C. and was especially interested in astronomy (wrote a commentary on Aratus' *Phaenomena*) and meteorology. In philosophy he was a Stoic, but not an orthodox one.

(2) The second was a Peripatetic philosopher of the age of Augustus who wrote commentaries on Aristotle.

Boio

A Delphic priestess, who was supposed to have written a work entitled *Ornithogonia* or transformations into various birds. Date unknown.

Bolus

Egyptian writer of works on miracles and magic, in the 3rd or 2nd cent. B.C. See Paradoxographers.

Book of Jubilees

See Pseudepigrapha.

Books

All through the classical and Hellenistic periods, books were made of papyrus rolls glued together, and written in columns. Many of these have been found in Egypt, where the aridity of the climate helped preserve them. Parchment or vellum is supposed to have been invented at Pergamum ca. 200 B.C. but was not in common use before the 4th cent.

A.D. Our earliest and best vellum MSS (Codices), the Vatican and Sinaitic Codices of the Greek Bible, come from the 4th cent.

Botany

See Aristotle, Theophrastus, Crateuas, Dioscorides, *Rhizotomikon.*

Briseis

The concubine of Achilles in Homer's *Iliad* (q.v.). Agamemnon's taking her away from Achilles started the great quarrel on which the whole plot of the *Iliad* turns. As part of the reconciliation she was returned.

Bryennius, Nicephorus (1062-1137)

Son-in-law of the emperor Alexius, husband of Anna Comnena (q.v.). Led the defense of Constantinople against Godfrey de Bouillon in 1097. Wrote a history of the years 1070-79.

Bryson

A Sophist, best known for his attempt to square the circle.

Bucephalus

("Ox-head") The beloved horse of Alexander the Great. It died in 326 B.C. and he built the town of Bucephala to commemorate it.

Bucolica

Pastoral poetry. See Theocritus, Moschus, Bion.

Busiris

In mythology, an Egyptian king who killed all foreigners. He in turn was slain by Heracles. Herodotus, Euripides, and others mention him.

Byzantine Literature

In the field of literature, the Byzantines were not nearly so spontaneous as they were in art. Language difficulties (i.e. the distinction between the classical, the Romaic or Demotic, and the learned Greek) constantly stood in the way of development. The classical tradition was never lost, however, as the libraries of Photius and Bessarion reveal. The savants of Byzantium read and knew all the classical authors, and, indeed, Greek literature was the basis of Byzantine education. The whole of Byzantine society was permeated with the classical spirit. On the other hand, the Christian tradition was equally strong.

The chief forms of literature were as follows: *History* (In all periods there were Byzantine historians, and some very good ones, too: e.g. Procopius, Psellus, Nicetas, Bryennius, Anna Comnena, Constantine Porphyrogenitus, Acropolites, John Cantacuzenus, and others too numerous to mention here); and the closely allied field of *Chronicles* (cf. Malalas, Symeon Magister, Glycas, Skylitzes, et al.) *Theology* (always a favorite subject with the Byzantines; the list is long, but see, e.g. Maximus the Confessor, John of Damascus, Acominatus, Bessarion, Photius, Arethas, Psellus, etc.); *Philosophy* (Psellus, Italus, Gennadius, Bessarion, etc.); *Rhetoric* (Photius, Psellus, and many others). It will be noticed that the same names appear under several headings. Indeed, many of the Byzantines were extremely versatile men, excelling in history, rhetoric, science, poetry, theology, etc. In the field of *Poetry* the lack of creativity is naturally more apparent, except in the field of hymnology (cf. *Acathistus*, Romanus). The favorite metrical form was the 15-syllable "political" verse, with the epigram a close second. One really fine epic (or chanson de geste) was produced: *Diogenes Akritas* (q.v.). In drama, the only significant item is the *Christos Paschon* (*Christus Patiens*). In *Philology* some important names are Photius, Suidas, Arethas, Eustathius, Planudes, Psellus, Tzetzes, and Moschopolus. In addition there were writers on medicine (e.g. Alexander Tralles), military tactics (e.g. Leon the Isaurian), and other subjects. Generally, the 5th and 6th centuries represented one high point, full of Classical influence, followed by about three centuries of Dark Ages, with a renaissance in the 10th, 11th, and 12th centuries. The *Greek Anthology* was compiled at Constantinople (see *Anthology,* Agathias, Planudes, Cephalas). *Miscellaneous works:* accounts of monuments, commentaries, dialogues, novels or romances, children's animal stories, and innumerable collections of letters. For full account, Krumbacher is still indispensable, but books on Byz. Civilization (e.g. Diehl, Runciman) are useful.

Byzantium

Founded in 667 B.C. Named New Rome in 330 A.D., but the name was quickly changed to Constantinople, after its "founder," Constantine.

C

Cabasilas, Neilus

Metropolitan of Thessalonica in the 14th cent. Theological and polemical writer. Wrote on the *Procession of the Holy Ghost.*

Cabasilas, Nicholas

Byzantine theologian and mystic of the 14th century (d. 1371). Probably the last of the important Byzantine mystics. Wrote 7 books on the *Life of Christ.*

Cabiri

Phrygian deities sometimes confused with the Dioscuri (q.v.)

Cadmus (1)

In mythology, the founder of the city of Thebes. He killed a dragon and sowed its teeth behind him. These turned into armed warriors whom he then set to fighting against each other. The five who survived were the ancestors of the Theban nobility. His children were Ino, Semele, Autonoë, and Agave. Cadmus is supposed to have introduced the art of writing into Greece.

Cadmus (2) of Miletus

An early logographer (q.v.) who wrote one of the first collections of town-histories.

Caecilius of Calacte

A rhetorician at Rome during the Augustan Age. Wrote

a work on the Ten Attic Orators, on history, a *techne,* on figures, on Asianism, etc.

Caelo, de

Aristotle's treatise on astronomy.

Calchas

Chief soothsayer for the Greeks at Troy. In Homer's *Iliad.*

Calecas, Manuel

Byzantine theologian of the 14th century, who wrote on the Hesychasts, and on the Procession of the Holy Ghost.

Callias (1)

Athenian comic playwright, victorious in 446 B.C. Probably not the same as Callias (2) who wrote a *Grammatike tragodia.*

Callias (2)

Wrote a history of Agathocles of Syracuse in 22 books.

Callicles, Nicholas

Byzantine professor of medicine and poet, ca. 1200 A.D. Wrote a dialogue between a stranger and the grave; and various epigrams and epitaphs.

Callimachus of Cyrene (ca. 304-240 B.C.)

One of the most important writers of later antiquity; certainly the greatest of the Alexandrian poets. His longest and most famous poem: the *Aitia* (q.v.) Other works include: *Acontius and Cydippe,* the *Lock of Berenice, Pollis' Banquet, Iambi,* the *Ibis,* Hymns to Zeus, Apollo, etc., a *Funeral Ode for Arsinoe,* and *epyllia* (e.g. the *Hecale).* In addition, he wrote tragedies, comedies, satyr-plays, and prose (encyclopedias on nymphs, birds, games, winds, rivers, etc.), a *Chronological List of the Athenian Dramatists,* and numerous other works. He was as learned as he was prolific. From the translations and reconstructions by Catullus and Ovid of some of his works, we can form a fairly good idea of their contents and style. According to Suidas, he wrote over 800 works. His writings are always characterized by versatility, grace, originality, erudition, and good taste.

Callimachus and Chrysorrhoe

A Byzantine romantic poem in 2607 unrhymed "political" verses. About a king with three sons, all of whom have to perform heroic deeds. Callimachus slays a dragon and frees the maiden Chrysorrhoe. The story contains all the stuff of the genre, mysterious ailments, magicians, magic golden apples, and a happy ending for the good, the reverse for the wicked.

Callinicus of Petra

Historian of the Second Sophistic. Left various rhetorical and historical writings (on bad imitations, on Alexandria, etc.).

Callinus of Ephesus

Elegiac poet of the 7th cent. B.C. One famous long fragment is a call to arms, directed to a group of young men at a feast.

Calliope

See Muses.

Callippus

A great astronomer who proposed a 76-year cycle to correct the 19-year cycle of Meton (q.v.).

Callisthenes of Olynthus

(1) The nephew of Aristotle, who wrote works of history, and works about Alexander (by whom he was later executed for conspiracy). His writings included *Hellenica* and the *Deeds of Alexander.*

(2) To be distinguished from the later author (unknown date) who wrote, under the name of Callisthenes, one of the

earliest versions of the *Alexander Romance,* which had a vast influence on medieval literature.

Callistratus

The following are to be distinguished:

(1) A grammarian, pupil of Aristophanes of Byzantium. Edited Homer, wrote commentaries on Pindar, Euripides, Sophocles, comic poets, etc.

(2) Sophist of the 3rd or 4th cent. A.D. Wrote descriptions of statues.

(3) A comic poet (?) under whose name Aristophanes produced three early plays.

(4) An epic poet.

Callixenus of Rhodes

Fl. 155 B.C. wrote *Peri Alexandreias.*

Calypso

In mythology, the nymph who received Odysseus and kept him on her island for seven years. Though she promised to make him immortal if he would stay, he refused, and so (on Zeus' command) she sent him away, helping him to build a raft. (*Od.* V)

Camaterus, Andronicus

Byzantine polemicist of the 12th cent. At the request of the Emperor Manuel Comnenus he wrote a "Holy Arsenal" (*Hiera Hoplotheke*), as a companion-piece to the *Panoply* of Zigabenus (q.v.). The polemics are mostly directed against the Latins and Armenians.

Camaterus, John

12th cent. Byzantine clergyman and poet, author of two didactic poems on astrology.

Cameniates, John

Byzantine priest who wrote a description of his adventures at the sack of Thessalonica by the Saracens in 904.

Described as "a well-written vivid, and terrible story, coming from an opinionated and ignorant priest." (Runciman)

Canabutzes, John

A Grecized Italian from Chios who wrote, in the first half of the 15th century, an addition to Dionysius of Halicarnassus, which dealt with Greek migrations to Italy, the origin of the arts and sciences, jurisprudence, chemistry, metallurgy, etc. Useful for late Greek vocabulary, place-names, superstitions, etc.

Canon

In Alexandrian times, a popular form of endeavor was the establishment of Canons, or official lists, e.g. the canon of the Ten Attic Orators. Such lists were made of poets, prose writers, historians, iambographers, New Comedy writers, lyric poets, the Second Sophistic, the books of the Old Testament and later of the New Testament, etc.

Canones

Type of religious poetry inaugurated by Andreas of Crete (q.v.). Consists of lyrics of various meters, all strung together into one long work.

Cantacuzenus, John

See John Cantacuzenus.

Cantharus

Athenian comic poet who won the victory in 422 B.C. One of his plays was entitled the *Symmachia* and apparently dealt with the ostracism of Hyperbolus.

Cappadocians, the

See Basil the Great, Gregory of Nyssa, Gregory of Nazianzus.

Capture of Oechalia

A lost poem in the Epic Cycle (q.v.), attributed to either Homer or Creophylus.

Carcinus (1)

A tragic poet, lampooned by Aristophanes. Thucydides mentions a general by this name, and the two may well be identical.

Carcinus (2)

Grandson of the above. Also a tragic poet. It is said that he wrote 160 plays and won 11 victories. Aristotle mentions his recognition scene (*Thyestes*). He was known for his obscurity. Titles include: *Amphiaraus, Alope, Oedipus, Aerope, Medea, Orestes.*

Carcinus (3) of Naupactus

Epic poet of the 7th or 6th cent. B.C., who wrote (?) the *Naupactia* (Catalogue of famous women).

Carmina Figurata

See *Technopaegnia,* Figure-poems.

Carneades (ca. 214-128 B.C.)

Founder of the New Academy; the greatest systematic figure in ancient scepticism. Won great fame in Greece and Rome. No writings.

Carneiscus

An Epicurean of the 3rd-2nd cent. B.C. Author of a work on friendship (*Philistas*).

Carpocrates

Middle of the 2nd cent. Platonist and Gnostic (q.v.).

Carpus of Antiocheia (1)

Astronomer and writer on mechanics.

(2) There was another Carpus who was the author of a *Martyrium.*

Casia

The only really important Byzantine poetess. A nun who lived in the 9th cent., wrote both hymns and epigrams (on friendship, happiness, beauty, wealth, etc.). Distinguished by great originality, beauty, and feeling.

Cassandra

Trojan prophetess (also called Alexandra), daughter of Priam. Given the gift of prophecy by Apollo, she was then given the further gift of never being believed. In Homer she is *not* represented as possessed of prophetic powers; the first author who mentions them is Pindar. Aeschylus, in the *Agamemnon,* describes her death at the hands of Clytemnestra. In later authors (e.g. Vergil) she prophesies the fall of Troy and warns against the Wooden Horse. See *Oresteia,* Lycophron.

Cassius Dio

See Dio Cassius.

Cassius Dionysius of Utica

1st cent. B.C. Wrote a Greek translation of the work on agriculture by the Carthaginian Mago (88 B.C.); also a *Rhizotomika.*

Cassius Longinus

See Longinus.

Cassius "Iatrosophistes"

Author of medical works (Difficult cures, Problems, etc.) not earlier than the 3rd cent. A.D.

Castor and Pollux

See Dioscuri.

Castor of Rhodes

Rhetor, and author of *Chronika* (tables of Greek, Roman and Oriental history) which were used by later historians.

Castorion of Soli

Author of a *Hymn to Pan* (end of the 4th cent. B.C.). The hymn is in iambic trimeter, each dipody ending with a whole word.

Catalexis

The omission of a syllable at the end of a (trochaic) line. The most common use of this is in the Trochaic Tetrameter Catalectic, as in the familiar: "In the spring a young man's fancy / Lightly turns to thoughts of love."

Catalogue of Ships

A portion of Book II of the *Iliad* giving a catalogue of the Greek and Trojan forces at Troy. (T. W. Allen's *Homeric Catalogue of Ships* deals with this.)

Catalogue of Women

See Hesiod, *Ehoiai.*

Categories

See Aristotle. A discussion of the ten classes into which all predicables are to be divided.

Catenae

A collection (chain) of excerpts from ecclesiastical writings (exegetical, dogmatic, ascetic, etc.) usually from some individual viewpoint. So called because the excerpts form links in a chain. A favorite Byzantine form. (See Krumbacher)

Catharsis

A purging of the emotions of pity and terror, said by Aristotle to be one of the chief functions of tragedy (See *Poetics*).

Catholic Epistles

James I & II, Peter I-III, John and Jude; so-called because they are not addressed to a single church, but have a more general (catholic) destination.

Cavasilas

See Cabasilas.

Cabes

One of Socrates' pupils. The extant dialogue (*Kebetos*

Thebaiou Pinax) seems to have been ascribed to him by mistake. It dates probably from the 1st cent. A.D. and is an eclectic work, with Platonic, Aristotelian and Stoic overtones.

Cecaumenus

A professional soldier and historian (Byzantine) who wrote, in the 11th cent., a work on military tactics. It is full of anecdotes and advice from his own and others' experience.

Cecrops

Mythical first king of Athens. Said to have instituted monogamy, burial, writing, etc.

Cedrenus, George

Byzantine historian of the 12th cent. Wrote a *World Chronicle* from the Creation to 1057. The last 2½ centuries, however, are a repetition of the chronicle of Skylitzes.

Celaeno

See Harpies.

Celsus (1)

An Academic philosopher who wrote the first comprehensive polemic against Christianity (ca. 180 A.D.), called the *Alethes Logos*. Most of this is quoted in Origen's *Contra Celsum*. It was much used by Neoplatonics.

Celsus

Several others of the name are to be mentioned:

(2) A physician and medical writer.

(3) An Epicurean philosopher.

(4) Grammarian of Antiocheia, pupil of Libanius.

(5) A lyric poet.

Centaurs

In mythology, creatures with the upper part of a man, the lower part of a horse. Possible symbols of the wildness of water, possibly from the Thessalian horse-breeders (presumably, people who had never seen a man on horseback before might think the two were one). Individual myths concern Nessus and Chiron (qq.v.) the former a wicked, the latter a benign, centaur. They are usually barbaric, lustful, and bibulous. They occur very early in art and literature.

Cento

A literary patchwork made up of verses from existing works. Usually but not always humorous. Aristophanes uses it *(Peace* and *Frogs),* and Lucian mentions a funny song made up of excerpts from Pindar, Hesiod and Anacreon. Homeric centos (*Homerokentrones*) were popular in Byzantine times (See Eudocia).

Cephalas, Constantine

Compiled the Palatine Anthology (q.v.) in the 10th cent.

Cephalion

Rhetor of the time of Hadrian. Wrote a history in nine books, each named after one of the Muses, in imitation of Herodotus.

Cephisodorus (1)

Old Comedy writer, ca. 400 B.C. One play, the *Antilais,* lampooned a hetaera named Lais.

Cephisodorus (2)

A pupil of Isocrates, who wrote a history of the Sacred War, and a treatise against Aristotle.

Cerberus

The dog who guarded the entrance to the underworld. There was no general agreement about the number of his heads (Hesiod says 50; Euripides says three). Heracles captured him, showed him to Eurystheus, and then returned him to Hades.

Cercidas of Megalopolis (ca. 290-ca. 220 B.C.)

Cynic philosopher and poet. Only nine tiny fragments survive. His best-known work was the *Meliambi,* poems of a lyrical-satirical nature. He was also known as a lawgiver and politician.

Cercopes

A mock- or parody-epic in which people were turned into monkeys.

Cercops of Miletus

Epic poet of the 6th cent. B.C. (?) to whom the *Aegimius* was attributed.

Ceremonies, Book of

A work by the Byzantine emperor Constantine VII Porphyrogenitus. It is a handbook of protocol and court etiquette, of great length (ca. 800 pp.) and minute detail, and is of considerable importance for the cultural history of the Byzantine empire.

Cerinthus

One of the earliest of the Gnostics, ca. 100 A.D. It may be that the heresy denounced in the 1st Epistle of John was that of Cerinthus.

Cerularius, Michael

Patriarch of Constantinople 1043-58. Repudiated the claim of Pope Leo IX to the universal leadership of Christendom, and thus brought about the Great Schism (between East and West) of 1054.

Chaeremon (1)

Tragic poet of the 4th cent. B.C. Wrote *Centaur* and *Oeneus.*

Chaeremon (2)

Stoic, teacher of Nero. Wrote on grammar, history, astronomy.

Chaerephon

Friend and disciple of Socrates. In the *Apology* the story

is told of his going to the oracle at Delphi and learning that Socrates was the wisest of men. None of his works have survived.

Chaeris

Pupil of Aristarchus. Wrote on Homer, Pindar, Aristophanes, and a *techne grammatike*. All are lost.

Chalcocondyles (also called Chalcondyles)

These two writers should be distinguished:

(1) Byzantine historian (Laonicus). Wrote, in ten books, the history of the years 1298-1463. Important for the development of the Turkish power.

(2) His brother Demetrius is important for his edition of the *Iliad*.

Chamaeleon

A Peripatetic of unknown date (shortly after Aristotle). Wrote on drama, satyr-plays, Sophocles, Euripides, *Protrepticus,* on the gods, etc.

Characters

Work by Theophrastus (q.v.). Consists of 30 sketches of typical people, each with some vice or foible. Often very witty and satirical.

Charax of Pergamon

Author of a World History in 60 books. Also wrote *Chronica* and *Hellenica*. Date unknown.

Chareas and Callirhoe

See Chariton.

Chares

Three authors of this name are to be distinguished:

(1) Commentator on Apollonius.

(2) Writer of *Gnomai* or proverbs.

(3) Ch. of Mytilene, who wrote a history of Alexander the Great.

Charites

The Graces: Thaleia, Auxo, Kale, Euphrosyne, Aglaia, etc. Daughters of Zeus, but with various mothers. Their numbers vary, sometimes three, sometimes more. Also, title of a work by Theocritus.

Chariton

Author of a novel: *Chaereas* and *Callirhoe,* the earliest Greek novel. Chaereas searches for his wife Callirhoe, is captured, escapes, etc. Rhetorical style, happy ending.

Charmides

Title of a dialogue by Plato (q.v.).

Charon

(1) The ferryman of Hades.

(2) of Lampsacus, historian, author of *Hellenica, Persica, Journey Beyond the Pillars of Heracles, Magistrates of Lacedaemon.*

Charybdis

A whirlpool or maelstrom (Straits of Messina). Odysseus had to sail between this and Scylla (q.v.). Proverbially, any great danger.

Children of Heracles

See *Heracleidae.*

Children's Songs

Paidiai, songs and games (e.g. Blind Man's Buff, Prisoner's Base, etc.). Quoted by Julius Pollux.

Chiliades

See Tzetzes, Johannes.

Chilon

One of the "Seven Sages." A Spartan ephor 556/5 B.C.

Chimaera

A monster, part lion, part goat, part serpent. Killed by Bellerophon.

Chionides

One of the earliest comic poets. Titles: *Heroes, Ptochoi* (?), *Persai* or *Assyrioi.*

Chiron (Cheiron)

Wisest of the Centaurs. Teacher of Achilles, Jason, Asclepius. Accidentally killed by Heracles.

Choephori (Libation-Bearers)

The second play in Aeschylus' *Oresteia* trilogy. The title is taken from the chorus of Trojan slaves. In this play, Orestes returns, is recognized by his sister Electra, and after a long, lyrical chant (*commos*), they go about the business of the play, viz. the murder of Clytemnestra and Aegisthus. At the end of the play, Orestes begins to have hallucinations in which he sees the Furies. The material in this play was also dealt with in the *Electras* of Sophocles and Euripides. Especially effective is the *Stichomythia* between Oerstes and Clytemnestra, just before the murder.

Choerilus

(1) of Samos. Epic poet, friend of Herodotus.

(2) of Iasos, epic poet, contemporary of Alexander. Known as a bad poet.

(3) An early Athenian tragic poet. Only one title is known: the *Alope.*

Choeroboscus, George

Byzantine grammarian, of uncertain date. Wrote on orthography, etc.

Choerosphactes, Leo

Byz. Ambassador of the Ninth Century. His *letters* are of great importance for the picture of his times.

Choliambics (or Scazons)

See Meter. A line of five iambic feet and one trochee. As if Antony had said: "I come to bury Caesar, not to praise *Brutus.*"

Choregus

"Producer" of plays or dithyrambs at Athens. A form of tax (leitourgia) imposed on wealthy citizens. On his liberality a good deal of the success of the play depended. The choregus won a prize if the play was successful.

Choricius of Gaza

Pupil of Procopius, sophist and rhetor. Wrote Declamations, etc.

Chorizontes

Those who believe the *Iliad* and *Odyssey* were by different authors. See Homeric Question.

Chortasmenus, Ignatius

Byzantine scholar of unknown date. Wrote a commentary on the *Progymnasmata* of Aphthonius.

Chortatzes, George

See *Erophile.*

Chorus

An essential element of Greek drama. The chorus might take a more or less active part in the play (In Aeschylus, for example, they are usually actively involved in the plot, e.g. *Suppliants, Eumenides;* in Euripides, they are usually bystanders, and sometimes embarrassing ones, though on occasion, even Euripides used an integrated chorus, e.g. *Bacchae, Troades*). The chorus had the following functions: to act as a link between the drama and the audience, to act as the sounding-board of public opinion, or the Ideal Spectator; to provide a lull in the action, to provide necessary exposition; as a mouthpiece for the ideas and philosophy of the author; to give actors time to change costumes and parts.

All these, however, are ancillary to the chief function of the chorus: to enhance the total aesthetic effect of the drama with its lyrics, chanting, movement; to provide the "melody" and "spectacle" that Aristotle calls the "pleasurable accessories" of the play. The play is often named after the chorus (*Choephori, Eumenides, Trachiniae, Bacchae, Troades,* etc.). In comedy, the chief purpose of the chorus is to provide lyrical beauty. Most of the extant comedies of Aristophanes are named after the chorus (*Frogs, Wasps, Clouds, Birds, Acharnians, Knights,* etc.). In New Comedy, the chorus is nearly always divorced from the action, and finally it disappears altogether.

The chorus sings the odes that form the break between the episodes; the leader of the chorus may also speak as an individual; and they take part in the commos (lamentation) in concert with one or more characters. According to one authority (Kitto, *Gk. Tragedy)* the so-called unities are due to the necessity of the chorus' dispersing at the end of the day, hence, when there is no such necessity (e.g. Eumenides), the "unities" are freely violated. The tragic chorus numbered 12 or 15; the comic chorus 24 (two semi-choruses).

Chreia
A collection of witty or useful sayings. Theocritus (2), Demetrius of Phalerum, Machon (qq.v.) made such collections. The largest extant collection is the *Gnomologium Vaticanum.*

Chrestomathia
A collection of excerpts from other authors, such as that of Proclus (q.v. v) and Helladius. Much of our information about the Epic Cycle is derived from the *Chrestomathia* of Proclus.

Christian Literature
See Bible, New Testament, Gospels, Apocrypha, Clement, Irenaeus, Justin Martyr, Eusebius, Origen, the Cappado-

cians, et al. Works dealt with apologetics, polemics, exegesis, hagiography, mysticism, sermons, hymnography, apocalyptic works, etc.

Christian Topography

See Cosmas Indicopleustes.

Christophorus of Mytilene

One of the best of the Byzantine poets. Ca. 1000-1050. Imperial secretary. Wrote occasional poetry, epigrams, religious poetry (Calendar of Saints) and an invective against mice.

Christus Patiens (or Christos Paschon)

A play describing the Passion of Christ, supposedly by Gregory of Nazianzus, but probably by an unknown Byzantine author of the 11th or 12th cent. It contains lines from Euripides, Aeschylus, and Lycophron, and has been useful for the recovery of portions of the lost end of the *Bacchae* (q.v.).

Chronology

See Eratosthenes, Apollodorus (5), Castor of Rhodes.

Chryseis

Daughter of the priest Chryses, in Homer's *Iliad.* The epic begins with her father's prayer to Apollo for her return, the god's sending a plague upon the Achaeans, and Agamemnon's being compelled to restore her to her father. In turn, this leads to Agamemnon's taking Achilles' prize Briseis, and the quarrel between them. (*Iliad,* Book I)

Chrysippus

Stoic philosopher and teacher. Became head of the Stoa in 232 B.C. Known for his harsh, obscure style.

Chrysippus

Several others of the name are to be distinguished:
(2) C. of Acraiphia, an epic poet.

(3) A grammarian, who wrote a commentary on Pindar.
(4) C. of Cnidus, a physician.
(5) A Presbyter, from Cappadocia.

Chrysoberges, Lucas

Patriarch of Constantinople, 1156-69. Wrote a didactic poem on fast days.

Chrysoberges, Nicephorus

Byzantine author of the 12-13th century. Author of speeches, rhetorical Progymnasmata, fables, etc.

Chrysostomos ("Golden-Mouth")

See Dio, John.

Chrysothemis

In mythology, daughter of Agamemnon, sister of Electra (qq.v.).

Chumnos, Nicephorus

Byzantine author of the 13th cent. Wrote on philosophy and theology (against the Neoplatonics), on rhetoric, and Letters.

Cimmerians

A legendary people in Asia Minor, where the sun never shines, according to Homer.

Cinaedic Poetry

Of a scurrilous and satirical character, recited by *kinaidolgoi* (e.g. Sotados and Timon of Phlius).

Cinaethon of Lacedaemon

An epic poet of unknown date, supposed to have written a *Telegony, Oedipodea, Little Iliad,* and *Heraclea.* See Epic Cycle.

Cincius

An early Roman historian (2nd Punic war) who wrote in Greek.

Cinesias

A dithyrambic poet, frequently lampooned by Aristophanes.

Cinnamus, John

Private secretary of the emperor Manuel. Wrote a history of the years 1118-1176, in seven books. Only an epitome remains.

Circe

An enchantress, in the *Odyssey* who changes men into swine, with the exception of Odysseus, who is able to resist her spell with the aid of a charm. Odysseus remains with her for a year, after which she gives him directions for his journey home.

Circle

See *Cycle,* Agathias.

Claudius Aelianus

See Aelian.

Claudius Ptolemaeus

See Ptolemy.

Cleanthes (331-232 B.C.)

Disciple of Zeno, and his successor as head of the Stoic school. Author of a famous *Hymn to Zeus.*

Clearchus (1)

Middle comedy poet. Wrote a play entitled *The Corinthians.*

Clearchus (2) of Soli.

Miscellaneous writer, fl. ca. 250 B.C. Wrote biographies, paradoxes, an encomium of Plato, on zoology, flatterers, skeletons, mystical works, etc. Seems to have been a Peripatetic.

Cleidemus (or Cleitodemus)

Author (ca. 350 B.C.) of an *Atthis* (q.v.) of which some fragments survive.

Cleitarchus

Wrote a history of Alexander, probably in the 3rd century B.C. From all accounts it was probably a very inferior one.

Cleitomachus (187-110 B.C.)

Carthaginian Academic and Sceptic, pupil of Carneades, later head of the Academy. Said to have written about 400 books (notes of Carneades' lectures, etc.).

Clement of Alexandria (born ca. 150 A.D.)

Author of many works on Christianity. Although much has been lost, the following survive: *Protrepticus* (Exhortation) to the Greeks; the *Paedagogus* (an exposition of the teachings of Jesus); the *Stromateis* (Miscellanies); and fragments of other works. He died in about 215 A.D. His writing, though perhaps too much influenced by Hellenism, is clear, serene, and charming. One homily is extant: *Quis Dives Salvetur?*

Clement of Rome

Probably author of the Epistle to the Corinthians (the first, not the second, which is spurious), which is said to have been read publicly in the assemblies of the early Christians, and given the same prominence as the Scriptures themselves.

Cleobuline of Lindos (or Eumetis)

Greek poetess, known for her skill in composing riddles. Supposed to have been the daughter of Cleobulus (q.v.).

Cleobulus

One of the Seven Sages, credited with the saying "metron ariston" (the mean is best).

Cleodemus (or Malchus)

Wrote a *History of the Jews* mixed with Greek mythology (e.g. Heracles married the granddaughter of Abraham, etc.)

Cleomachus

Hellenistic poet, who imitated Sotades. The Ionic dimeter was named after him.

Cleomedes

Writer on astronomy and optics, probably ca. 150-200 A.D. One title: *Kyklike Theoria Meteoron* (On the Revolutions of the Heavenly Bodies).

Cleonides

(2nd cent. A.D.) Author of an *Eisagoge Harmonike,* which is one of our best sources for the harmonic theory of Aristoxenus.

Cleophon

Athenian tragic poet. Some titles, no fragments. Aristotle mentions him for his prosaic style and lack of idealism.

Cleostratus of Tenedos (6th cent. B.C.?)

Mathematician and astronomer. Probably the one who imported the knowledge of the signs of the Zodiac from the Babylonians.

Clio

See Muses.

Clitopho (Cleitophon)

A work ascribed to Plato, but of doubtful authenticity.

Clotho

One of the three Fates (q.v.).

Clouds, the (Nephelai)

Comedy of Aristophanes, produced in 423 B.C. It only won third prize, and a new version was produced with a new parabasis. Basically, the play is an extremly witty lampoon on the Sophists, their religious scepticism, legalistic quibbles, grammatical hairsplitting, etc., in short, a diatribe against the New Education. An old Athenian, Strepsiades, sends his son to the "Thinkery" (*Phrontisterion*) of Socrates to learn the New (Unjust) Reasoning of the Sophists, so that he may avoid paying his debts. The Agon of the play consists of a debate between Just and Unjust Reasoning, won by the latter. The son, having graduated with honors, gets the father out of his debts, and then, in a fine comic peripety or reversal, beats up his father, justifying his actions with the very same New Reasoning. Plato represents Socrates as saying that much harm was done him by the sort of prejudice represented in this play.

Clytemnestra

In mythology, the sister of Helen of Troy, and wife of Agamemnon (q.v.), whom she kills, together with his concubine Cassandra. In various accounts of the story, she shares the guilt in varying proportions with her lover Aegisthus: In Homer, she is the weak accomplice of Aegisthus, who is the real villain; in Aeschylus, she is the leader, while Aegisthus is a blustering coward. In Euripides, she is sorry for what she has done. In all versions, she is killed by Orestes, her son.

Cocceianus, Dio

See Dio Chrysostomus.

Codex Alexandrinus

Fifth century MS of the Greek Bible, almost complete. Now in the British Museum.

Codex Bezae

Fifth or Sixth cent. MS of the four Gospels, with the Greek on the left-hand page, and the Latin on the right. Now in Cambridge University.

Codex Ephraemi

Fifth cent. MS of the Greek Bible. Now in the Bibliothèque Nationale in Paris.

Codex Sinaiticus

4th century MS of the Greek Bible, second only to the Codex Vaticanus. Preserves the N.T. complete, with about one-third of the O.T.

Codex Vaticanus

4th cent. MS of the Greek Bible. Our most valuable text.

Codinus, George

Byzantine author, of unknown date, to whom were attributed works dealing with the foundation, topography, monuments, public buildings, churches, etc. of Constantinople, including Hagia Sophia. Under his name a work on the court officials appears, (see Pseudo-Codinus).

Colchis

A region at the eastern end of the Black sea, home of Medea, and goal of the Argonauts' expedition.

Colluthus

One of the revivers of the epic in the 5th cent. A.D. Wrote a short poem entitled *The Rape of Helen,* in simple style.

Colonus

A hill near Athens where (see *Oedipus at Colonus*) Oedipus found asylum and burial. Sophocles' birthplace was there.

Colors, on

Title of a work in the Aristotelian corpus, wrongly attributed to him. May be by Straton or Theophrastus.

Colotes of Lampsacus (4th-3rd cent. B.C.)

Pupil of Epicurus. Wrote works *Against Plato's Lysis, Republic, Gorgias,* etc.

Comedy

1. *Old Comedy.* Two types: Sicilian and Attic. Sicilian comedy did not have a chorus or political satire, and seems to have anticipated New Comedy in its use of type-characters. Of Attic Comedy we have the eleven plays of Aristophanes. Frank personal abuse was one of its chief characteristics, and the *parresia* (freedom of speech) of the age guaranteed the poet's right to this. Not only political figures (Pericles, Cleon, etc.) but also literary ones (Euripides, etc.) were considered fair game. The plays began with the exposition of a "Happy Idea" which was then developed to its logical, or rather illogical, conclusion. Fantasy and mythological burlesque were also not uncommon. The *Agon* or set debate was a feature of most of the comedies.

2. *Middle Comedy.* It is not easy to draw the line between Old and Middle Comedy. The transition is apparent in the *Plutus* of Aristophanes. The wild extravagance and obscenity of Old Comedy are for the most part gone. Comedy of types and manners is more frequent, although, since we have not a single Middle Comedy, it is very difficult to reconstruct the plots. We have the names of 57 poets and we know of about 800 plays from this period.

3. *New Comedy.* Again, the development is a continuous one. The chief practitioners are Menander, Diphilus, and Philemon, and we have considerable remains of Menander (q.v.) as well as many Roman comedies that were imitations or translations of the Greek ones. Stock characters are more frequent (e.g. parasites, soldiers, cooks, irate old men, lovesick youths, etc.). The chorus has almost nothing to do with the plot, and is merely used for lyric interludes. Love stories are very common, and the influence of Euripides is frequently seen in the seriousness of the treatment, the type of prologue, etc. We have the names of about 70 New Comedy writers. For further references see Schmid-Stählin, Rose, OCD.

Cometas

Poet of the 9th cent. A.D. Author of epigrams in the Palatine Anthology, one of which deals with the *Raising of Lazarus.*

Commos (Kommos)

A lamentation in tragedy, in which there is alternate chanting between the chorus and one or more characters. A good example is the long chant in the *Choephori.*

Comnenus (Comnena)

Imperial family of Byzantium in the 12th cent. See Anna Comnena.

Comnenus, Isaac

Byzantine prince who wrote commentaries on Homer.

Complutensian Polyglot

See Polyglot Bibles.

Comus (Komos)

A performance by a band of revellers, out of which comedy grew. It is thought that the chorus were frequently dressed as animals (cf. *Frogs, Wasps, Birds,* etc.). The form probably goes back to a time before the introduction of the worship of Dionysus, into which it was later incorporated. The use of phallic symbols testifies to the fertility aspect of the *Komos.*

Confessor

See Maximus (3), Theophanes (2).

Confutation of Zeus

See Lucian.

Conon (1) of Samos. 3rd cent. B.C.

Matehematician and astronomer who discovered the new constellation known as the *Berenikes Plokamos* (Lock of Berenice). Also wrote a work on astrology or astronomy, and one on conic sections.

Conon

The following should also be mentioned.

(2) A mythographer who wrote 50 tales *(diegeseis).*

(3) An epic poet.

(4) A rhetor of the Asianist school.

Consolation

See Plutarch.

Constantine (1) VII, Porphyrogenitus

Byzantine emperor 944-959; author of a *Book of Ceremonies* (q.v.) and a work on the *Administration of the Empire.* A man of broad learning and tremendous curiosity. A great Encyclopedia of history was compiled under his administration, as well as works on tactics, collections of excerpts, etc. Also wrote a life of his grandfather Basil I.

Constantine (2) the Rhodian

10th cent. Byzantine poet, who wrote a description of the mosaics of the Holy Apostles, in 981 trimeters.

Constantine (3) the Sicilian

Byzantine poet of the circle of Leo the Wise. Wrote anacreontic love-poetry, an elegy on the death of his family in a storm at sea, and an alphabetic acrostic.

Constantinople

The center of the later Roman Empire. Founded as New Rome in 330 A.D. by the emperor Constantine, after whom it was renamed. See Byzantium.

Constitution of Athens

A work in the Aristotelian corpus; one of the large collections of Constitutions (*Politeiai*); found in a papyrus in 1891. It may be by Aristotle or by one of his pupils. It is to be distinguished from the work by the "Old Oligarch" (q.v.).

Constitution of Sparta (Lakedaimonion Politeia)
Title of a work by Xenophon (q.v. 1).

Contest between Homer and Hesiod
See *Agon Homeri et Hesiodi.*

Corax of Syracuse
Wrote the first manual of rhetoric (5th cent. B.C.), in which the speech is divided into three parts, the prooemium, agones, and epilogue.

Corinna of Tanagra
Lyric poetess, contemporary of Pindar, to whom she is supposed to have given advice. Some titles: *Seven against Thebes,* the *Return of Orion, Iolaus,* etc. Some fragments survive.

Corinthian Epic, Corinthian History
Lost works, the former ascribed to Eumelus, dealing with the legendary history of Corinth (Medea, etc.); the latter a prose work of unknown date.

Cornaro, Vincent
See *Erotocritus.*

Cornutus, L. Annaeus
Teacher of the Roman poet Persius, whose 5th Satire is dedicated to him. We have one work by him, in Greek: a Stoic exposition of Greek myths, with allegorical interpretations.

Corona, de
The most famous speech of Demosthenes (*On the Crown*). Probably the greatest piece of oratory to come down to us from antiquity. A spirited defense of the anti-Macedonian policy of Demosthenes and his party, as well as a reply to the charge against Ctesiphon and a bitter personal attack on Aeschines (q.v.). The "crown" in question was a garland

which Ctesiphon had proposed for Demosthenes, and which Aeschines had declared was illegal on three counts.

Coronistae

See Phoenix (2).

Coryphaeus

The leader of the chorus in Greek tragedy and comedy. In tragedy, he speaks as a character, and in comedy, he delivers the *parabasis* (q.v.).

Cosmas (1) Indicopleustes (6th cent. A.D.)

Author of a work entitled *Christian Topography,* ca. 550 A.D. As the name implies, it is a work of geography, with Christian interpretations, Biblical explanations, etc. Interesting for its zoölogical descriptions, and details of monuments he described. Cosmas also wrote a (lost) work on astronomy.

Cosmas (2) of Jerusalem

Byzantine religious poet of the 8th cent.

"Cranes of Ibycus"

See Ibycus.

Crantor (ca. 335-275 B.C.)

Philosopher of the Old Academy. Wrote a commentary on Plato's *Timaeus* which is probably the first Platonic commentary. Also wrote a work *On Grief,* the prototype of the ancient Consolatio, which later became very popular.

Craterus

Probable author or compiler of a collection of Athenian decrees (*Psephismaton Synagoge*) with commentary, ca. 300 B.C.

Crates (1)

Athenian comic poet, the first to dispense with personal invective. Fl. ca. 450 B.C. The following titles survive:

Geitones, Heroes, Theria, Pedetai, Lamia (Vampire), *Samioi.* Fragments are too scanty for any reliable estimate of his merit.

Crates (2) of Thebes (ca. 365-285 B.C.)

Cynic philosopher. Wrote many poems, revised existing poems to give them a Cynic slant, and is said to have written tragedies. The letters that have survived under his name are not genuine. See also *Pera.* The general name for his verses was *Paignia* (trifles).

Crates (3) of Mallos

Librarian of Pergamum in the middle of the 2nd century B.C. Wrote on Homer, Hesiod, Euripides, Aristophanes, Aratus. He was an anomalist (see Analogy and Anomaly).

Crateuas

A pharmacologist at the court of Mithridates. Wrote a great work entitled *Rhizotomikon,* on drugs and Materia Medica, and a work which was of great importance since it contained illustrations of plants. His works influenced Dioscorides and all later medicine and pharmacology.

Cratinus (1) ca. 484-ca. 419 B.C.

The greatest of the Athenian comic poets after Aristophanes. His plays were personal or political satires, and mythological burlesques. Titles: *Nemesis, Odysseus, Thrattai, Satyrs, Cheimazomenoi,* etc. Enough fragments have been preserved to indicate a direct and vigorous style.

Cratinus (2) the Younger

Middle comedy poet who attacked Plato in his writings.

Cratippus of Athens

Continued the history of Thucydides. Some have thought he was the author of the *Hellenica Oxyrhynchia* (q.v.).

Cratylus

Dialogue of Plato (q.v.) dealing mostly with etymology.

Creon

(means "ruler" or king). In mythology, he is (1) the king of Corinth in the *Medea* of Euripides (q.v.) (2) The uncle and brother-in-law of Oedipus. He appears in all three of the Sophoclean plays about Oedipus and his descendants, but his character undergoes a remarkable transformation. In the *Oedipus Rex* he is a kindly and wise person; in the *Antigone,* an Aristotelian tragic hero; and in the *Oedipus at Colonus,* he is the nearest thing we have to a villain in Greek tragedy.

Creophylus of Samos

Reputed author of a poem on the epic cycle: the *Capture of Oechalia (Oechaliae Halosis).*

Crinagoras (born ca 70 B.C.)

Elegiac poet, from Mytilene. We possess several of his epigrams, which are variously described as "beautiful" and "undistinguished."

Critias (ca. 460-403 B.C.)

One of the Thirty Tyrants at Athens. Wrote elegiac poetry and tragedies. Titles: *Sisyphus, Pirithous.*

Critias

Title of an unfinished dialogue of Plato (q.v.).

Criticism

See Literary Criticism.

Crito (1)

One of the most famous of Plato's (q.v.) dialogues. Socrates is in prison and Crito comes to him with plans for an escape. Socrates, however, refuses to cooperate in breaking of the law. Crito is also referred to in the *Apology, Phaedo,* and *Euthydemus.* He was supposed to have written 17 dialogues.

Crito (2)

New Comedy poet of the 2nd cent. B.C. Titles: *Ephesians, Aitolos, Philopragmon* (the Busybody).

Crito (3)

Neo-Pythagorean of the 1st cent. B.C. or the 1st cent. A.D.

(4) Physician, ca. A.D. 100. Galen preserves fragments of his works.

Critobulus

Byzantine historian of the 15th cent. Wrote a history of the Sultan Mohammed II.

Critolaus

Peripatetic philosopher of the 2nd cent. B.C. One of the famous embassy to Rome.

Croesus

King of Lydia in the middle of the 6th cent. B.C. The story told by Herodotus of his conversation with Solon on the subject of happiness can hardly have taken place. When Cyrus conquered Lydia, Croesus was captured and put on a funeral pyre, but miraculously saved by Apollo's intervention. This is one of the many legends told about him.

Cronus (Kronos)

Son of Heaven and Earth, and father of Zeus. Overthrew his father and in turn, he was overthrown by Zeus. Presumably a pre-Hellenic deity who was later worked into the Olympian pantheon.

Crown, on the

See *Corona, de* and Demosthenes.

Ctesias

Greek physician at the Persian court who assisted Artaxerxes. Wrote a history of Persia, and an *Indica* (probably the first such work).

Ctesibius of Alexandria

3rd cent. B.C. (?) writer on mechanics, much used by later writers although nothing of his has come down to us.

Ctesiphon

See Aeschines, Demosthenes, *Corona, de.*

Curmudgeon, the

See *Dyscolus.*

Cybele

A mother-goddess of Asia Minor, worshipped with Attis, a vegetation-god. Her cult was known in Greece as early as the 5th cent. B.C. and was associated with the worship of Demeter.

Cycle (or Circle)

Volume of contemporary verse issued in the time of Justinian. Included the works of Agathias (q.v.), Paulus Silentarius, Julian, Leontius, Macedonius, etc.

Cyclic poets

See Epic Cycle.

Cyclopes

A race of one-eyed giants, the most famous of whom was Polyphemus. Homer tells of Odysseus' adventures with the latter. In Hesiod they are makers of thunderbolts; in Homer they are savage cannibals. Later legends tell of a more amorous side to Polyphemus.

Cyclops

The one extant satyr-play; by Euripides, and consequently of great historical value, aside from any question of its literary merit. It deals, essentially, with the episode from Book xi of the *Odyssey* describing the blinding of Polyphemus by Odysseus. A chorus of Satyrs, and the elderly Silenus as well as Odysseus and Polyphemus are characters.

The satyric element is best seen in the episode where Odysseus gets the Cyclops intoxicated. This is more important in the play than the details of the cannibalism and blinding. This semi-comic treatment of a serious, if not tragic, subject may be taken to be typical of the satyr play.

Cydones, Demetrius

Byzantine essayist of the 14th cent. Wrote many works on theology, rhetoric, letters, and a *Monody on the Casualties at Thessalonica.* He took Plato as his model, not without success.

Cyllenius

Wrote a history of the wars of the emperor Julian. Otherwise unknown.

Cynaethus

A rhapsode, supposedly the author of the Homeric *Hymn to Apollo.*

Cynegetica

Books on hunting-dogs; see Oppian, Xenophon (1).

Cynics

Followers of the philosopher Diogenes of Sinope. They advocated complete self-sufficiency. See Antisthenes, Crates (2), Onesicritus, Bion and Menippus.

Cyparissiotes, John

Byzantine theological writer of the 14th century, who was one of the first to establish a systematic body of dogma on the pattern of the Western Scholastics. Opponent of Palamas (q.v.).

Cypria

One of the poems in the Epic Cycle (q.v.), telling the events leading up to the Trojan War. Supposed to have been composed by Hegesias or Stasinus.

Cyranides

Title of a work on magical cures deriving from plants, animals, stones, etc.

Cyrenaics

School founded by Aristippus (q.v.) which advocated pleasure as the chief goal in life (i.e. hedonism).

Cyril (1) of Alexandria (376-444)

Theological writer, patriarch of Alexandria, ca. 412. His rivalry with the Antiochians brought him into conflict with Chrysostom. Wrote works against the Nestorians, letters, sermons, exegetical works, and a polemic against the emperor Julian ("the Apostate").

Cyril (2) of Jerusalem (ca. 315-386)

Bishop of Jerusalem ca. 350 A.D. Wrote sermons on dogma, and 24 catecheses.

Cyril (3) of Scythopolis

One of the chief hagiographical writers of the 6th century.

Cyriotes, John

Metropolitan, late 10th century. Wrote epigrams, hymns, and occasional poetry, as well as panegyrics.

Cyropaedia

Work by Xenophon (q.v.), an idealized biography of Cyrus the Elder.

D

Dactyl

See Meter.

Daedalus

Legendary artist and inventor, said to have invented various tools (e.g. saw, ax,) parts of ships (mast and yards), to have built the famous labyrinth at Cnossus, and the wings with which he and his son Icarus escaped from prison. He arrived safely in Sicily, but his son flew too near to the sun, with the result that the wax of his wings melted, he fell into the sea, and was drowned.

Daimachus (1) of Plataea (4th cent. B.C.)

Possibly the author of the *Hellenica Oxyrhynchia* (q.v.).

Daimachus (2)

Wrote a work entitled *Indica* in the 3rd cent. B.C. Often confused with Daimachus (1).

Daimon

Used variously to mean a god, a spirit, any supernatural power, or even Fate. Heraclitus, for example, says that a man's character is his "daimon." The modern connotation of the word "demon" is because of the Christian attitude towards the pagan gods. The "little voice" that Socrates spoke of, his divine sign or warning, is called a *daimonion*.

Damagetus

Epigrammatic poet of the third or second century B.C.

Damascius

One of the last of the Neoplatonic philosophers; follower of Proclus and Iamblichus. Wrote a commentary on Plato's *Parmenides,* and a work entitled *Questions and Answers.* Also wrote poetry.

Damastes of Sigeum

An early logographer (q.v.). Pupil of Hellanicus and contemporary of Herodotus. Wrote on *Events in Greece, Poets and Sophists, Peoples and Cities,* and *Ancestors of those who Fought at Troy.*

Damocles

A Sicilian courtier who, when he praised the happiness of the tyrant Dionysius I, was made to sit at a banquet with a sword suspended by a hair above his head. Hence the proverbial expression "Sword of Damocles," used of any precarious situation or imminent danger.

Damon (1)

A Pythagorean from Syracuse, famous for his friendship with one Phintias (*not* Pythias).

Damon (2)

Or Damonides. A musician of Athens, teacher of Pericles, ostracized for his influence on the latter. He was also a sophist, and possibly teacher of Socrates.

Damoxenus

A New Comedy playwright. Scant fragments remain.

Danaans

One of Homer's names for the Greeks, whom he also called Argives and Achaeans.

Danaë

The mother of Perseus (q.v.). Zeus visited her in the form of a shower of gold.

Danaë

Poem by Simonides, preserved by Dionysius of Halicarnassus (qq.v.).

Danais

A long epic poem (6500 lines) dealing with the story of the fifty daughters of Danaus. The work is lost, and the date and author are unknown.

Danaus

In mythology, son of Belus, brother of Aegyptus. Fled with his fifty daughters to Argos. The story of the daughters and their murder of the sons of Aegyptus (with the exception of Hypermestra, who spared the life of Lynceus) was told in a trilogy by Aeschylus, of which the first play, the *Suppliants,* survives.

Daphnis and Chloë

See Longus.

Daphnopates, Theodore

Byzantine who compiled a collection of Chrysostomus' sermons, in 48 *Eklogai* 10th century.

"Dares Phrygius"

A priest of Hephaestus at Troy, supposed to have been the author of a pre-Homeric account of the Trojan War. This work is lost (if indeed it ever existed) but a Latin "translation" exists, which was the basis for much of the knowledge of the Trojan War during the Middle Ages. (cf. "Dictys Cretensis")

Definitions

A pseudo-Platonic (q.v.) work, presumably a product of Plato's Academy.

Deianira

In mythology, the wife of Heracles. See *Trachiniae.*

Deinarchus

See Dinarchus.

Deipnosophistai

Variously translated as: "Specialists on Dining" (i.e. gourmets), "Doctors at Dinner," and the "Learned Banquet." See Athenaeus (1).

Delphi

Site of the famous oracle of Apollo, where the Pythian priestess gave out her ambiguous answers. It was a pre-Olympian shrine dating from the remotest antiquity. The old theory of intoxicating vapors accounting for the frenzy of the priestess has been rendered untenable, and much remains to be explained about the answers of the oracle. It enjoyed a unique and universal prestige all through the classical and post-classical period, and was finally closed by the emperor Theodosius in 390 A.D.

Delphic Hymns

Fragments of two hymns were discovered at Delphi, with musical notation, extremely important for our knowledge of Greek music. The first, by Limenius (q.v.) in the 2nd cent. B.C. is in the Lydian mode with indications of instrumental score; the second, of unknown author and date, is in the Phrygian mode.

Demades (fl. ca 350 B.C.)

Athenian rhetorician and politician. Nothing has survived of his speeches.

Demeter

The Greek goddess of grain, identified with the Roman Ceres. The last two syllables of her name almost certainly mean "mother." Her mysteries were celebrated at Eleusis. The story of her daughter Persephone is one of the most familiar of the etiological myths. The festival of the *Thes-*

mophoria was also in honor of Demeter, and it commemorated the introduction of laws and civilization (i.e. agriculture.) See Rose in OCD.

Demeter, Hymn to
See Homeric Hymns.

Demetrius (1) of Phalerum (born ca. 350 B.C.)
Athenian writer and statesman. Wrote moral treatises, histories, literary criticism, letters, fables, proverbs, declamations, etc.

Demetrius (2)
Old Comedy writer, ca. 400 B.C. One title: *Sikelia.*

Demetrius (3) of Scepsis (born ca. 214 B.C.)
A grammarian and polymath. Wrote 60 books on the Homeric *Catalogue of Ships.*

Demetrius (4) Ixion
Grammarian and lexicographer. Compiled an *Attic Lexicon.* Contemporary of Aristarchus, with whom he disagreed on textual matters.

Demetrius (5) Lacon
Epicurean philosopher of the 2nd cent. B.C. Criticized Carneades' attack on the possibility of proof, and wrote on Epicurus.

Demetrius (6) (2nd or 1st cent. B.C.)
Author of a guide to letter-writing, enumerating 21 different types of letter, with examples.

Demetrius
The following should also be mentioned:

(7) D. of Magnesia, author of a work, *On Concord,* and one dealing with homonymous towns and writers.

(8) Author of a treatise on style. May be identical with (9).

(9) D. of Tarsus 1st cent. B.C. grammarian.

(10) D. of Troezen. 1st cent. A.D. Wrote on philosophers and sophists.

(11) A Jewish historian, the first to write Jewish history in Greek. 3rd cent. B.C.

(12) A historian.

(13) An editor of Homer. See Chalcocondyles (2).

(14) A Sophist, of Alexandria.

(15) A rhetor, from Syrus.

For complete list, see Schmid-Stählin and Krumbacher.

Demochares (ca. 360-275 B.C.)

Nephew of Demosthenes, himself an orator and statesman. Wrote speeches, and a history of Athens in more than 21 books, "rhetorical and lacking in objectivity."

Democles

(1) A logographer.

(2) An epic poet.

Democritus of Abdera (ca. 460 B.C.)

Adopted the atomic theory of Leucippus (q.v.) who was his teacher. His writings were extremely numerous, and covered the following fields: Physics, psychology, logic, ethics, mathematics, astronomy, music, and other fields. Aristotle thought very highly of Democritus. He was known as the "laughing philosopher."

Demodocus (1)

The blind bard of the court of Alcinous in Homer's *Odyssey* (Bk. viii) whose singing of the events of the Trojan War made Odysseus weep, and gave him the opportunity to tell of his adventures (*Od.* ix-xii).

Demodocus (2)

An early gnomic poet. A few fragments remain.

Demodocus

Title of a Pseudo-Platonic (q.v.) work.

Demon (ca. 300 B.C.)

Wrote an *Atthis* (q.v.) and a large collection of proverbs, which was widely quoted.

Demonax of Cyprus (2nd cent. A.D.)

A cynic philosopher who is known chiefly through the life ascribed to Lucian. Starved himself to death at an extremely advanced age.

Demophilus

The following should be mentioned:

(1) An astrologer.

(2) Son of Ephorus, who edited his father's history.

(3) Comic playwright.

(4) Neopythagorean philosopher.

Demosthenes (1)

The greatest of the Greek orators. Various legends are told of his efforts to surmount physical obstacles (e.g. speaking with pebbles in his mouth, shouting against the roar of the surf, etc.). Nearly all of his speeches are political in nature. He clearly saw the danger to Athens represented by the career of Philip of Macedon, and repeatedly warned of it. Most of his greatest speeches were delivered by himself, though he also wrote speeches for clients. Of the 61 speeches that have come down to us, about 36 are undoubtedly genuine. Some of the most important are: *On the Freedom of the Rhodians, On the Peace,* the *Philippics, On the Crown* (the most famous single speech), the *Olynthiacs, On the Embassy,* the speeches against Leptines, Aristocrates, Timocrates, etc. His fame rests on his sincerity and honesty, his singleness of purpose, and the lucidity of his style and arrangement. He uses metaphor only sparingly.

Demosthenes (2) of Bithynia

Epic poet of the 2nd cent. B.C. Wrote a *Bithyniaca.*

Descent into Hades

See Lucian.

Deucalion

In mythology, the Greek equivalent of Noah, On the advice of Prometheus his father, he built an ark. After the flood, he threw "the bones of his mother" (i.e. stones) over his shoulder and so the earth was repopulated.

Dexippus, Publius Herennius

Athenian sophist and statesman, who fl. ca. 250 A.D. Wrote a *Chronike Historia* in 12 books, a work on the Gothic Wars, a history of the Diadochi, and other works. His style was modelled on that of Thucydides.

Diadochi

The successors of Alexander the Great (Antigonus, Antipater, Ptolemy, Cassander, Lysimachus, and Seleucus). Histories of the Diadochi were written by Hieronymus of Cardia, Rexippus, Duris, Diyllus, and others.

Diagoras

Lyric poet of Melos in the 5th cent. B.C. An atheist who lost his faith in the gods because they did not punish someone who had broken his oath. This is not, however, apparent from the fragments.

Dialectic

Aristotle says that Zeno invented dialectic, but this is not true. Plato was the first extant author to use this means of arriving at the truth, following the example of Socrates.

Dialects

The main dialects are: Epic (mostly Ionic, with some Aeolic), used by Homer, and also Hesiod. Lyric dialect was largely the Aeolic dialect of Lesbos, as seen in the poetry of Sappho and Alcaeus. Other lyric poets used Ionic or

Boeotian, and artificial creations (mixing Aeolic, Ionic, epic and Doric elements). Prose first developed in the Ionic dialect. After the time of Alexander, the dialects merged into one common language, the *koine,* in which the Septuagint was written. Later, the classical revival strove to impose an archaistic Attic dialect, which even during the Byzantine period still kept its influence. Hence the modern Greek must learn the "purist" or *kathareuousa* dialect as well as the spoken or *demotike.*

Dialexeis

Or *Dissoi Logoi.* A short sophistic work written ca. 400 B.C.

Dialogue

The form was invented by Socrates, although certain passages in Herodotus foreshadowed the use by Socrates of the question and answer method of arriving at some important truth. Plato and Xenophon were the first to write works in dialogue form. Aristotle also wrote dialogues, which were famous in antiquity, but they have not survived. Later exponents of the form include Plutarch and Lucian, Julian and Synesius.

Dialogues of Courtesans, of Gods, of the Dead

See Lucian.

Diassorinus, Neilus

Byzantine scholar of the 14th century. Although he wrote on theological subjects, his secular works are more important. He wrote a work on grammar, metrics, rhetoric and philosophy, entitled *Pege Gnoseos* (Fountain of Knowledge). Also wrote on natural history, church history, and poetry.

Diatessaron

Harmony of the Gospels by Tatian (q.v.).

Diatribe

Characteristic of the Stoic and Cynic schools. See Epictetus, Teles.

Dicaearchus

Pupil of Aristotle, wrote voluminously; only fragments survive: Wrote the first universal history of Greek culture (*Bios Hellados*); *Politeiai* (constitutions); and other political works; Biographies and literary history (*Bioi* on the lives and works of Plato and others, on Alcaeus, on Homer), *Hypotheses* of the plays of Sophocles and Euripides; Philosophical works (on the soul, on the destruction of men, on divination, etc.); geographical works, and others. An extremely learned and imaginative man, who had a great influence on later authors, e.g. Cicero, Eratosthenes, Plutarch.

Dicaeogenes

Tragic poet of the 5th cent. B.C. Titles: *Medea, Cyprians.* Mentioned by Aristotle for his recognition scene.

"Dictys Cretensis"

Supposedly the author of a diary on the Trojan War, "discovered" during the reign of Nero and "translated" into Latin. Together with the work of Dares Phrygius (q.v.), this was the chief medieval source for stories of the Trojan War.

Didache

The *Teaching of the Apostles,* a short manual of church life and morals, written ca. 150 A.D.

Didactic Poetry

Hesiod provides the earliest example of Greek didactic poetry. Later examples are the *Sententiae Chironis* (lost), the works of Phocyclides and Xenophanes. Empedocles wrote a great poem *On Nature* (also lost), which must have been one of the outstanding works of all didactic poetry.

In Alexandrian times, such authors as Aratus, Nicander, and others are representative, and in Roman times, Dionysius Periegetes and Oppian. See under the individual names.

Didascalia

Means either the rehearsal or the performance of a play or a dithyramb. In the plural *(didascaliae)* the word refers to the records of public performances, including the names of actors, poets, etc. A lost work of Aristotle bears this title. The *didascaliae* were engraved on stone and large fragments survive, possibly based on Aristotle's work.

Didymus (1) ca 80-10 B.C.

Alexandrian scholar of tremendous erudition and even greater industry, said to have written 3500-4000 books! The list of works includes: textual criticism and recension of Homer, Commentaries on Homer, Pindar, Hesiod, the tragedians, comic playwrights, historians, orators, and lyric poets, with mythological, geographical, historical and biographical details; lexica, works on grammar, inflexions, analogy, polemics, and many other miscellaneous writings.

Didymus (2)

Atticist lexicographer of the 1st cent. A.D. Wrote on Thucydides, and a work comparing Greek and Latin.

Didymus (3) "The Blind"

Contemporary of Athanasius; wrote many exegetical works.

Diegesis Paidiophrastos ton Tetrapodon Zoon

(Children's Story about the Four-footed Animals) Children's poem about King Lion and his ministers, etc. In 1082 "political" verses. Probable date: 1365 A.D. After a bloody battle peace is restored among the animals. The work has both symbolic and satirical elements.

Dieuchidas of Megara

4th cent. B.C. Historian who wrote the annals of Megara.

Digenis Akritas

The great Byzantine epic. In ten books of "political" verse. Written some time during the tenth or eleventh century. A "chanson de geste" comparable to the *Song of Roland,* and possibly superior to it. The work reveals the border struggles between the feudal lords, heroes of chivalry and guardians of the marches, and the infidel.

Dike

Personification of Justice. Appears from Hesiod on, even in Christian lit.

Dinarchus (born ca. 360 B.C.)

The last of the Ten Attic Orators. We possess only three of his 60 speeches (all composed for delivery by others, as he was forbidden to speak in person, being a *metic* or foreigner). The speeches: *Against Demosthenes, Against Aristogiton, Against Philocles,* reveal careless structure, not much originality, and too much invective. He was imitative in style, and knew all the tricks of the trade. With his speeches begins the decline of Attic oratory.

Dinon

Wrote a history of Persia which was used by Plutarch.

Dio Cassius

(Cassius Dio Cocceianus). Fl. 200 A.D. Author of a *Roman History* from the beginnings to 229 A.D. Partly preserved, annalistic in arrangement, Thucydidean in style. Also wrote a life of Arrian and a work on dreams and portents.

Dio Chrysostomus (ca. 30-112 A.D.)

Philosopher and orator. Banished from Italy by the emperor Domitian for his role in a political intrigue, he wandered in Asia and the Balkans, turning to philosophy. Returned to Rome under Trajan. His philosophy is eclectic and unoriginal, but his oratory is powerful, his style excellent, and the philosophical basis sound. We possess about 80 speeches.

Diocles (1)

Comic poet, fl. about 400 B.C. Titles (*Bacchae, Thyestes, Cyclopes*) suggest mythological burlesque. He may be identical with the Diocles who invented a kind of harmonica.

Diocles (2)

Physician, contemporary of Aristotle. Wrote on anatomy, dietetics, physiology, prognostics, botany, etc. Influenced by Aristotle, Hippocrates, Empedocles, and Archidamus.

Diocles (3)

Mathematician of the first cent. B.C. Author of a work on burning-glasses. Invented the "cissoid curve" for doubling the cube.

Diocles

The following should also be mentioned:

(4) Author of a compendium of philosophers.

(5) Greek rhetor of the Augustan Age.

(6) An obscure historian, from Peparethos.

Diodorus (1) of Sinope

Middle or New Comedy playwright. Brother of Diphilus. Titles: *Mainomenos, Nekros.*

Diodorus (2) Cronus

Teacher of Zeno the Stoic. Denied the possibility of motion, repeating the doctrines of Zeno the Eleatic.

Diodorus (3) Siculus

Contemporary of Caesar and Augustus. Wrote a World History (*Bibliotheke*) from the earliest times to the Gallic Wars of Julius Caesar. The only important feature of the work, which is otherwise quite undistinguished, is his universal concept of history.

Diodorus (4) of Tarsus

Christian writer. Bishop of Tarsus in 378. Wrote dogmatic, polemic, apologetic, historical, and exegetical works; also on astrology. Against paganism and heresies, especially the Arian.

Diodorus

Mention should also be made of the following:

(5) Mathematician, author of a commentary on Aratus.

(6) Grammarian and poet, of Tarsus.

(7) Epigrammatist, from Sardes.

Many others. For complete list, see Schmid-Stählin.

Diodotus

See Ephemerides.

Diogenes (1) of Apollonia

Eclectic philosopher of the 5th cent. B.C. Wrote on Nature, Meteorology, the Nature of Man, etc. Revived the teaching of Anaximenes, i.e. that the primary element is Air.

Diogenes (2) of Sinope (ca. 400-325 B.C.)

Founder of the Cynic school. Lived in extreme poverty, advocating the virtues of self-sufficiency (*autarkeia)* and asceticism. Because of his "shamelessness" (*anaideia*) he was called *Kuon* or "dog" whence the name Cynic. He is said to have written tragedies and dialogues. He became proverbial for his caustic wit, and the subject of numerous collections of anecdotes.

Diogenes (3) of Babylon

Stoic philosopher, Pupil of Chrysippus, teacher of Panaetius. His works, all lost, include writings on grammar, divination, Athens, dialectics, etc.

Diogenes (4) of Tarsus
Epicurean philosopher of unknown date.

Diogenes (5) of Oenoanda
Epicurean of the 2nd cent. A.D. who had a huge Epicurean inscription made, including principles of physics and ethics, and the following, which might be called the cardinal doctrines of Epicureanism: "God is not to be feared; Death cannot be felt; the Good is attainable; Evil is endurable."

Diogenes (6) Laertius
Author of a compendium of ancient philosophy (3rd cent. B.C.). The work is preserved, and is of great importance, as from it comes most of our knowledge of the lives of ancient philosophers.

Diogenes
Also, mention should be made of the following:
(7) Diogenes or Diogenianus of Cyzicus, a grammarian.
(8) An author of Satyr-plays.
(9) D. of Tarsus, tragic playwright.
(10) D. of Thebes. Also a tragic playwright.

Diogenianus (1) probably 2nd cent. A.D.
An Epicurean, quoted by Eusebius for his anti-Chrysippus polemics.

Diogenianus (2) of Heraclea. 2nd cent. A.D.
Compiled geographical indexes, proverbs, and made an alphabetically arranged epitome of the *Lexicon* of Pamphilus, which was used by Hesychius.

Diomedes
(1) in mythology, a Thracian, owner of man-eating horses captured by Heracles.
(2) Son of Tydeus, one of the greatest Greek heroes of the Trojan War. He wounded Aphrodite and Ares, and conquered many Trojans, but refused to fight Glaucus because

of the hereditary tie of hospitality. He figures conspicuously in the post-Homeric Trojan saga.

Dionysalexandros

A comedy by Cratinus, based on the Judgment of Paris, who in this version is replaced by the god Dionysus.

Dionysia

The festival of Dionysus at Athens at which the dramatic performances took place, beginning ca. 535 B.C.

Dionysiades of Tarsus

Tragic poet of the 3rd cent. B.C. One of the *Pleiad* (q.v.)

Dionysiaka

A miscellany of mythology, centering on the career of Dionysus. See Nonnus.

Dionysius (1) Aelius

A lexicographer of the 2nd cent. A.D. Compiled 10 books of *Attikai Lexeis.*

Dionysius (2) of Alexandria (died 265 A.D.)

Pupil of Origen, bishop of Alexandria. Opposed the doctrines of the Atomic materialists, Chiliasm, etc. Wrote on the Gospels.

Dionysius (3) the Areopagite

An Athenian converted to Christianity by St. Paul. To him were attributed works *On the Celestial Hierarchy, On the Divine Names, On Mystical Theology,* and others, now believed to date from the 5th cent., and they may be either deliberate forgeries, or Neo-Platonic writings somehow confused with the original Dionysius. They had a great influence on Christian theology during the Middle Ages.

Dionysius (4) of Byzantium (fl. ca 175 A.D.)

Wrote a description of a *Voyage on the Bosporus,* which survives in part in a Latin translation.

Dionysius (5) Chalcus

5th cent. B.C. poet, and the man who introduced bronze currency into Attica.

Dionysius (6) of Halicarnassus

Historian and rhetor who taught at Rome in the 1st cent. B.C. His works include *On the Arrangement of Words, On the Ancient Orators, On Mimesis, On Thucydides,* etc. D. was an excellent literary critic. He also wrote a historical work: *Roman Antiquities (Romaike Archaiologia).*

Dionysius (7) of Halicarnassus

Author of a textbook on music. See Aelius Dionysius.

Dionysius (8) of Heraclea (ca. 328-248 B.C.)

A prolific Stoic writer. Wrote poetry, a tragedy, and numerous other works.

Dionysius (9) of Miletus

A logographer, author of a *Persica,* the first work on Oriental history.

Dionysius (10) Periegetes

Wrote a *Periegesis* (description) of the world, for schoolboys. Also wrote on stones, birds, etc.

Dionysius (11) of Philadelphia

Reputed author of a poem on birds (*Ornithica*) which may be by Dionysius (10).

Dionysius (12) of Samos

Wrote a *Kyklos Historikos* in 7 books, which was either a mythological handbook or a romance.

Dionysius (13) Scytobrachion

Alexandrian grammarian of the 1st or 2nd cent. B.C. who wrote a mythological romance dealing with the Argonauts, the Trojan War, etc.

Dionysius (14) of Sinope
Obscure Middle Comedy poet.

Dionysius (15) of Thebes
Poet and teacher of Epaminondas.

Dionysius (16) Thrax
Grammarian and teacher, author of an extant *Techne Grammatike* which had a tremendous influence in antiquity, especially on Latin grammar, and thus on modern grammar. Included classification of the parts of speech, cases, moods, paradigms, etc.

Dionysius
Many others of the same name are listed in Schmid-Stählin and Krumbacher, including an alchemist, a letter-writer, an astronomer, a geographer, a rhetor, an ascetic, a commentator on Euripides, an epic poet, a physician, and various poets, philosophers, clergymen, sophists, and miscellaneous writers. For complete list, see Schmid-Stählin and Krumbacher.

Dionysodotus
A Spartan poet who wrote choral lyrics. Nothing survives.

Dionysus
God of vegetation, wine, and of religious ecstasy. Hardly mentioned in Homer. Worshipped by women with rites of an orgiastic nature, which included tearing an animal to pieces (see *Bacchae*). His other names include Bacchus, Zagreus, Bromius, Iacchus. His festival, the Dionysia, was the scene of the dramatic presentations at Athens. His devotees, the Maenads, were commonly clad in fawn-skins and carried the sacred wand or *thyrsus*. His worship is believed to have come from Phrygia. For full discussion, see Rose and Nilsson in the OCD.

Dionysus, Hymn to
See Homeric Hymns.

Diophantes of Alexandria (fl. 250 A.D.)

Mathematician, the first to invent a system of algebraic notation. Wrote an *Arithmetica* in 13 books, 6 of which survive. Also a work on *Polygonal Numbers,* and a *Porismata.*

Dios

Author of a *History of Phoenicia* mentioned by Josephus.

Dioscorides (1)

Last of the great Alexandrian poets. 40 epigrams in the Anthology are by him. The style is sharply epigrammatic, the subject is love, hate, etc.

Dioscorides (2) Pedianus

Physician of the 1st cent. A.D. Wrote a work on *Materia Medica,* listing plants, drugs, and remedies, arranged into careful subdivisions. The work superseded all earlier writings on the subject, and had enormous influence on later times.

Dioscuri (or Sons of Zeus)

Castor and Pollux (Polydeuces), the brothers of Helen. Twin gods, protectors of sailors. One myth deals with their alternating immortality. Identified with the constellation Gemini.

Dioscurides (1st cent. B.C. or 1st cent. A.D.)

Author of a book *On Customs in Homer,* as well as the following: *Recollections* of sayings of famous men, *Spartan Constitution,* etc. They may not all be the work of one author, however. Schmid-Stählin lists several authors of this name.

Diotimus of Thrace (fl. 250 B.C.)

Author of 10 epigrams in the Anthology.

Diphilus of Sinope

New Comedy poet who wrote about 100 plays. We have

about 60 titles and considerable fragments. Plays of his were the original for Plautus' *Rudens* and *Casina.* Judging from the Latin plays and the fragments he must have been a witty and vigorous writer.

Diphilus

The following should be mentioned:

(2) Egyptian poet of the 4th cent.

(3) Writer of Choliambics.

(4) Epic poet, writer of a *Theseid.*

(5) Author of a commentary on Nicander.

See Schmid-Stählin.

Dirge

There were two types, one sung over the body of the dead, the other in his memory. Simonides and Pindar wrote both kinds. Homer in the *Iliad* gives examples (Bks. xviii and xxiv).

Discourses

See Epictetus.

Dissoi Logoi

See *Dialexeis.*

Distaff

See Erinna.

Dithyramb

The word first appears in Archilochus, referring to a choral song in honor of Dionysus. Many poets, e.g. Simonides, Pindar, Bacchylides, et al. wrote dithyrambs. It is hard to judge, from the surviving fragments, exactly what they were like. See article by Bowra in the OCD for further information.

Divination

Some common forms of divination were from dreams, animals, birds, flour, eggs, soothsayers, weather, sneezes, lots, and random opening of books. Dreams were probably the most primitive. Examination of the liver and entrails of sacrificial animals was an important method.

Diyllus of Athens

Author of a *Universal History* in 26 books. Used by Diodorus and Plutarch.

Docianus, John

Byzantine rhetor of the 15th century, and author of an encomium on Constantine IX, the last emperor.

Dodona

Seat of an important oracle of Zeus in Western Greece.

Dorotheus (1) of Sidon

Astrological poet of the 1st or 2nd cent. A.D.

Dorotheus (2) (ca. 700 A.D.)

Byzantine scholar and author of works on the ascetic life and renunciation of the world, dress of monks, etc.

Other writers by this name include (3) An Alexander-historian, (4) a grammarian, from Ascalon, (5) a 4th century poet. See Krumbacher.

Dosiadas

Wrote a poem called *Bomos* (altar) because of its shape. See *Technopaegnia.*

Dositheus (1) of Pelusium (fl. ca. 230 B.C.)

Astronomer, wrote on meteorology and the calendar.

Dositheus (2) Magister (4th cent. A.D.)

Author of a bilingual *Ars Grammatica,* for Greeks to learn Latin from. Probably an interlinear translation.

Dositheus (3) the Gnostic

See Gnostics.

Douris (Duris) of Samos (ca 340-ca 260 B.C.)

Pupil of Theophrastus, author of historical and critical

works on painting, music, literature. History: *Hellenica, Samian Chronicle, History of Agathocles.* He was a tyrant of Samos.

Doxographers

Authors who wrote on the doctrines of philosophers. Aristotle was the first to write this type of literature. Others were Theophrastus, Diocles of Magnesia, Diogenes Laertius, Arius Didymus, etc. (qq.v.).

Doxopatres, John

Byzantine monk of the 11th century. Wrote Homilies, Prolegomena, commentaries on Hermogenes.

Dracon of Stratonicea

Wrote a number of works on grammar, metrics, lyric poets. However, the extant work attributed to him (on poetic meters) is a 16th century forgery.

Drama

See Comedy, Tragedy.

Dreams, works on

See Antiphon (2), Panyassis, Aristander, Artemidoms (3).

Drosilla and Charicles

See Eugenianus.

Ducas

15th century Byzantine author of a historical work on the last century of Byzantine history, up to the fall of Constantinople.

Duris

See Douris.

Dyscolus

See Apollonius (5).

Dyscolus (The Grouch)

If this, the only complete (or almost complete) play of

Menander is a typical one, his popularity seems a little surprising. It is a simple rustic comedy about a bad-tempered old man. It is full of slapstick and good-natured low comedy—a pleasant play, but by no means a great one. There is no chorus as such, but the papyrus indicates Choral Interludes between the scenes.

E

Easter Chronicle (or Paschal Chronicle)

A Byzantine history or chronicle from Adam to the year 627 A.D.

Ecclesiastical History

See Eusebius.

Ecclesiazusae

Comedy by Aristophanes (391 B.C.) The plot is as follows: women seize the Athenian government and introduce a form of communal life. This is so close to the situation described in *Plato's Republic* that there may be some connection. The date of the play makes the nature of such a connection uncertain, however. Perhaps Plato had written or discussed some of the ideas in the Republic before its publication. Perhaps it is mere coincidence, added to the fact that these ideas were topics of common discussion in the beginning of the 4th cent. The slight amount of personal satire and the relative unimportance of the chorus in this play are arguments in favor of its classification with Middle, rather than Old, Comedy.

Eccyclema

A platform on wheels that was rolled out from within the skene to reveal the interior in Greek tragedy. It is used in the *Agamemnon* of Aeschylus to reveal the bodies of Agamemnon and Cassandra, who have been murdered offstage; and similarly in the *Choephori.*

Eclecticism

In philosophy, the selection of doctrines from different schools. Became common in the 2nd cent. B.C.

Eclogarius Casauboni

An anonymous Byzantine historical epitome, important for the restoration of Eusebius.

Ecphantides

According to Aristotle, the earliest of the comic poets, who won his first victory ca. 457 B.C. Five fragments and two titles: *Satyroi* and *Peirai.*

Education

Varied according to the state and time. In Sparta, for instance, education consisted of military training and discipline and little else. The Ionian education stressed science, philosophy and art, i.e. the education of the "whole man." In the Hellenistic period, the rhetorical training instituted by the Sophists (q.v.) was continued, with a greater tendency to specialization in certain intellectual areas. In Athens a boy's elementary education (age 6-14) consisted of reading, arithmetic and music, and physical training in the palaestra or gymnasium. Secondary school (14-18), which was only for the wealthy, consisted of mathematics, literature, and rhetoric. Higher education was supplied either by wandering Sophists, or schools of philosophy, like Plato's Academy or Aristotle's school. There was no fixed period for this training; Aristotle was Plato's student for 20 years. The schools at Athens were closed by Justinian. In the Dark Ages that followed, education was largely private, until it was taken over by the Church (e.g. Pachomius in the 8th cent. deplored the "profane science" which leads men astray from the "true science" of Theology). Later education at Constantinople was based on a study of the classics (cf. Prodromus, who studied grammar, rhetoric, Aristotle, and Plato). Libraries were located in churches and monasteries, but they seem to have been largely theological, except for the private libraries. During the last days of the Byzantine Empire, education flourished as never before, and combined the best of classical and theological learning, even including the Western Scholasticism and Oriental knowledge. Constantinople was the center of (Greek) education until the end. By the 8th century, the "language of the Romans" was Greek, hence the term Romaic.

Ehoiai (or Eoiai)

See Hesiod.

Eirenaios

See Irenaeus.

Eirene

See *Peace* (Aristophanes).

Ekphrasis

A literary description of a work of art, monument, landscape, etc. such as the description by Paulus Silentarius of Santa Sophia.

Eleatic School

Founded by Xenophanes ca. 540 B.C. Chief exponents were Zeno, Parmenides and Melissus. Its teaching was that of materialistic monism, denying the evidence of the senses, or the existence of plurality or change.

Electra

(myth.) The daughter of Agamemnon and Clytemnestra, and the subject of dramas by all three of the great tragedians. In the *Choephori* of Aeschylus, she does not actually take part in the murder, but is represented as a poor Cinderella-like character. In the Sophocles *Electra* she is a much more spirited individual, who, when she hears her mother's death-cry, shouts: "Strike again, if thou canst!" (cf. "Triff noch einmal!" in the Strauss-Hofmannsthal opera), and who resolves to kill her mother alone, when she thinks Orestes is dead. In this play, her character is beautifully contrasted with that of her timid, "normal" sister Chrysothemis, in much the same way as the characters of Antigone and her "weak sister" Ismene had been contrasted in the *Antigone*. In the *Electra* of Euripides, she is a neurotic person who insists on going about in rags and revels in her humiliation (she has been married off to a peasant in this play, so that no offspring of hers can ever claim succession to the throne). In the Euripides play, furthermore, she not only lures Clytemnestra to her death by pretending to have had a baby, but takes active part in the murder, after which, however, she goes nearly mad with remorse. In this play, the Dioscuri, Clytemnestra's brothers and Electra's uncles, appear at the end to point out that Apollo was wrong in demanding the act of matricide. In the *Orestes* of Euripides, Electra is the nurse and keeper of her insane brother, and joins in his mad deeds (e.g. arson); in this play she marries Pylades. Elsewhere (Hyginus) she nearly kills her sister Iphigenia, thinking the latter has killed Orestes. The idea that her name means "unwedded" is nothing more than a bad pun (a-lektron) probably originated by Xanthus.

Elegiac Poetry

A development of the epic hexameter, consisting of one line of hexameter, followed by a "pentameter" or two half-hexameters. See Callinus, Archilochus, Mimnermus. It probably began in Ionia in the 8th cent. B.C. and was used for flute-songs, military poems, inscriptions, epitaphs, laments, etc. Later, it was a popular form of literary exercise. See Agathias, *Anthology*. For fuller treatment, see Bowra in the OCD.

Elements

Euclid's great work, called "the most widely read and studied book in Western Civilization, except the Bible."

Elements of Theology

See Proclus (2).

Elysium

The idea of Elysian fields appears only once in Homer (Od. iv, 561) and may be a Minoan influence. See After-life.

Embassy, On the

See Aeschines, Demosthenes.

Embassy to Gaius

See Philon (3).

Empedocles (fl. 440 B.C.)

Philosopher, orator, statesman, poet, scientist. Wrote two philosophical poems: *On Nature* and *Purifications.* Although Aristotle says in his *Poetics* that Empedocles does not deserve to be ranked as a poet, the fragments that we have appear to possess considerable literary merit. His philosophy was a pluralistic one, based on the four elements of earth, water, air, and fire, which mix and separate according to the opposite impulses of Love and strife (i.e. attraction and repulsion). Empedocles was one of the few Greeks to perform actual experiments. In the *Purifications* he writes about the Orphic doctrine of transmigration, which he presumably reconciled with his teachings in physics. The importance of E. in Greek thought is great, and the loss of his works is an irreparable one.

Empusa

A sort of amorous bogey-woman, like the Lamiae.

Enchiridion

The *Handbook* or *Manual* of Epictetus, by Arrian (qq.v.) The simplest exposition of the Stoic doctrine, it advocates man's concentrating his will on things in his power, and forgetting about things not in his power. It advocates a complete self-sufficiency and harmony with Nature. Nothing is intrinsically evil, not even pain or death. Possessions are all very well, but man should not strive for them or lament their loss ("You can't take it with you" might be the Stoic's motto). Treat property, relations, etc. as "passers-by treat an inn." The alternation between optimism and pessimism is one of the Stoic paradoxes, but a practicing Stoic would be incapable of unhappiness, for he would never lose his peace of mind.

Enchiridion of Hephaestion

A Byzantine work on metrics.

Encomium

The word is first used by Pindar. In prose it is usually either the eulogy of a real person, or an appreciation of a legendary one. The *Encomium of Helen,* supposedly by Georgias, is an example. Isocrates (q.v.) wrote encomia on *Helen* and *Busiris;* Polycrates one on *Mice;* Lucian on the *House-Fly.*

Encyclopedia of History

A Byzantine collection of excerpts made from such historians as Herodotus, Thucydides, Xenophon, Polybius, Diodorus, Dio Cassius, et al. The work was compiled under the emperor Constantine (q.v.) Porphyrogenitus.

Encyclopedic Learning

The Sophists were the first to claim all knowledge for their domain. Although the Greeks attached much importance to encyclopedic learning, they did not compose any encyclopedias (as did the Romans). For examples of polymaths, see Aristotle, Eratosthenes, Posidonius, Photius, Tzetzes, and Psellus.

Endymion

(Myth.) A beautiful youth to whom the boon of everlasting sleep was given. He was beloved by the Moon, who bore him 50 daughters, according to one version of the story.

Enneads

See Plotinus, Porphyry.

Eoiai (Ehoiai)

See Hesiod.

Eos

Goddess of Dawn, described by Homer as "rosy-fingered" (*rhododaktykos*) and "saffron-robed" (*Krokopeplos*).

Epaphroditus of Chaeronea

Grammarian of the 1st cent. A.D. Wrote commentaries on the *Iliad* and *Odyssey;* and on Hesiod and Callimachus.

Ephemerides

The word means diaries, but especially the Official Diaries of Alexander the Great, kept by Eumenes and Diodotus. These were probably the basis for the later *Alexander-Histories* (e.g. Arrian's).

Ephesiaka

See Xenophon (2). Ephesiaka is the alternate title of Xenophon's novel *Anthia and Habrocomes.*

Ephialtes

(1) A giant who was slain by Apollo.

(2) A demon.

(3) A traitor who showed the Persians the pass by which they were enabled to outflank the Spartans at Thermopylae.

(4) An Athenian statesman.

Ephippus (1)

Middle Comedy poet, author of a *Busiris* and other plays.

Ephippus (2)

A contemporary and enemy of Alexander, who wrote a rather malicious pamphlet which started the legend of Alexander's excessive drinking.

Ephorus of Cyme (ca. 405-330 B.C.)

(1) Wrote a *Universal History* in 30 books, the chief source for Diodorus. Also *History of Cyme, On Style,* and other works.

(2) Another Ephorus of Cyme was a historian in the 3rd cent. A.D.

Ephraim (1)

Patriarch of Antioch. Wrote many religious works. Only fragments.

Ephraim (2) Bishop of Cherson.

Ephraim (3) 14th cent. Byzantine historian, who wrote a versified chronicle of Roman and Byzantine history from the time of Julius Caesar until the recovery of Constantinople in 1261. The work was written in about 1315, and consists of 9564 trimeters.

Epic Cycle

Collective term for early epic poems not by Homer or Hesiod. Included the following: Before the *Iliad, a Theogony, Titanomachy,* and the *Cypria.* Between the *Iliad* and the *Odyssey,* the *Aithiopis,* the *Little Iliad,* the *Iliu Persis* (Sack of Troy), and the *Nostoi* (Returns). After the *Odyssey* came the *Telegony,* describing the death of Odysseus. There were other "cycles" besides that dealing with the Trojan War. There was an early *Thebaid,* an *Oedipodea (?),* an *Amphiarai Exelasis,* and an *Epigonoi,* all dealing with the Theban cycle. Poems about Heracles included a *Heraclea, Minyas,* and *Oechaliae Halosis;* in addition there were poems on the Argonauts, on Theseus, and others. These poems were attributed to various authors (e.g. Arctinus, Eumelus, Carcinus, Cercops, Creophylus, and others, as well as to Homer and Hesiod). Strictly, only the first group should be listed under the *Epic Cycle* heading, but the others were loosely (and disparagingly) called Cyclic as well.

Epic Poetry

In Book viii of the *Odyssey* we see the minstrel Demodocus singing at a public gathering. This must have been the beginning of the epic. We have no pre-Homeric works, although the *Iliad* and *Odyssey* must have had a long list of predecessors. Other poets, filled in the gaps between the *Iliad* and *Odyssey* (See Epic Cycle), as follows: The *Cypria* told the events leading up to the *Iliad,* the *Aethiopis* told of Achilles' death, the *Little Iliad* and *Iliu Persis* the end of the War, the *Nostoi* the fate of the other heroes on their return home (e.g. the death of Agamemnon, etc.), and the *Telegony* told of the death of Odysseus at the hands of his (unknown to him) son Telegonus. Other poems dealt with other cycles of legend (the Oedipus story, the Quest for the Golden Fleece, Heracles, Theseus, Perseus, etc.). Hesiod wrote a *Theogony* in the epic meter, but this belongs under the heading of didactic poetry, rather than epic. Later epic poetry, e.g. in the Alexandrian period, was designed to be read, rather than heard (e.g. the *Argonautica* of Apollonius of Rhodes). For later works, see Quintus Syrnaeus, Colluthus, Tryphiodorus; Musaeus (*Hero and Leander*) and Nonnus (*Dionysiaca*). The impact of Homer on the form is shown by the fact that all the later practitioners imitate him in respect to meter (dactylic hexameter) and other features. Even Lucretius, writing a work on the Atomic Theory, begins with an invocation to a goddess, because Homer did. For Byzantine epic, see *Digenis Akritas.*

Epicaste

Another name for Jocasta. See Oedipus.

Epicharmus

Sicilian writer of comedy, 5th cent. B.C. His plays differed from those of Aristophanes in that they had (apparently) no chorus, and hardly any personal satire. 35 titles survive. Some are mythological burlesques or Homeric parodies, some farces. They seem to have been directed at an intellectual audience. Epicharmus is also supposed to have written treatises on physics, medicine and ethics.

Epicles

Author of an epitome of a Hippocrates-Lexicon.

Epicrates

Middle Comedy poet, from Ambracia. In one fragment he makes fun of the scientific research of Plato and his pupils.

Epictetus (ca. 55-135 A.D.)

Stoic philosopher. A freed slave, he taught philosophy in Rome, then at Epirus, when the philosophers were banished by Domitian. Arrian (q.v.) collected his lectures in the *Discourses* and the *Enchiridion* (q.v.). Unlike earlier Stoics, his works were for the masses. He believed in, and taught, the common brotherhood of man. Happiness depends on each person's striving after only those things which are in our power. Death, illness, pain, loss of family, etc. are all matters of indifference to us, as they are not in our power to change or prevent. These things belong to the external world, and are caused by Divine Providence. Evil does not exist unless we think it does.

Epicurus (342/1-271/70 B.C.)

Athenian philosopher. Influenced by Democritus and his (and Leucippus') atomic theory, he incorporated this doctrine into his ethics, teaching that the chief evil is the superstitious fear of death and of the gods. If people could understand the physical laws of the universe, they would be free from these fears. Everything is due to the movement of the atoms in the void; at a man's death, he simply breaks up into atoms. Pleasure (i.e. freedom from physical and especially mental pain) is the chief goal in life. This was apparently misunderstood by those who identified him with a philosophy of pure pleasure or hedonism. His preserved works include *Letters to Herodotus, Pythocles,* and *Menoeceus,* the *Kyriai Doxai* (Principal Doctrines), and the *Sententiae Vaticanae.* His style is obscure, crabbed, and difficult. The Roman poet Lucretius is a better spokesman for his doctrines than Epicurus himself.

Epigenes (1) of Sicyon

Said to have been the first tragic poet. Nothing known about him.

Epigenes (2)

Middle Comedy Poet.

(3) Astrologer.

(4) A grammarian.

Epigonoi

The sons of the Seven Against Thebes (q.v.). A poem was written about their exploits. See *Epic Cycle.*

Epigram

Originally, an inscription, then, a metrical inscription. The earliest verse-epigrams are in hexameters, iambics, or elegiacs. It is not until the Hellenistic period that the form takes on its literary, artificial aspect, often emotional, dealing with love, etc. almost invariably in elegiac couplets. Invective epigrams were also common, beginning in the 3rd cent. B.C. See *Anthology,* Meleager, Agathias, *Cycle, Garland.* Highet's article in the OCD is concise and informative.

Epigraphy

The study of inscriptions on hard material (e.g. stone or metal).

Epilycus

Old or Middle Comedy author. Nothing known about his work except what Athenaeus tells us (one title: *Koraliskos*).

Epimenides

Cretan religious teacher and miracle-worker. Supposed

to have written a *Theogony, Cretica,* and *Katharmoi.* Various legends are told about him, including that of a 57-year-long sleep.

Epimerismoi

Explanations of difficult or obscure passages in ancient authors.

Epimetheus

In Mythology, the brother of Prometheus (q.v.). See also Pandora.

Epinician Odes

Poems written to celebrate a victory in the Olympian, Pythian, etc. games. See Pindar, Bacchylides.

Epinicus

New Comedy poet. Nothing known about the man or his works.

Epinomis

A Platonic or pseudo-platonic supplement to the laws. Diogenes Laertius says it is the work of Philip of Opus.

Epiphanius (ca. 315-403 A.D.)

A fourth century bishop of Cyprus. Violently opposed to all heresies (including the teachings of Origen, which he thought heretical and dangerous). Wrote *Panarion, Ancoratus.* The former is a description and refutation of about 80 heresies, the latter a treatise on Christian doctrine.

Epiphanius

The following should be mentioned:

(2) An 8th century hagiographical writer (Life of St. Andrew).

(3) Commentator on Hermogenes.

(4) A Sophist, pupil of Aeneas of Gaza.

For complete list, see Schmid-Stählin and Krumbacher.

Episode

The division or "act" of a drama. Episodes are usually separated from one another by choral odes or *stasima.*

Epistle

See Plato, New Testament, Apocrypha, John, Peter, Jude, James, Barnabas, Clement, Ignatius, etc.

Epistolai Agroikikai

See Aelian (1).

Epistolography

See Letters.

Epitaphius

A funeral speech. The most famous is that of Pericles, given by Thucydides (q.v.). Other examples: Hyperides, Lycurgus, Gorgias (fragment). Socrates in Plato's *Menexenus* recites a funeral speech.

Epithalamium

Song sung by young men and girls outside of the bridal-chamber. Examples in Sappho, Theocritus (*Epithalamium of Helen,* Theo. xviii).

Epitome

A summary of a longer work. Pamphilus' *Glossary* was reduced from 95 books to 30 to 5. Strabo and Aristotle were often epitomized, and the first two books of Athenaeus survive only in epitome. Of especial importance is the epitome of Proclus of the *Epic Cycle,* preserved by Photius. This is an extremely important source of mythology.

Epitrepontes

(*The Arbitration*). A play of Menander, most of which (ca. two-thirds) has been preserved. Plot is very involved, dealing with a girl (Pamphila) who had been ravished by a youth (Charisius) who subsequently married her, neither being aware of the other's identity. An exposed child is found with trinkets, and the Arbitration is a question of custody. The child turns out to be Pamphila's and Charisius', and everything is known at the (happy) end of the play. Until the appearance of the *Dyscolus* (q.v.) this was the most nearly complete example of New Comedy.

Eponymoi

Those who give their name to a place, e.g. Gods (Athena-Athens), heroes (e.g. Colonus), magistrates, etc.

Epops

The Hoopoe, see Aristophane's *Birds.*

Epyllion

Diminutive of Epic. A favorite form in Alexandrian times, when everything tended to run to extremes. Usually 100-600 hexameter lines. For examples, see Theocritus, Callimachus, Moschus, Bion, Euphorion. Formal artistry, learned allusions, and romantic themes are typical of the epyllion.

Er, Vision of

See Plato's *Republic.*

Erasistratus of Cos

Alexandrian physician, 3rd cent. B.C. His works were popular for many centuries. Performed post-mortem dissections. He explained all disease by the "plethora" theory.

Erato

See Muses.

Eratosthenes (1) (ca 275-194 B.C.)

Head of the Library of Alexandria, one of the greatest scholars of antiquity, certainly the most versatile of his time. Wrote on literary criticism, comedy, constellations, chronology, Olympic victories, geography, mathematics. Perhaps most famous is his calculation of the circumference of the earth, and the size and distance of the sun and moon. Also wrote poetry, philosophy, etc. In some ways, he best typifies Alexandrian scholarship. His nickname was "Beta" because he was second in poetry to Callimachus, in philosophy to Chrysippus, in astronomy to Aristarchus, in mathematics to Archimedes, in scholarship to Zenodotus. In geography and chronology, however, he was second to nobody.

Eratosthenes (2)

Historian, who wrote a *Galatica.*

Erechtheus

Legendary king of Athens, son of Earth, reared by Athena.

Eretria, school of

School of philosophy founded by Menedemus. It was a continuation of the Eleatic school.

Erinna of Telos (end of 4th cent. B.C.)

Called by Suidas a contemporary of Sappho, but this is most unlikely. A poetess, who wrote a work called the *Distaff,* a poem in 300 hexameter lines, in memory of her friend Baucis. She herself died at the age of 19. Only very few fragments survive.

Erinyes

Avenging spirits who pursued those who had killed blood-relatives. See *Oresteia, Eumenides.* In Aeschylus they are pictured as hideous, blood-sucking creatures, who have hatred for the newer gods for usurping their prerogatives. Aeschylus describes their transformation to the Eumenides (who were originally different deities confused with the Erinyes).

Eriphus

Middle Comedy Poet. Titles: *Aeolus, Meliboea.*

Eris

Goddess of Discord, who stirs up the trouble that results in the Trojan War, by throwing a golden apple inscribed "to the Fairest." This leads to the Judgment of Paris, the abduction of Helen, etc.

Erophile

Work by George Chortatzes in the 15th or 16th century. A tragedy dealing with the unhappy love of the king of Egypt.

Eros

God of Love. Does not occur as a god (although the word *eros* meaning "love" does occur) in Homer. Early linked with Aphrodite. Appears in the lyric poets of the 7th and 6th centuries. Euripides is the first to mention his bow and arrows. In Hellenistic literature, the playful rather than terrible aspect is emphasized.

Erotianus

Compiler of a glossary to Hippocrates.

Erotic Fragment

Found in an Oxyrhynchus papyrus. 40 lines of a "Maiden's Lament" at being jilted by her lover. The style is reminiscent of Sappho, though it must be much later.

Erotocritus

("Test of Love") A long poem (11,400 rhymed political verses) by Vincent Cornaro, in the last period of Byzantine literature. Best classified as a romantic epic. The work was very popular, and Cornaro was called the "Homer of Folk-literature."

Erucius (Erykios)

Author of 14 epigrams in the Anthology. He imitated Vergil (a very unusual thing for a Greek poet to do).

Eryxias

A popular pseudo-Platonic (q.v.) work.

Escurial Collection

An important collection of rhetorical and other works, made in the 13th century. Valuable source of knowledge of Byzantine literature. Includes sacred and profane speeches, essays, letters, etc. and throws considerable light on the political and religious, as well as literary history of the times.

Esdras (Ezra)

Important apocryphal work. Various books, popularly attributed to the prophet Ezra, are known as the Books of Esdras. Books I and II appear in the Septuagint and the Vulgate. Two other non-canonical works, III and IV Esdras, are included in the Vulgate. The confusion arises from the fact that these two are sometimes known as I and II Esdras, while the other two are called Ezra and Nehemiah. IV Esdras is an apocalyptic work, probably written during the first century A.D.

Eteocles

In Mythology, the elder (but in *Oedipus at Colonus,* the younger) son of Oedipus (q.v.). Dies fighting for the city of Thebes at the hands of his brother Polynices, whom he kills.

Eternity of the World, on

See Philon (3).

***Ethics, Nicomachean* (Aristotle)**

See *Nicomachean Ethics.*

Ethiopica

See Heliodorus (4).

Ethnica

See Stephanus of Byzantium.

Ethopoiia

Character-delineation, an important attribute for an orator, who would often have to write speeches for others to deliver; it was important for the speech to be appropriate to the speaker. Lysias (q.v.) was considered an expert in this. Also see Nicephorus Chrysoberges.

Etiological Myth

Any myth invented to explain some phenomenon. Greek mythology is particularly rich in such myths. Cf. the tree- and star legends, the stories of Niobe, of Midas, of Phaethon, of Io, etc.

Etymologica

Earliest etymological studies are in the philosophers. Heraclides Pontus was the first to use the title *Peri Etymologias* (lost). In Alexandrian times, the Atticizing influence led to the flourishing of etymological studies, which continued in Byzantine times. See *Etymologicum Magnum.*

Etymologicum Magnum

An extant lexicon of unknown date, based on earlier compilations of the 9th century, completed under Photius.

Euagon of Samos

Minor historian or logographer. May be identical with Eugeon (q.v.).

Euagrius (1) or Evagrius, ca. 346-99

Prolific writer on religious subjects, although little remains in Greek. Works include *Antirrhetikos* (a collection of Biblical excerpts arranged according to the deadly sins); *Sententiae, Problemata,* (now only in Syrian and Armenian), Letters, monastic treatises, etc.

Euagrius (2) ca. 536-600

Byzantine advocate and historian. Wrote a Church History in six books, important for the history of dogma in the 5th and 6th centuries.

Euaion (or Bion?)

Son of Aeschylus, who also wrote tragedies.

Euangelus

New Comedy poet. One fragment preserved from a work called *Anakalyptomene.*

Eubulides of Miletus

Teacher of Demosthenes, famous for an anti-Aristotelian satire or lampoon, and for his sophistic arguments.

Eubulus (1)

Middle (or Old?) Comedy poet. Wrote 104 plays and won six victories. Titles seem to indicate a preference for mythological burlesque *(Anchises, Auge),* but also type-comedy, etc. Considerable fragments, including a catalogue of women, riddles, Euripidean parody.

Eubulus (2)

A minor philosophical writer on Plato and Aristotle.

(3) Religious historian who wrote on Mithraism.

Eucleides

See Euclid.

Eucleides (1) of Megara

Disciple of Socrates, founder of the Megarian School. May have developed a Theory of Ideas similar to, but antedating that of Plato, but this is rather unlikely.

Eucleides (2)

Grammarian, writer of a work on Poetics.

Euclid (Eucleides) of Alexandria. Fl. 300 B.C.

Most famous for his *Stoicheia* (Elements) in 13 books, of which the first six deal with plane geometry, 7-9 on the Theory of Numbers, 10 on irrationals, 11-13 on solid geometry. "Book 14" is not by Euclid but by Hypsicles, and "Book 15" a compilation. Other works of Euclid include *Data, Pseudaria, Divisions, Porismata, Conics, Optics,*

Phaenomena (an extant work on astronomy), and a work on music. Euclid was chiefly important as an organizer and arranger of previous mathematical knowledge, although he added much that was his own.

Eudaemonism

The theory that happiness is the *summum bonum* for mankind. Not to be confused with *hedonism,* which holds that pleasure is the chief good.

Eudemian Ethics

See Aristotle.

Eudaimon

The following are to be distinguished:

(1) A poet, from Egypt.

(2) A grammarian, from Pelusium.

(3) A sophist, from Antiocheia.

Eudemus (1)

Peripatetic philosopher, pupil of Aristotle. Wrote works on the history of science and civilization, including works on arithmetic, geometry, astronomy, and a paraphrase of Aristotle's *Physics*. Edited the *Eudemian Ethics*.

Eudemus (2)

Historian, from Lindos.

(3) Logographer, from Paros.

(4) Rhetor, and source for Suidas. There is some confusion here, and two people may be involved. (See Krumbacher)

Eudocia

Byzantine empress, wife of Theodosius II (5th cent.) Wrote hymns, poetic paraphrases of the Old Testament, Homeric centos, and a hexameter poem on her husband's Persian War.

Eudorus of Alexandria

Fl. 25 B.C. An eclectic philosopher who wrote commentaries on Plato's *Timaeus,* Aristotle's *Metaphysics,* Aratus' *Phaenomena,* etc.

Eudoxus (1) of Cnidos (ca 409-355 B.C.)

Mathematician and astronomer. Wrote works on *The Mirror, Phaenomena,* and a work on concentric spheres, to explain the movements of the sun, moon, and planets. Also wrote on geography, and an eight-year cycle (*Octaeteris*). He influenced Euclid, with regard to the theory of proportions.

Eudoxus (2)

Historian, from Rhodes (fl. ca. 200 B.C.)

(3) There was also a comic poet of the same name.

Euenus

See Evenus.

Euetes

Either a tragedian or a writer of comedy. Suidas says the latter, but this is probably a confusion with the tragedian of this name.

Eugammon of Cyrene

Epic poet of the 6th cent. B.C. Reputed author of the *Telegonia* in the Epic Cycle (q.v.).

Eugenianus, Nicetas

Author of a verse novel in nine books, entitled *Drosilla and Charicles,* in the second half of the 12th cent.

Eugenicus, John

Byzantine author, first half of the 15th cent. Wrote *Ekphraseis* or descriptions (e.g. of Trebizond).

Eugenicus, Marcus

Byzantine theological writer of the 15th century, brother of John Eugenicus. Wrote polemical works against Bessarion, and against union with the Latins.

Eugenius of Augustopolis

Grammarian at the University of Constantinople under the emperor Anastasius I (ca. 500 A.D.). Wrote on the meters of Aeschylus, Sophocles and Euripides; also a Lexicon, and works on orthography, etc.

Eugeon of Samos (or Euagon?)

A logographer who wrote a history of Samos.

Euhemerus of Messene fl. ca. 300 B.C.

Author of a travel-book called *Hiera Anagraphe* (Sacred Scripture) chiefly known for its theory of the origin of the gods. Euhemerus said that they had formerly been great conquerors and kings, who were later worshipped by people as a sign of gratitude. More popular with the Romans than with the Greeks. Especially used by Christian authors like Lactantius. The word "euhemeristic" is used of mythological interpretations which account for gods such as Asclepius, by presuming them to be of mortal origin.

Euhippus

Comic poet of the 4th century B.C.

Eukleides

See Euclid.

Eumelus of Corinth

Epic poet of the 8th century B.C. (?) who wrote a *Corinthiaca* (dealing with the story of Medea, etc.) and other works, possibly a *Titanomachia.*

Eumenes

See Ephemerides.

Eumenides

The third play in Aeschylus' trilogy *Oresteia.* The title means "the Kindly Ones"— a euphemism for the Erinyes or Furies who constitute the chorus. Central part of the play is the trial scene in which Orestes is exonerated by a jury of Athenian citizens. Athena herself is the judge, and a not unbiased one. Apollo is the attorney for the defense. The end of the play shows Athena placating the Furies and inducing them to become gentler deities (Eumenides). The etiology of the Areopagus—the court for trying cases of homicide—is an important feature of the play, which ends with a long choral ode of rejoicing, similar to a "Hallelujah" chorus.

Eumetis

See Cleobuline.

Eumolpus

Legendary ancestor of the Eumolpidae and founder of the Eleusinian mysteries.

Eunapius of Sardes (346-415)

Wrote a history (*Hypomnemata Historika*) covering the years 270-404, and *Lives of the Sophists*. Source for many later historians, who quoted excerpts from it.

Euphantus of Olynthus

Author of a treatise *Peri Basileias* (on Monarchy), as well as contemporary history and tragedies.

Euphorion (1)

Son of Aeschylus, who produced plays of his father, and also wrote some of his own.

Euphorion (2) of Chalcis. b. ca. 276 B.C.

Philosopher and poet, author of numerous works in prose and verse. Prose: *On the Isthmian Games, On the Aleuadae*. Verse: epigrams, epics or epyllia (*Thrax, Chiliades, Curses, Replies to Theodoridas,* and other works). Unfortunately there are only very few fragments, so that any critical estimate is difficult. He had a considerable influence on later poets, especially the Romans (the name *Cantores Euphorionis* was applied to a school of Roman poets).

Euphron

Comic poet of the third cent. B.C. Author of New Comedies. Titles include *Theon Agora, Theoroi, Mousai* and indicate a penchant for mythological burlesques.

Euphronius (1)

Teacher of Aristarchus, author of commentaries on comedy and on metrics.

(2), (3) There were also a tragic and a comic poet of the same name.

Eupolemus

A Hellenized Jew who wrote, ca. 150 B.C. a popular history of the Jews *(Peri ton en te Ioudaian Basileion).*

Eupolis (fl. 430-410 B.C.)

One of the greatest writers of Old Comedy. We know of 17 plays of his, and he won seven victories. His *Parasites* was judged better than Aristophanes' *Peace*. Titles include: *Aiges, Baptai, Demoi, Androgynoi, Autolycus,* and others. Like Aristophanes, he dealt mainly with personal and political satire. Fragments are too scanty for any valuable critical estimate. According to one (apocryphal) story, Alcibiades was so enraged with him that he threw him into the sea.

Euripides (1) 485?-406? B.C.

The third of the great Athenian playwrights. Euripides was not popular in his own day, to judge from the four or five victories he won (Sophocles won over 20), and from the merciless satire in Aristophanes. Among other things, Euripides was accused of being a misogynist. This is patently ridiculous; Euripides had probably a greater insight into and sympathy for the suffering of women than any other dramatist who ever lived—his female characterizations are masterpieces of shrewd psychological insight, and far surpass the male characters. In succeeding generations, Euripides became the most popular of the ancient dramatists, which is why 19 (?) plays of his are preserved, as compared with only seven each of the other two tragedians. In some ways, he was ahead of his time, challenging some of the old beliefs on religion, morality, war, etc. More than the other tragedians, Euripides was a product of the new education of the Sophists (q.v.). At his worst, his plots are weak, episodic, his style over-rhetorical, and there seems to be too much striving for pathetic effect. In matters of plot structure, he was certainly not the equal of Sophocles. But at his best (e.g. *Medea, Hippolytus, Bacchae,* etc.) he ranks with Sophocles, Aeschylus and Shakespeare as one of the greatest dramatists of all time. Besides the above, the extant plays include: *Alcestis, Troades, Electra, Helen, Orestes, Iphigenia in Tauris, Suppliants, Heracleidae, Iphigenia in Aulis, Hecuba, Andromache, Hercules Furens, Ion, Phoenissae.* Also a satyr-play, *Cyclops,* and a *Rhesus,* the subject of much controversy (See under the individual titles for discussion of these plays). Lost works include *Cressae, Alcmeon, Telephus, Dictys, Philoctetes, Sisyphus, Chrysippus, Stheneboea, Hypsipyle, Antiope, Ixion, Reapers, Lamia, Eurystheus, Aegeus, Phaethon,* etc. As can be seen from the titles, Euripides was almost predominantly interested in the problems and suffering of women. His *Troades* is probably the greatest anti-war play ever written. He was free with his dramatic invention, sometimes making fun of his two predecessors for their adherence to convention. As for his plots, they usually begin with a long, formal prologue, often spoken by a god, which tells the audience all they need to know. The epilogue is often delivered by a *deus ex machina.* His choruses are usually not well integrated into the plot, serving rather as lyrical interludes (but not so in *Troades* and *Bacchae*). He strives for effect, and to this end, frequently introduces children on the stage (cf. *Troades, Medea, Alcestis,* etc.) for pathetic effect, and he was greatly criticized for introducing characters in rags (cf. *Electra*). This undoubtedly influenced Sophocles (cf. *Philoctetes*).

Euripides influenced all later writers, not only of tragedy, but even of comedy. Many of the romantic conventions (e.g. the love-triangle) originated with him, and he is the first to represent Eros with bow and arrows. As inventor of the romantic drama of love, he stands as the ancestor of New Comedy. Many of his plays are sometimes classified as melodrama or tragi-comedy, instead of tragedy. Aristotle says of him (Poetics): "Even if his execution be faulty in every other point, (Euripides) is seen to be nevertheless the most tragic certainly of the dramatists."

Euripides (2)

The son of the playwright (or possibly his nephew; there is some confusion here) who produced a play of his father (uncle?) posthumously, and wrote plays himself. There may be two people involved, but this is unlikely.

Europa

In mythology, the daughter of Agenor (or Phoenix). Beloved by Zeus, who sent, or appeared as, a bull, which carried her off to Crete, where she became the mother of Minos, Rhadamanthus, and according to some accounts, Sarpedon.

Europa

An epyllion, or toy epic, by Moschus (q.v.) in 166 hexameters, describing the Rape of Europa. The model for Catullus' *Peleus and Thetis.*

Eurycleia

The old nurse of Odysseus, who recognized him from an old scar. She assists in the slaughter of the Suitors by keeping the maids in their quarters.

Eurydice

(1) The wife of Orpheus. Fatally bitten by a snake, she was allowed to return to the upper world (because the play-

ing of Orpheus so charmed the infernal powers) if he did not turn to look at her. He did so, however, and she was lost. In the Gluck opera *Orfeo ed Eurydice,* she was redeemed a second time for a happy ending. The story has obvious parallels to that of Lot's wife.

(2) Wife of Creon in the *Antigone* of Sophocles. Commits suicide on the death of her son Haemon.

Eusebius (1) of Caesarea (ca. 260-340 A.D.)

Prolific Christian author. Wrote *Chronica, Church History, Life of Constantine, Preparation of the Gospel, Against Hierocles,* as well as exegetical works, speeches, letters, commentaries, apologetic and dogmatic works. Jerome said his works were "innumerable." It is chiefly as a church historian and scholar that he is known today.

Eusebius

The following should also be mentioned:

(2) Sophist, from Alexandria.
(3) Another sophist, from Antiocheia.
(4) Historian under Diocletian.
(5) Poet of the 4th cent. A.D.
(6) Neopythagorean, from Myndos.
(7) Bishop of Nicomedea, teacher of the emperor Julian.
(8) Philosopher, author of proverbs in Ionic.

Eustathius (1) of Antiocheia

Bishop of the 4th cent. Wrote on the Arians, on the Witch of Endor, on the Soul.

Eustathius (2) of Thessalonica

12th cent. Byzantine scholar. Wrote a commentary on Pindar, a paraphrase of Dionysius Periegetes, Commentaries on the *Iliad* and *Odyssey,* a treatise on Monastic Life, a history of the Norman Conquest of Thessalonica, speeches, sermons, letters, and other works. One of the greatest scholars of his age.

Eustathius

Others of this name include:

(3) a historian, from Epiphaneia.

(4) a Neoplatonic philosopher, author of a commentary on Hermogenes.

(5) a Sophist in Tyre.

Eustochius of Alexandria (3rd cent. A.D.)

Physician; pupil of Plotinus, whose works he edited.

Euterpe

See Muses.

Euthycles

Writer of Old or Middle Comedy. Only two titles: *Asotoi* or *Epistole* and *Atalante.*

Euthydemus

(1) Sophist ridiculed by Plato in the dialogue *Euthydemus.*

(2) Phoenician rhetor.

Euthymius Zigabenus

See Zigabenus.

Euthyphro

Dialogue of Plato (q.v.). Deals with definition of piety.

Eutocius

Matematician, born ca. 480 A.D. Wrote commentaries on Archimedes and Apollonius of Perga.

Eutropius

Historian of the 4th cent. A.D. Wrote a (Latin) history which was translated into Greek by Paeanius.

Eutyches

Denied the two natures of Christ, holding that only the divine nature existed. Condemned and excommunicated by the Council of Chalcedon in 451. See Monophysitism.

Evagrius
See Euagrius.

Evenus (Euenus) of Paros
Poet and Sophist mentioned by Socrates in the *Apology*.

Exagoge
See Ezechiel.

Exegesis of the Law of Moses
See Aristobulus (2).

Exhortation
See Clement of Alexandria, Iamblichus.

Exodos
The final portion of a Greek tragedy, wherein the chorus leaves the stage.

Ezechiel
Greek-Jewish author of a drama *Exagoge* on the Exodus from Egypt. Over 200 lives survive. The style is reminiscent of Euripides.

Ezra
See Esdras; Apocrypha.

F

Fabius Pictor

One of the earliest Roman historians. Wrote a history of Rome from its legendary founding to the Second Punic War, in Greek.

Fable

The term usually means a little story about animals with a moral implication for men. Hesiod and Archilochus use the fable, but not Homer. By the 5th century, the collection of fables was attributed to Aesop (q.v.). The earliest extant collection is that of Babrius. In Byzantine times the fable was also popular.

Fall and Recapture of Constantinople

Byzantine poem by an unknown author, of little historical, but some literary value.

Fate

In Homer, Fate is regarded as both coming from Zeus and as superior to him, in a sense. There must have been an evolution from an abstract noun to a personification, then to a deity, then to three. Words for Fate are: *aisa* (a man's lot), *moira* (lot, or destiny), and *ananke* (necessity). Although Moira may be practically equated with death, she is regarded as distinct from Thanatos. The notion of the "spinners" is an early one. Homer mentions them, but does not give their names. Hesiod, however, does: Lachesis, who assigns the lot, Clotho, who spins the thread, and Atropos, who cuts it. The question of the relationship of the Fates to the gods is a difficult one, as is the question of fate versus free-will, e.g. in the Oedipus story. He is regarded as somehow being responsible for what was "fated." (For the best discussion of the problem, see Greene, W. C., *Moira: Fate, Good and Evil, in Greek Thought.*)

"Father of History"

See Herodotus. ("Father of Medicine"—Hippocrates)

Favorinus (ca. 80-150 A.D.)

A Gaul, rhetor, historian, and hermaphrodite. Wrote many works, most of which are lost: *Miscellaneous History,* an encyclopedia, memoirs, *Pyrrhonian Modes,* and speeches. Two of the speeches under the name of Dio Chrysostom have been assigned to Favorinus.

Festivals

Sacred rites repeated at yearly (or other) intervals. Usually of agricultural origin. At the Dionysia and Lenaea the dramatic performances took place in Athens.

Figure poems

Poems in different shapes, like the "Mouse's Tale" in *Alice in Wonderland.* Examples: the *Pan-Pipe* of Theocritus, the *Axe, Wings,* and *Egg* of Simmias, the *Altar* of Dosiadas (also one of the same name by Besantinus). The Greek term for the form is *Technopaegnia.*

Firmilianus

Author of a letter (middle of the 3rd cent. A.D.) on the Baptism of Heretics.

Firminius

Sophist of the 4th cent. A.D. Known from the letters of Libanius.

Flavius

See Clement.

Flavius Josephus

See Josephus.

Folk-Tales

Themes from the folk-tale, or Märchen, are frequent in classical literature: the Home-comer's Vow, involving the sacrifice of the first living thing he sees (e.g. his child); the Invulnerable Hero; the husband who returns in time to stop his wife from marrying someone else, the beast-fable, etc. See Rose in OCD.

Forgeries

See Pseudepigrapha. The difference is that in the case of forgeries, the substitution is intentional, but it is very difficult to determine whether there was intent to deceive, in many cases of real or supposed forgery.

"Fortunate Isles"

(Isles of the Blessed). Identified with Madeira or the Canaries. Mentioned as early as Homer, also in Hesiod, Pindar, etc. Mythical home of the happy dead.

Fountain of Knowledge

See John of Damascus, Nilus Diassorinus.

Frogs, the

Comedy by Aristophanes (405 B.C.). Dionysus, god of Tragedy, goes down to Hades to bring back Euripides, who has just died. Since Heracles succeeded in bringing back Cerberus, the god dresses in the lion-skin and club of the hero. After the famous "croaking chorus" of the Frogs: "Brekekekex co-ax co-ax," the central part of the play consists of a long debate *(agon)* between Aeschylus and Euripides, which contains much brilliant parody, some shrewd literary criticism, and a lot of fun. Aeschylus, of course, wins (Dionysus tells Euripides: " 'Twas but my tongue, and not my soul, that swore," quoting the famous line from *Hippolytus*), but only after the comic business of both poets speaking words into a giant scale. Although the chief target for lampoons is Euripides (as frequently in Aristophanes), Aeschylus does not get off scot-free, and his refrains, long words, etc. are satirized. The wit in this comedy is generally on a high intellectual level, though there is also some slapstick and indecency, as always in Aristophanes.

Furies

See Erinyes.

G

Gaia (Ge)

The Earth, offspring of Chaos, Uranus (Heaven) is her child and husband. Titans, Cyclopes, Erinyes, etc. are her children.

Galatea

A sea-nymph loved by Polyphemus, but in love with Acis. Polyphemus kills Acis. Story told by various pastoral writers. In antiquity the name Galatea does not appear as the name of Pygmalion's statue.

Galen of Pergamum (129?-199 A.D.)

Philosopher and physician. An eclectic writer, equally great in theory and practice. Wrote many works on physiology, anatomy, pathology. He proved that the arteries carry blood, and did much physiological research based on experiment. Also wrote on pharmacology, dietetics, and other medical subjects; as well as works on philosophy, philology, rhetoric, commentaries on Hippocrates, hygiene, etc. For complete list, see Schmid-Stählin. Galen may be compared to Aristotle for his summarizing, classifying, and explaining all existing knowledge in his field, and his influence on later generations was also comparable to that of Aristotle.

Galeomyomachia

(Battle of the Cats and Mice) See Prodromus.

Ganymede(s)

A beautiful Trojan youth, carried off by the gods to be

the cupbearer for Zeus. According to some accounts it was an eagle that snatched him away.

Garden (Kepos)
The school of Epicurus (q.v.).

***Garland* (of Meleager)**
See *Anthology,* Meleager.

Gelasius (1)
Bishop of Caesarea, d. 395. Wrote a continuation of Eusebius (q.v. 1) of which only fragments survive.

(2) Another Gelasius, of Cyzicus, a century later, wrote on the Nicene Council.

Geminus of Rhodes
(1) Stoic philosopher of the first century B.C. Wrote a treatise on mathematics, which included a complete classification of the mathematical sciences. Also wrote *Introduction to Phaenomena,* an elementary astronomy textbook.

(2) Another Geminus wrote a work on dreams.

Generatione Animalium, de
See Aristotle.

Genesius, Joseph
Byzantine historian of the 10th century. Commissioned by the emperor Constantine Porphyrogenitus, he wrote an Imperial History in 4 books, covering the reigns of Leo V, Michael II, Theophilus, Michael III, Basil I (813-886). It is full of miracles, gossip, etc.

Gennadius (1)
Patriarch of Constantinople 458-471 A.D. Wrote polemics, homilies, letters. A bitter opponent of Origen, he wrote a polemic against the Apology of Pamphilus and Eusebius, also polemics against Apollinarius, and Cyril of Alexandria.

Gennadius 2 (Georgius Scholarius) d. 1468

The first patriarch after the fall of Constantinople, and the last of the great Byzantine polemicists. Wrote against the Latins, but also interested in Western scholasticism. Translated some of Thomas Aquinas into Greek, and helped to introduce Plato to the West. Also wrote polemics against the Jews and Islam.

Gentilianus Amelius

Student of Plotinus 246-269. Wrote many works; nothing survives.

Geographical Lexicon

See Stephanus of Byzantium.

Geographica

See Strabo.

Geography

The Greeks were the first people to write on geography as a science. Works include reports on areas, maps, manuals for travellers, and descriptions (*periegeseis*). Aristotle proved that the earth is round. Dicaearchus and Eratosthenes (qq.v.) made important calculations. Ptolemy, in his *Geographike Hyphegesis,* used curved lines of latitude and meridians of longitude. The work of Strabo (q.v.) includes physical topography, mathematical geography, and political and historical information. See also Aristarchus, Agatharchides, Nearchus, Posidonius, Arrian, *Periplus,* and Dionysius Periegetes.

Geometrus, John

Byzantine writer of epigrams. Wrote on the disasters of the second half of the Tenth Century.

Geoponica

Work on agriculture by the Carthaginian Mago, translated into Greek by Cassius Dionysius. It became the standard work on the subject.

Georgillas

See Limenites.

George (1) of Cyprus

Wrote, in the 7th cent. a description of the Eastern Empire, like the *Synekdemos* of Hierocles (q.v. 2).

Georgius (2) Monachus (George the Monk)

Byzantine chronicler ca. 850 A.D. Wrote a *World Chronicle* from Adam to the year 842.

Georgius (3) Pachymeres

See Pachymeres.

George (4) the Patriarch

An important Byzantine writer of the 13th century. Wrote an autobiography, encomia, proverbs, speeches, letters, and other sacred and profane works.

George (5) of Pisidia

Wrote epigrams in iambic trimeters—7th century A.D.

Georgius (6) Scholarius

See Gennadius (2).

Georgius (7) Syncellus

Byzantine chronicler, secretary to the Patriarch Tarasius (784-810), who wrote a *World-Chronicle* from the Creation to the time of Diocletian. Also wrote chronological tables with interspersed commentaries.

Georgius (George)

(8) Patriarch of Alexandria, hagiographer.

(9) Commentator on Hermogenes.

(10) G. of Nicomedia, panegyrist and writer of sacred poetry.

(11) Bishop of Naxos, hagiographer.

Many others. See Krumbacher for complete list.

Germanicus Caesar

Translated Aratus (q.v.); wrote Greek poetry and comedies.

Germanus (1) d. 733

Metropolitan of Cyzicus, later patriarch of Constantinople in the 8th century. Involved in the Iconoclastic Controversy. His works were burned by the emperor Leo. Wrote a polemic against Origen and Gregory of Nyssa, also dialogues, letters, etc.

(2) Patriarch of Constantinople 1222-40. Letters, sermons.

(3) Church poet.

(4) Patriarch of Nicaea.

Several others. See Krumbacher for complete list.

Giants

Mythological race, sons of Ge. See Gigantomachy, Ephialtes, etc.

Gigantia

Epic by Scopelianus (q.v.).

Gigantomachia

Lost poem on the battle of gods and giants. Also, a parody by Hegemon (q.v. 1).

Gitiadas

Spartan poet after Alcman. Wrote choral lyrics. Nothing is preserved.

Glaucon

(1) of Ephesus, tragedian.

(2) Plato's brother, a character in the *Republic.*

Glaucus (1)

In the *Iliad,* a Lycian ally of the Trojans. He meets Diomedes on the battlefield and they exchange armor, because of their hereditary guest-friendship. Glaucus gets the worst of the exchange, giving gold armor for bronze.

Glaucus (2) ca. 400 B.C.

Wrote a work on ancient poets and musicians, a source for Plutarch. Others of the same name include:

(3) A writer on Aeschylus.

(4) A grammarian, from Samos.

(5) Author of an *Arabica.*

(6) Writer of epigrams.

Glossa, Glossary

Glossai were words belonging to a literary dialect rather than to the spoken language. Homeric glosses, or collections of words and dialectical forms, were made, also collections from Old Comedy, Alcman, etc. In the Alexandrian period, collections were made of all sorts of special vocabularies (e.g. lists of fishes, winds, etc.) Many of these collections are preserved in extant scholiasts and lexicographers. See *Onomastikon.* Aristophanes of Byzantium (q.v.), Artemidorus, and others made collections of glosses. By the first century, compilation takes the place of research.

Glycas, Michael

Byzantine author of the 12th century. Tried for political reasons, imprisoned and blinded. Wrote a chronicle from the Creation to the year 1118, full of scientific, theological and miscellaneous information.

Glycon

An unknown poet to whom the invention of the Glyconic meter was attributed.

Glycys, John

Patriarch of Constantinople in the 14th cent. In addition to his theological writings, he wrote a voluminous work on syntax.

Gnome

A proverb, or pithy expression. They occur all through Greek literature and thought. Examples: *Gnothi seauton*

(Know thyself), *Meden agan* (Nothing in excess). Hesiod is full of these gnomic utterances, so are the dramatists, especially Euripides. See *Chreia* for collections of gnomes.

Gnosticism

"The acute Hellenization of Christianity." Tended towards a repudiation of the Old Testament. Both dualistic and monistic. For a list of Gnostic writers, see Schmid-Stählin, Ferm, *Encyclopedia of Religion* and OCD.

Gods, Olympian

See Zeus, Poseidon, Apollo, Hephaestus, Ares, Hermes, Hera, Aphrodite, Artemis, Athena, Demeter, Hestia. Other deities include Hades, Persephone, Dionysus, Eros, and such personifications as Nemesis, Eris, Ate, etc.

Gorgias (1) of Leontini (ca. 483-376 B.C.)

One of the most important of the Sophists (q.v.), usually designated as the father of artistic prose. Wrote a philosophical treatise, maintaining that nothing exists; if anything does exist, it cannot be known; if it can be known, it cannot be communicated.

Gorgias (2)

Athenian rhetor and Atticist of the first cent. B.C. Teacher of Cicero's son, and author of a treatise *Peri Schematon.*

Gorgias

Title of a dialogue by Plato (q.v.).

Gorgon (or Medusa)

A monster whose sight turned men into stone. Killed by Perseus (q.v.), Pegasus, the winged horse, sprang from her blood. There were also other Gorgons.

Gospels

Mark's was the earliest. The purpose of the Gospels was primarily apologetic and didactic. The Canon of the four gospels (Mark, Matthew, Luke and John) was formed ca. 150 A.D. The first three of these are called the Synoptic Gospels. See New Testament, *Koine.*

Graces

See *Charites.*

Graeae

In mythology, three sisters, old hags who shared a common eye and tooth. Perseus (q.v.) stole their eye and thus forced them to tell him where to find the Gorgon. Daughters of Phorcys.

Grammar

The study of grammar beings with the Sophists of the 5th century. Democritus wrote a (lost) work on cacophonous and euphonious letters. Plato distinguishes *rhemata* and *onomota* (predications and designations). Protagoras and Aristotle classified words into parts of speech, according to their functions. The Stoics (e.g. Chrysippus, etc.) continued with the classification of parts of speech and cases and tenses. Further study, classification, and codification took place in Alexandrian times (see Aristarchus, Dionysius Thrax, etc.) Apollonius Dyscolus (q.v.) had a tremendous influence on later grammarians. See also *Philology.*

Greek Anthology

See *Anthology.*

Gregoras, Nicephorus (1295-1360)

One of the last of the great Byzantine polymaths. Wrote numerous works on theology, philosophy, astronomy, history, rhetoric, grammar, etc. In 1325 he proposed a calendar reform, but in vain. One of his most important works is the *Roman History* in 37 books (1204-1359; with emphasis on the last 40 years of this period).

Gregory Acyndinus

See Acyndinus.

Gregory (1) of Agrigentum

Ecclesiastical writer of the 6th century. Wrote on fasts, an *Encomium of Peter, Panegyrics,* a commentary on Ecclesiastes, etc.

Gregory (2) Patriarch of Antiochia 570-93

Writer of sermons on the Passion, Resurrection, etc.

Gregory (3) of Corinth (ca. 1300 A.D.)

Grammarian, wrote commentaries, and a work on dialects.

Gregory (4) of Cyprus

Byzantine theologian of the 13th century. Opponent of Beccus (q.v.), against whom he wrote a polemic.

Gregory Mammas

See Mammas.

Gregory (5) Nazianzus (ca. 326-390)

One of the greatest of the Church Fathers. Wrote 45 speeches, 243 letters, as well as poetry. Most of the speeches are on theological subjects (e.g. the Trinity), holidays, etc. The letters to his friends are masterpieces of epistolary style. The *Christus Patiens,* attributed to him is probably of much later date.

Gregory (6) of Nyssa (died 395)

Bishop of Nyssa in Cappadocia. Great theologian and versatile writer. Wrote speeches, letters, exegetical and dogmatic works, etc.

Gregory, Palamas

See Palamas.

Gregory (7) Sinaites

Monk at the Sinai monastery, ca. 1300 Wrote works on monastic life, asceticism, etc.

Gregory (8) Thaumaturgus (ca. 213-272)

Was converted to Christianity after hearing Origen. Became a bishop in Pontus. Wrote sermons, letters, speeches.

Gregory

For complete list, which includes hagiographers, polemicists, poets, ascetics, etc. see Krumbacher.

Grote, G.

Greek historian, partly responsible for the *Achilleis* (q.v.) theory.

Grouch, the

See Dyscolus.

Gymnasium

Place for exercise and physical training, consisting of a track and palaestra. Very important for Greek education.

H

Habron (1) of Phrygia

Grammarian of the first century A.D. Wrote *Peri Antonymias,* cited by Apollonius Dyscolus.

(2) Habron of Bate, exegetical writer.

Hades

Means "the unseen." God of the underworld, son of Kronos. Not the name of a place, except as one would say: "Let's go to Joe's." (i.e. Joe's house.) Thus heroes are spoken of as going to (the realm of) Hades. He is grim, but not evil. He does not torment the souls of the dead. The most familiar of his myths is the Rape of Persephone (q.v.).

Hadrian

Roman Emperor 117-138 A.D. An extremely literate and cultivated man, who wrote Greek epigrams and other verse.

Haemon

Son of Creon (q.v., see also Antigone). According to a later version of the story (Apollodorus) he was killed by the Sphinx.

Hagia Sophia

The great cathedral of Constantinople, rebuilt by Justinian. Usually known by the Latin name of Santa Sophia. See Paulus (1).

Hagias (or Agias)
Reputed author of the *Nostoi* (See Epic Cycle).

Hagiography
That branch of literature that deals with the lives of saints and martyrs. Byzantine writers on hagiography were extremely numerous, including the following: Cyril of Scythopolis, John Moschus, Sophronius, Leontius, Epiphanius, Symeon Metaphrastes, Planudes, Xanthopulos, Neilus, Philotheus, Nicephorus Gregoras, etc. (vid. Krumbacher, s.v. and passim).

Halicarnassus
Town in Southwestern Asia Minor, the site of the famous Mausoleum built by Queen Artemisia for her husband Mausolus. Halicarnassus was the birthplace of Herodotus.

Halieutica
Title of a work on fishing. See Oppian, Numenius (2).

Hamartia
The "error in judgment" or the "tragic flaw" that Aristotle says is necessary for the downfall of the ideal tragic hero. Considerable debate has arisen over the precise meaning of the term, which originally comes from archery and means a "missing of the mark." It makes a great difference whether this is simply a mistake, or a character flaw. Conceivably, it could mean both, the latter causing the former.

Hanno of Carthage
Wrote a work on Africa, probably in the 5th century B.C. The work was written in Punic, but a Greek translation survives. It is the first work to mention gorillas.

Hapax Legomenon
A word that appears only once. See Lycophron.

Haplucheir, Michael
Byzantine poet, end of the 12th cent. Wrote a *Drama-*

tion (playlet or Comedietta) in 122 trimeters. The characters are: a farmer, a wise man, Tyche (Fortune), the Muses, and a chorus.

Harmonics

See Aristoxenus, Euclid, Plutarch, Music.

Harmony of the Gospels

See Tatian, *Diatessaron.*

Harpies

Winged monsters who seize (*harpazo*) food from people. Their names are Aello, Ocypete and Celaeno. They snatch the food from the blind Phineus, defiling with excrement what they leave. Dawson's explanation is that Apollonius, who mentions them in his *Argonautica,* had heard of the Indian bats, which are voracious, dirty, fruit-eaters. In art they were represented as birds with the faces of women; so in Vergil.

Harpocration, Valerius, of Alexandria. Unknown date

Lexicographer, author of a *Lexicon of the Ten Orators,* a valuable source of information, not only on oratory, but on such subjects as legal, religious, artistic, constitutional, matters.

Others of the same name include:

(2) Egyptian author of a Hermetical work.

(3) Author of a *Techne,* works on falsehood in Herodotus, on Xenophon, Antiphon, etc.

(4) Pupil of Numenius; a philosopher.

For complete list, see Schmid-Stählin.

Hebe

Daughter of Zeus and Hera, cup-bearer to the gods. Married to Heracles. Her name means "youthful beauty."

Hecabe

See Hecuba.

Hecale (Hecaline)

A goddess or old woman who entertained Theseus. Callimachus wrote an epyllion entitled *Hecale,* dealing with Theseus and the Bull of Marathon, and telling how he was entertained by a poor but hospitable old woman.

Hecataeus (1) of Miletus

Logographer, used by Herodotus. He wrote two works, each the first ever written: (1) *Genealogiae* (or Histories), (2) *Periegesis* (Voyage around the World, including a map).

Hecataeus (2) of Teos or Abdera

Author of an *Aegyptiaca,* or popular history of Egypt, written ca. 300 B.C.

Hecate

A Chthonian goddess. She does not occur in Homer. She is frequently associated with ghosts, and worshipped at the crossroads. She also has associations with sorcery and black magic.

Hecaton of Rhodes

A Stoic philosopher of the 2nd century B.C. Wrote on ethics (*Peri Agathon, peri Areton, peri Paradoxon,* etc.) Some of his arguments are preserved by Cicero.

Hecatoncheires

Hundred-handed monsters who helped Zeus in his war with the Titans. Their names are Cottus, Briareus, and Gyes.

Hector

In mythology, the eldest son of Priam, and chief defender of Troy. Virtually all we know about him comes from Homer. He is noble, generous, brave (although he runs from Achilles). He is killed by Achilles, who drags his body around the walls of Troy. His body is ransomed by Priam, and the Iliad ends with his funeral, and the laments of Andromache, Hecuba and Helen. His farewell to Andromache in Book vi of the *Iliad* is one of the most touching scenes in literature.

Hecuba

(Hecabe) Wife of Priam, mother of Hector. A dignified but pathetic figure in Homer.

Hecuba

Play by Euripides. Tells of the sacrifice of Hecuba's daughter Polyxena, by the Greeks, to appease the shade of Achilles; and of Hecuba's vengeance upon Polymestor, king of Thrace (he had murdered her son Polydorus, and she killed his children and blinded him). It is not one of Euripides' best plays, and falls into two parts. The speech of the herald Talthybius, telling of the death of Polyxena, is rather fine. The play contains the curious prophecy, by Polymestor, that Hecuba will turn into a bitch before her death.

Hecyra

A mimodrama; also a play by Apollodorus (q.v.2) which was the original of Terence's comedy of the same name.

Hedylus (fl. 270 B.C.)

Greek epigrammatist, author of three fine poems in the *Anthology*.

Hegemon (1) of Thasos

A writer of parodies, or of Old Comedies. He is said to have raised Parody to an independent form of literature, with its own place in competitions. He won one such competition with his parody *Gigantomachia*.

Hegemon (2)

Alexandrian epic poet, author of a *Darcanica*.

Hegemonius

A Syrian of the 4th century, who wrote an *Acta Archelai*. Nothing else known about him.

Hegesander of Delphi

Wrote memoirs (*Hypomnemata*) in the 2nd century B.C. as well as a collection of anecdotes.

Hegesias (1)

Epic poet, reputed author of the *Cypria* (see Epic Cycle, *Cypria*).

Hegesias (2) of Cyrene, (Peisithanatos)

Head of the Cyrenaic school; advocated suicide, hence the nickname. Expelled from Alexandria because of his lectures. Wrote *Apokarteron.*

Hegesias (3) of Magnesia Fl. ca. 250 B.C.

Wrote speeches, and a *History of Alexander.* Arch-corrupter of style, and one of the first Asianists (See Asianism). Faults in his style were: short sentences, unnatural word-order, over-bold metaphors, etc.

Hegesippus (1) of Sunium

Orator and contemporary of Demosthenes. Supporter of the Anti-Macedonian policy. Nicknamed "krobylos" because he wore his hair in a top-knot. The speech *De Halonneso* (formerly attributed to Demosthenes) was made in answer to Philip's offer to give (or return) to Athens an island that neither side really wanted.

Hegesippus (2)

A New Comedy poet. One fragment is about a conceited cook.

Hegesippus (3) (fl. ca. 300 B.C.)

Epigrammatist, author of eight poems in the *Greek Anthology.* Mostly inscriptions for votive tablets and tombs, they are in a formal and archaic style.

Hegesippus (4) of Mecyberna

Writer of an Alexander-history.

Hegesippus (5) ca. 180 A.D.

Author of a book of *Memoirs,* the earliest Christian history after the *Acts of the Apostles.* The work is lost, but fragments are preserved in Eusebius.

Helen

Daughter of Zeus and Leda, a "faded goddess" according to H. J. Rose; In Homer, she is the wife of Menelaus, carried off to Troy by Paris. In the *Iliad* she is the wife, not the mistress of Paris, and consequently, feels quite ambivalent about the war. After the fall of Troy, there was a reconciliation with Menelaus, and they lived "happily ever after." According to other versions of the story, she never went to Troy at all, but to Egypt (see Stesichorus; Euripides' *Helen*), and Zeus sent a phantom of her to Troy with Paris. In either case, she was the cause of the Trojan War.

***Helen* (412 B.C.)**

A romantic melodrama by Euripides, who uses the Stesichorus (q.v.) version of the Helen story, in which the real Helen has gone to Egypt, a phantom of her having gone to Troy. The Egyptian king Theoclymenus wants to marry her; meanwhile Menelaus with the phantom Helen has been shipwrecked nearby. The play ends, after various intrigues, with the escape of Menelaus and Helen to Sparta. Not a great play, but has some good features.

Helenus

Son of Priam, warrior and seer. He was captured by Odysseus and prophesied the fall of Troy if Philoctetes (q.v.) came with his bow. After the war, Neoptolemus gives him Andromache as his wife, and they settle in Epirus, where Aeneas visits them, and Helenus tells Aeneas of his future wanderings.

Helicon

A mountain of Boeotia, known in antiquity as the home

of the Muses, whose shrine was located there. At its foot was Ascra, the home of the poet Hesiod.

Heliodorus (1) ca. 150 B.C.

Author of *Anathemata,* works on the treasures of the Acropolis.

Heliodorus (2)

Wrote a work on *Meters* (1st century A.D.), and edited the comedies of Aristophanes, with metrical signs, commentary, etc. Preserved in the scholia to Aristophanes.

Heliodorus (3)

Physician, ca. 100 A.D., belonging to the pneumatic school, mentioned by Juvenal. Wrote on surgery, phlebotomy, bandages, etc.

Heliodorus (4) of Emesa

Author of a novel called *Aethiopica* or *Theagenes and Chariclea.* It is a romantic love-story, full of masquerades and mistaken identities, hairbreadth escapes, pirates, separations and reunions, with the inevitable "happily ever after" ending. The main plot is enlivened with sub-plots and stories; the style is rhetorical but not bad, and this is probably the best of the extant novels. It exercised a considerable influence on later romance and drama.

Heliodorus

The following should also be mentioned:

(5) An alchemist.

(6) A peripatetic philosopher, from Alexandria.

(7) A Sophist, from Arabia.

(8) An Astrologer.

(9) A Mathematician, from Larissa.

(10) A Neoplatonist and astronomer.

For complete list, see Schmid-Stählin.

Helius

The sun-god. Not one of the Olympian gods. His chief

myth is the story of Phaethon (q.v.). Identified with other gods, especially Apollo.

Helladius

See *Chrestomathia.*

Hellanicus of Mytilene

Born ca. 500 B.C. Wrote works on history and mythology of countries and cities, in prose and verse. The mythology is better than the history, which was full of guesswork and errors.

Hellenes

The national name of the Greeks from the seventh century onwards. Homer does not mention Hellenes, but once, in the Catalogue of Ships, he refers to the Panhellenes.

Hellenica

Title of a history by Xenophon, continuing that of Thucydides, and going down to the battle of Mantinea (362 B.C.). Works of this title were also written by Callisthenes, Theopompus, Ephorus, Duris, Neanthes, and Anaximenes.

Hellenica Oxyrhynchia

About 900 lines from a lost history were discovered at Oxyrhynchus in Egypt in 1906. Apparently a continuation of Thucydides. The question of authorship has been much debated, the work having variously been assigned to Theopompus, Ephorus, Cratippus, Daimachus.

Hellenistic Literature

After the time of Alexander the Great, Greek culture was diffused through the known world. This diffusion, combining with the existing cultures, is known as Hellenistic (Greek-like) rather than Hellenic or Greek. The *Koine* begins to supersede other dialects. Emphasis is placed on learning and scholarship: it is the age of the grammarians, philologists and polymaths (See Aristarchus, Eratosthenes, Callimachus, Zeonodotus, etc.). When the "Canons" were formed, when Homeric scholarship and recension took place. Alexandria and other cities replaced Athens as cultural centers. It was an age of cosmopolitan, rather than national feeling. It was the age of the epigram and the epyllion (toy epic). Jewish and Christian works were written in Greek. Generally, the Hellenistic period may be considered as ending with the Greco-Roman (ca. 150 B.C.).

Heniochus

Middle Comedy author. Some fragments survive. One title: *Polyeuctus.*

Hepatoscopy

One of the commonest forms of divination, consisting of the inspection of the liver of sacrificial animals.

Hephaestion (1)

A writer on metrics in the 2nd cent. A.D. His *Peri Metron* was originally in 48 books, but the extant one is an abridgement or *encheiridion.* His chief use is not in the field of metrics *qua* metrics, but for his preservation of fragments of lost poems.

(2) A sophist, probably of the 4th century A.D.

(3) A Theban astrologer.

Hephaestus

God of fire and the forge, associated with volcanoes, and identified with Vulcan. He is represented as being lame, and married to Aphrodite. The Cyclopes are his workmen. He made the wonderful shield of Achilles, Agamemnon's scepter, etc. He is both the god of craftsmen and the craftsman of the gods.

Hera

The queen of the gods; both sister and wife of Zeus.

Goddess of marriage and of women. Originally worshipped in Argos and Samos. Homer pictures her as a nagging wife of Zeus. She was identified with the Roman Juno.

Heraclea

Title of a work or works on Heracles. See Peisander (1), Panyassis, Rhianus.

Heracleidae

Play by Euripides, ca. 427 B.C. Probably the earliest of the "political" plays. It is a rather poor play. Plot is concerned with the children of Heracles, who take refuge at Marathon from the enmity of Eurystheus. One of the daughters offers herself as the necessary sacrifice for the victory of the Athenians. Eurystheus is defeated and promises posthumous aid against the descendants of the Heracleidae (i.e. the Spartans) if he is given proper burial.

Heracles (or Hercules)

The most popular of the Greek heroes. Myths deal with his birth, his madness and death (and apotheosis), and especially with the Twelve Labors: The Nemean Lion, the Lernaean Hydra, the Erymanthian Boar, the Ceryneian (or Arcadian) Stag, the Stymphalian Birds, the Augean Stables, the Cretan Bull, the Horses of Diomedes, the Girdle of Hippolyta, Geryon, Cerberus, and the Apples of the Hesperides. In addition, Heracles figures in other myths: he takes part in the expedition of the Argonauts, he rescues Alcestis by wrestling with Death, he gives his bow to Philoctetes, etc. The ancients thought that he was not one but several persons, because of the diversity and variety of the myths. He is sometimes pictured as a tragic figure (cf. the *Heracles* of Euripides and the *Trachiniae* of Sophocles); sometimes as a gluttonous, or bibulous, semi-comic figure.

Heracles

Play by Euripides; date unknown. Does not follow the

Sophoclean version (see *Trachiniae*) but the "Theban version." Lycus, the tyrant of Thebes, has captured the wife and children of Heracles, and is about to kill them, along with the hero's "father" Amphitryon. Heracles returns from Hades just in time to save them, but then he goes mad and kills his wife and children, driven by the hostility of Hera. One choral ode, dealing with the miseries of old age, has suggested to some that this is a late play; Wilamowitz places it in the 420's. The play, which is frequently known by its Latin title, *Hercules Furens,* has some very fine passages.

Heraclides (1) Ponticus

Philosopher and polymath of the 4th century B.C. (ca. 490-410 B.C.) None of his works has been preserved. A partial list of the lost works includes books on molecular theory, astronomy, history, physics, ethics, grammar, music, and rhetoric. It is in the first two of these fields that his chief contributions were made.

Heraclides (2) Ponticus, the Younger

A grammarian, pupil of Didymus. Taught at Rome in the middle of the first century A.D. Wrote erudite and obscure books of Sapphic hendecasyllables, called *Leschae;* also epic poems and *Pyrrichae.*

Heraclides (3) of Cyme

Author of a Persian history (*Persica*) used by Plutarch. The work was written in the middle of the 4th century B.C.

Heraclides (4) Lembus

Alexandrian writer of the second century B.C. Wrote histories, epitomes, a life of Archimedes (?), and other miscellaneous works. Sometimes confused with Heraclides (2).

Heraclides (5) of Tarentum

Physician, contemporary of Cicero. Praised by Galen

for his skill and objectivity. Practiced dissection, and wrote on pharmacology, therapeutics, and dietetics. Galen preserves some fragments.

Heraclides

The following should also be mentioned:

(6) H. of Athens, author of Satyr-plays.

(7) H. of Heraclea, author of *Phlyakes.*

(8) H. of Lycia, a sophist.

(9) H. of Miletus, a grammarian.

(10) Sophist, editor of the speeches of Nicetes of Smyrna.

Heraclitus (1)

One of the greatest of the Pre-Socratics. Fl. ca. 500 B.C. Among his doctrines the following are most important: Everything is in a state of flux (*panta rhei*); all things are "an exchange for fire"; he was the first to explore the nature of the knowledge and the soul, the founder, therefore, of epistemology. Like Anaximander, Heraclitus thought of the world as a conflict of opposite forces. The only eternal thing is Logos. Nature becomes, the Logos is. The Stoics followed his belief that the universe is controlled by a divine Fire.

Heraclitus

Mention should also be made of the following:

(2) Elegiac poet, from Halicarnassus.

(3) A mythographer.

(4) Physician, from Rhodes.

(5) Christian author of a work on the Apostles.

(6) Platonist, of Tyre.

Hercules, Hercules Furens

See Heracles.

Herennius (1) Philo of Byblos (1st cent. A.D.)

Author of a work on the Jews, and various other grammatical and scholarly works.

(2) A Neoplatonic philosopher, supposed author of a commentary on Aristotle's *Metaphysics.*

Heresiologist

One who writes about (against) heresies. Cf. Hippolytus (2), Irenaeus, Dionysius of Alexandria, Epiphanius, et al.

Herillus of Carthage

Stoic philosopher, disciple of Zeno, and the founder of a separate Stoic sect (the Herilleioi) which did not last long.

Hermagoras (1) of Temnos

Rhetor, fl. ca. 150 B.C. Noted for his casuistry. Wrote six books of *Technai Rhetorikai.*

(2) Rhetor of the 2nd century A.D.

(3) Stoic philosopher, from Amphipolis.

Hermarchus of Mytilene

Epicurean philosopher, succeeded Epicurus as head of the school in 270 B.C. Wrote on Plato, Aristotle, Empedocles, etc., all polemics.

Hermas, Shepherd of

The longest of the writings included in the collection of the Apostolic Fathers. The author, a Roman Christian, describes in three sections (Visions, Mandates, Similitudes) the message brought by Jesus in the guise of a shepherd. Chief object of the work is to ensure a second repentance for sins committed after baptism.

Hermeias (1)

Choliambic poet of the 3rd century B.C.

(2) Christian apologist, author of *Diasurmos ton exo philosophon.*

(3) Neoplatonist of Alexandria.

(4) Epic poet, from Hermupolis.

(5) Historian, from Mytilene.

(6) Stoic, writer on Homeric tactics.

(See Schmid-Stählin).

Hermes

One of the Olympian gods. Guide of the dead to Hades, messenger of the gods (identified with the Roman Mercury). God of travellers, inventor of the lyre. The conventional representation of the Hermae emphasizes also the sexual, or fertility aspect of the god. Carries a magic wand. Also associated with oratory and athletics.

Hermes, Hymn to

One of the Homeric Hymns, of unknown author and date.

Hermes Trismegistus

"Thoth the very great" (Thoth was identified with Hermes), supposed author of a collection of philosophical and religious treatises known as *Hermetica,* also works on magic, astrology, and alchemy. These are generally late (third or fourth centuries A.D.), and embodied a conglomeration of Greek, Egyptian, Platonic, and Christian elements.

Hermesianax of Colophon

Alexandrian poet, born ca. 300 B.C. Wrote a collection of elegies, named for his mistress Leontion. Also wrote a *Persica.*

Hermione

In mythology, the daughter of Menelaus and Helen. Betrothed at different times to both Orestes and Neoptolemus. In the *Andromache* of Euripides, she was married to Neoptolemus, who was murdered by Orestes. Other authors say she married Orestes, except for one, who says she married Diomedes.

Hermippus (1)

Athenian comic poet of the 5th century B.C. Author of an *Agamemnon* which may have been a parody of Aeschylus; he also parodied Homer, wrote mythological burlesques, political plays (*Moirai, Stratiotai,* which are anti-Pericles plays).

Hermippus (2) of Smyrna

Peripatetic biographer of the third century B.C. Used by Plutarch. He is supposed to have deliberately falsified history, in search of the sensational.

Hermippus (3)

Author of a book on dreams.

(4) Author of *Phaenomena.*

Hermocles of Cyzicus

Poet, ca. 300 B.C. Author of hymns and paeans.

Hermogenes (1) of Tarsus

Sophist and rhetor, author of many technical writings: *Progymnasmata, peri ton Staseon, peri Ideon,* etc. He established Plato and Demosthenes as models of style. His influence was great, especially in the Byzantine period.

Hermogenes (2) of Ephesus

Eclectic, and teacher of Plato.

(3 of Smyrna, a physician.

(4) of Priene, an architect.

(5) of Tarsus, the Elder, author of *Peri Koiles Syrias.*

Hermoniacus

Author of a vernacular translation of the *Iliad,* in the 14th century.

Hero of Alexandria

See Heron.

Hero and Leander

Romantic poem, probably of the 5th century A.D. by Musaeus (q.v.3). Leander, a youth of Abydos, swam the Hellespont to visit Hero. When he drowned, she threw herself into the sea.

Hero-Cult

Worship of real or imaginary men (e.g. Theseus, Heracles, etc). Best treatment of the subject is Farnell's *Greek Hero-Cults*. See also: Rose (OCD).

Herodas (or Herondas?)

Writer of *Mimiambi* (literary mimes), of the third century B.C. Subjects: *The Bawd, the Pimp, the Schoolmaster, Female Worshippers, the Jealous Mistress, the Shoemaker,* etc. They are short, realistic pieces, possibly intended for solo-performance.

Herodes Atticus (101-177 A.D.)

Famous sophist and patron of learning of the second century A.D. Wrote letters, diatribes, a literary diary (*Ephemerides*). Chief exponent of the New Sophistic. The Theater of Herodes Atticus in Athens is still in existence, and ancient plays are still performed there.

Herodian (1) (Aelius Herodianus)

Grammarian in the time of Marcus Aurelius; son of Apollonius Dyscolus. Wrote on the *Accentuation of the Iliad and Odyssey*. In his *Katholike Prosodia,* he is said to have discussed the accentuation of 60,000 words. Also wrote on quantities, breathings, enclitics. Disagreed with his father on the subject of Analogy. The two of them rank among the greatest of ancient grammarians.

Herodian (2) of Syria

Wrote, in the third century, a history covering the period from 180 to 238 A.D. Title: *Tes meta Markon Basileias Historiai.*

Herodicus of Babylon

Author of *Komodoumenoi* (People satirized in comedy), *Symmikta Hypomnemata,* and *pros ton Philosokraten*. Date: probably second century B.C.

Herodorus of Heraclea

Logographer. Wrote a work on Heracles and one on the Argonauts.

Herodotus (1)

The "Father of History." Born "a little before the Persian War." Died ca. 425 B.C. Travelled all through Greece, southern Italy, Egypt, Babylon, Scythia, gathering material for his researches (*Historiai*). His *History of the Persian War* is epic in scope, covering lands, centuries, and subjects that are not strictly relevant to his story, but he says that his aim is to record the traditional of the greater and lesser nations alike, because those that were powerful are now weak, and vice versa. In the Ionic dialect, and in a lucid, simple style, he carries on his narrative, which is linked by the theme of Hybris and Nemesis (i.e. nations are ill-adapted to withstand too much good fortune, and so they are struck down, Lydia by Persia, Persia by Greece, etc.). Herodotus is one of the world's supreme story-tellers. He has been criticized by many, beginning with Thucydides, for his credulity, but this is not entirely fair. He repeatedly says that the reader is not bound to believe his tales, and even intimates that he does not always believe them himself. He combines an encyclopedic interest and omnivorous curiosity with sympathy, humor, and tolerance. He has a child-like enthusiasm for wonders and novelties. His industry, honesty, and piety are tremendous. Military details and other facts have been questioned as to their accuracy (e.g. it is extremely unlikely that Solon and Croesus could have met; battle statistics are probably somewhat erroneous, etc.). His purpose, he says, is to "prevent the great deeds of the Greeks and Barbarians from losing their due meed of glory." There is a note of tragedy and pathos, as well as one of comedy and charm, in Herodotus, but the latter is more often remembered than the former.

Herodotus (2)

Physician of the Pneumatic school, in the Flavian period (second half of the first century A.D.). Works: *Iatros, peri Boethematon,* and *Diagnosis peri ton oxeon kai chronion nosematon* (Diagnosis of Acute and Chronic Diseases). The latter is extant.

Two others of the name are to be mentioned:

(3) Compiler of a Hippocrates glossary.

(4) H. of Tarsus, a Sceptic.

(See Schmid-Stählin).

Heroikos

See Philostratus (2).

Heron (1) of Alexandria (also called Hero)

Great mathematician, but chiefly known as "The Mechanic." Invented many "modern" devices, such as slot-machine vendors, siphons, water-organs, and various contrivances operated by water, steam, and compressed air. Wrote on geometry (mensuration of figures, definitions, commentaries on Euclid, etc.) and other mathematical subjects. Also wrote *Pneumatica, Automaton-Making, on Mirrors,* and other works.

Heron

Several others of the same name:

(2) a mathematician, teacher of Proclus.

(3) a Deacon, of Antiochia.

(4) of Athens, author of memoirs, studies or commentaries on Herodotus, Thucydides, Xenophon, and Dinarchus. See Schmid-Stählin.

Herondas

See Herodas.

Herophilus of Chalcedon

Physician of the third century B.C. Studied the brain,

pulse, etc. Probably wrote a comprehensive work on anatomy, based on dissections and studies of the human cadaver.

Hesiod (Date unknown. 8th or 7th cent. B.C.)

Earliest Greek poet whose works are extant, except for Homer. Native of Cyme, lived in Ascra in Boeotia. Works: *Works and Days* (Erga kai Hemerai) a didactic poem, dealing with farm life, moral precepts, mythology (Five Ages of Man), description of a year's work on a farm, folk-lore, and miscellaneous advice and superstitions; *Theogony*. On the universe and the genealogy of the gods. The authenticity of this work has been doubted, but without good reason. *The Shield* (Aspis). Chiefly a description of the shield of Heracles. (Also of doubtful authenticity). Lost Works include *Ehoiai, Catalogues, Astronomia, Idaean Dactyls, Aigimios, Maxims of Chiron,* etc. Some fragments exist, but again, the authenticity is doubtful. Hesiod is superstitious and narrow, but honest and realistic. The *Works and Days* is tinged with pessimism, especially the part about the Ages of Man (Golden, Silver, Bronze, Heroic, and Iron—the worst of all). The Loeb edition is very useful, for it contains all the fragments.

Hesione

(1) An Oceanid, wife of Prometheus.

(2) Mother of Palamedes.

(3) Daughter of Laomedon, rescued by Heracles from a sea-monster, given to Telamon as a prize, mother of Teucer.

Hestia

Goddess of the hearth (Identified with Vesta). Little mythology. Not mentioned by Homer at all.

Hesychius (1) of Alexandria

Lexicographer, probably of the 5th cent. A.D. His lexicon is known from a badly preserved 15th century manuscript, and is based on the lexica of Aristarchus, Heliodorus, and others. It is valuable for the study of rare words, dialects, inscriptions, etc.

Hesychius (2) of Jerusalem

Exegetical writer. Numerous works include commentaries on Isaiah, Job, the Minor Prophets.

Hesychius (3) of Miletus (6th cent. A.D.)

Author of a *Word History,* and account of the reign of Justin and the first years of Justinian, an *Onomatologos,* etc.

For others of the same name, including an Egyptian bishop, a physician et al., see Schmid-Stählin.

Hexaemeron

A poem on the Creation by Pisides (q.v.).

Hexameter, Dactylic

The meter of Homer, and, therefore, of all ancient epic poetry, even didactic poems like that of Lucretius. Consists of six feet, of which the first four are dactyls or spondees, the fifth usually a dactyl, and the sixth a spondee or trochee. (cf. "This is the forest primeval, the murmuring pines and the hemlocks.")

Hexapla

Origen's monumental edition of the Bible, which included, in six parallel columns, the Hebrew original, a Greek transliteration, and four Greek translations (the *Septuagint,* and the translations of Aquila, Symmachus, and Theodotion).

Hiatus

A gap between one word ending with a vowel and the following word beginning with a vowel. Studiously avoided by Gorgias, deprecated by Isocrates. Mostly avoided by Demosthenes, allowed by Thucydides.

Hicetas of Syracuse

A Pythagorean, said to have been the first to teach that the earth rotates.

Hierocles (1)

Stoic of the 2nd century A.D. Wrote *Elements of Ethics* and other works.

Hierocles (2)

Grammarian of Justinian's time, author of *Synekdemos,* a description of the Eastern Empire, including 64 provinces and 912 cities or towns.

Others of the same name (see Schmid-Stählin) include a Neoplatonic, a rhetor, a lawyer and sophist, etc.

Hieron

Title of a work by Xenophon. Hieron was the tyrant of Syracuse, and his court was frequented by poets and philosophers (e.g. Aeschylus, Pindar, Bacchylides, Simonides, etc.) There was also a historian of the name. Hieron II of Syracuse wrote works on agriculture.

Hieronymus (1) of Cardia

Wrote a history of the Diadochi. Called one of the greatest of the Greek historians. Source for Arrian, Diodorus and Plutarch. It is impossible to form any estimate of his value, since almost nothing remains.

Hieronymus (2) of Rhodes

Peripatetic philosopher, and founder of an eclectic school. Works include historical memoirs, letters, *on Isocrates, on Poets, Symposium,* and others.

Hilarodia

Type of mime (q.v.).

Hilarotragodiai

See *Phlyakes.*

Himerius of Prusa (315-386)

Sophist and rhetor. 24 of his 80 speeches survive.

Hipparchia

Greek poetess of the 4th century B.C. Said to have been the first female philosopher.

Hipparchus (1)

New Comedy poet, fl. 250 B.C.

Hipparchus (2)

The greatest of Greek Astronomers (b. ca. 190 B.C.) Adhered to the geocentric hypothesis. Wrote a commentary on Eudoxus and Aratus, also on geography, algebra. Estimated the sizes and distances of the sun and moon, calculated the length of the year, etc. Procession of the Equinoxes his great discovery.

Hipparchus (3)

A rhetor who distinguished five kinds of style. Date unknown.

Hippes

See *Knights* (Aristophanes).

Hippias of Elis

A Sophist, younger contemporary of Protagoras. Had great fame and wealth. Taught mathematics, astronomy, grammar, poetry, music, history, handicrafts. Made several mathematical discoveries (unless this is a different Hippias). Wrote a *Synagoge, Troikos Logos,* and other works, including a list of Olympian victors.

Hippias Major and Minor

Two dialogues in the Platonic corpus. The former is of doubtful authenticity.

Hippiatrici

Veterinarians. The *Corpus Hippiatricorum Graecorum* is a ninth century compilation. Xenophon and Aristotle (?)

also wrote on the subject, Xenophon's work (*peri Hippikes*) dealing mostly with horsemanship. An Athenian, Simon of the 5th cent. also wrote on horses and horse-breeding.

Hippo

See Hippon.

Hippobotus

Philosopher and historian of the 3rd century B.C. Wrote *Peri Haireson* and *Philosophon Anagraphe.*

Hippocrates (1) of Cos

Almost legendary physician, contemporary of Socrates. Although his works are all lost, something of his doctrine and method are known. He considered the body as a whole. Many works are preserved under his name, dealing with all aspects of medicine: prognostics, surgery, pharmacology, etc., but it is not likely that any are genuine. (See Edelstein in OCD).

Hippocrates (2) of Chios. 5th cent. B.C.

Mathematician, the first person to write an *Elements of Geometry*. Dealt with the problems of squaring the circle and doubling the cube.

Hippodromus of Larissa

Sophist of the Greco-Roman period. Wrote lyric poetry.

Hippolytus (1)

In mythology, son of Theseus and the Amazon Hippolyta. Subject of extant tragedy by Euripides, in which H. is a young man devoted to Artemis and obsessed with chastity, to the point where he refuses to recognize Aphrodite. Phaedra, his stepmother, is violently in love with him. On being repulsed, she commits suicide, leaving a note accusing Hippolytus of violating her. Theseus thereupon banishes Hippolytus and asks his father Poseidon to bring about the death of Hippolytus. The god sends a sea-monster which frightens the horses of H., he is thrown from the chariot and dies. Artemis tells Theseus the truth, but it is too late. The nurse of Phaedra is an interesting figure; trying to do the right thing (i.e. tells H. of Phaedra's love) she unwittingly brings the tragedy about. One of the best plays of Euripides, noted for the beautiful, romantic choral odes, and for the portrait of Phaedra, as well as that of H.

Hippolytus (2) ca. 160-235 A.D.
A heresiologist. Wrote *Refutation of Heresies* in 10 books, and other exegetical and homiletic works.

Hippon or Hipponax
Philosopher of the Age of Pericles. Believed water to be the chief element. Mentioned disparagingly by Aristotle.

Hipponax
Iambic poet, of Ephesus, in the 6th cent. B.C. Invented the scazon, or choliambic line, consisting of five iambic feet, followed by one trochee. Known for his satire and invective, and his vivid style. Said to have been the inventor of parody.

Hippys of Rhegium
Logographer, ca. 500 B.C. Wrote on Italy and Sicily.

Historia Animalium
Work on zoology by Aristotle. Some of it may not be genuine.

Historical Commentaries
Lost work in 43 books by Strabo.

Histories of Individual places
There were many such histories (cf. Atthidographers, who wrote on Attica). Examples: Argos (Deinias, Ister, Socrates of Argos), Elis (Ister, Hieronymus), Laconia (Proxenus, Persaeus), Megara, (Dieuchidas, Hereas). For complete list, see Schmid-Stählin.

Historiography
The Ionian logographers (prose, as opposed to epic

writers) were the first writers of history. The greatest of these was Hecataeus. Followers of Hecataeus were Xanthus, Hellanicus, Scylax, and Herodotus. Thucydides and the writers who continued his history (Xenophon and Theopompus), relied less on hearsay and more on first-hand evidence. Xenophon wrote historical memoirs and romance. Ephorus was the first to treat of all Greek history from the mythological period to the time of Philip of Macedon. In the Hellenistic period, histories and romances about Alexander were popular. Polybius and Plutarch, Diodorus and Dionysius of Halicarnassus, Josephus and Arrian are examples of later historiography, which showed several tendencies: universal history, epitomes, histories of individual peoples and rulers. In the Byzantine period, Procopius, Agathias, Anna Comnena, Nicetas, Acropolites, Psellus, Bryennius, John Cantacuzenus, Cinnamus, Ducas, Phrantzes, etc. are examples. See under the individual names.

Holobolus, Manuel

Byzantine poet of the 13th cent. Wrote hymns and devotional poetry, as well as letters, scholia and commentaries on Aristotle and Boethius.

Homer (1)

Nearly all the ancients believed that one man was the author of the *Iliad* and the *Odyssey,* but there are no facts about his life, date, place, etc. Probably he lived in the 8th century B.C. Although the poems may have originated in a collection of shorter Lays, the unifying force of the complete works seem to bespeak a single genius who impressed both the *Iliad* and *Odyssey* with the stamp of his own personality. To be sure, there are important differences in the style, manner, and certain details, but perhaps no more so than between *Othello* and *As You Like It, Moby Dick* and *Typee, Salome* and *Lady Windermere's Fan.* It seems pretty clear that the *Odyssey* was written as a sequel to the *Iliad,* as all the significant intervening events are told, so that we have a continuous story. The characters, language and structure of both works are quite similar, and both have the universal qualities of sympathy, humor, love for nature and mankind. The differences are not to be ignored, i.e. treatment of the gods, women's status, familiarity with iron, etc. but they seem to be far outweighed by the similarities. When compared with other folk-epics (e.g. *Beowulf*) Homer has far more literary self-consciousness, but when compared with literary epics (e.g. the *Aeneid*), Homer has more of the improvised folk-quality coming from an oral tradition. Noteworthy are the long, vivid similes, drawn from nature, and the short, graphic stock-epithets (e.g. "rosy-fingered dawn"). Like Shakespeare, Homer created the language he used. It is because of the language, the perceptive characterizations, the all-embracing picture of society, the blending of pathos and humor, the universal emotions and problems with which he deals, and above all, the living, three-dimensional people he has created, that Homer, the earliest of all Greek authors who have come down to us, is also the greatest. See *Iliad, Odyssey,* Achilles, Homeric Question, etc.

Homer (2) of Byzantium

Tragic poet of the third century B.C. Member of the *Pleiad* (q.v.).

Homeric Epigrams

A collection of epic hexameters of unknown author and date.

Homeric Hymns

A group of hexameter hymns, of different dates and varying merit. Included are hymns to Pan, Demeter, Dionysus, Apollo, Hermes, Aphrodite, and many others (33 in all). The style of these hymns is carefully modelled on that of Homer. Especially lovely is the *Hymn to Demeter.* The *Hymn to Hermes* is in a comic or burlesque style. The *Hymn to Pan* is notable for the beauty and freshness of its descriptions of nature. Many of the hymns are very brief and almost perfunctory. The Loeb edition of Hesiod contains the Homeric Hymns.

Homeric Question

The problem of single or multiple authorship of the *Iliad* and *Odyssey*. In modern times, the question was raised by Wolf, because of various inconsistencies. Theories range from the Grote hypothesis of an *Achilleis* which furnished the nucleus of the *Iliad,* and to which interpolations and additions were made, to the theory of many separate lays, all collected under Pisistratus, and the hypothesis of whole, complete poems by different authors. (For fuller discussions see Rose, and Bowra's article in the OCD. Lattimore's *Introduction* also has pertinent discussion). The question is by no means resolved, although the decipherment of Linear B may throw new light upon it, at least as regards the difficulty of one person's remembering such long poems. The present editor firmly believes that the similarities outweigh the differences, and that one Homer is responsible for the *Iliad* and the *Odyssey,* which was the belief of most people in antiquity, who knew of only one Homer.

Homeridae

Rhapsodes, the "descendants of Homer" who spread the knowledge of Homer's poems through the Greek world. At first the title was restricted to the actual descendants, but afterwards extended to others.

Homoeomeries

See Anaxagoras.

Homiletics

See Glycys, Neilus, Modestus, Andreas of Crete, Nicetas David, Leo the Wise, George of Antioch, Xiphilinus, and see Krumbacher, passim.

Honestus of Corinth

Author of 10 epigrams in the *Anthology,* and some recently discovered inscriptions in Boeotia. Middle of the first century A.D.

Horae

Goddesses of the Seasons, daughters of Justice. Associated with Demeter, Apollo, Dionysus, etc.

Hyacinthus

A beautiful youth, loved by Apollo, accidentally killed by the god; from his blood the flower sprang. Actually, H. is probably a pre-Hellenic god.

Hybrias

Cretan poet of the 6th or early 5th century B.C.

Hybris or Hubris

Overweening pride, insolence or arrogance. One sin which is always punished in mythology and tragedy. Examples: Creon, Pentheus, Agamemnon (qq.v.). The agency for the punishment of Hybris is called Nemesis.

Hygieia

Personification of Health, daughter of Asclepius.

Hylas

A youth who took part in the Argonauts' expedition. Captured by nymphs who fell in love with his beauty, he was sought by Heracles. Probably connected with ritual search for a deity of vegetation (see Rose).

Hymenaeus, Hymen

It was customary to call "O Hymen" or "Hymen Hymenaie" at weddings. This was interpreted as an invocation to a god called Hymen or Hymenaeus, and so various stories were invented about him.

Hymn

A poetic address to a god, usually sung. See Homeric Hymns, Musaeus, Callimachus, Cleanthes, Romanus, etc. Some of the hymns had musical notation (e.g. those found at Delphi) and are valuable for the knowledge they give us on Greek Music.

Hypatia

Daughter of Theon, presided over the Neoplatonic school. Killed by the mob because of her alleged friendship with Orestes in 415 A.D.

Hyperboreans

A legendary race of worshippers of Apollo, who were thought to lead a blessed existence in the far North. See Abaris.

Hyperides 389-332 B.C.

One of the Ten Attic Orators. Only recently have any of his speeches been discovered: *Against Athenogenes, Lycophron, Philippides,* and *For Euxenippus.* Known for his excellent style, he was ranked by the ancients as second only to Demosthenes. He was the pupil of Isocrates.

Hypermestra

One of the daughters of Danaus. See *Suppliants* (Aeschylus) for the story. In the sequel, Hypermestra is the only one of the Danaids that does not murder her husband (Lynceus).

Hypnos

God of Sleep. A winged youth who lived in the Underworld.

Hypokrites

The first actor, introduced by Thespis, was called the "answerer" (*hypokrites*). The word did not originally have a pejorative connotation.

Hypomnemata

See Memoirs, Strabo, Aratus (2).

Hypothesis

Prefixed to editions of the plays were brief resumes of the plots, known as *hypotheses*. The dates and authorship of these are unknown, but they often contain valuable information about the play, other treatments of the legend, historical background, etc. Libanius wrote hypotheses of the speeches of Demosthenes.

Hypsicles of Alexandria

Wrote "Book XIV" of Euclid's *Elements*. Second half of the second century B.C.

Hypsicrates

Historian of the first century B.C.

Hypsipyle

In mythology, a Lemnian woman, the only one who did not take part in the general plot to kill all the males on the island; she hid her father Thoas and smuggled him out of the land. When the Argonauts came, the women of the island mated with them, and Hypsipyle had two sons by Jason.

Hyrtacenus, Theodore

Teacher of grammar and rhetoric in Constantinople, ca. 1300. Author of Declamations, letters, etc. Characterized by bad taste and poverty of ideas.

Hysmine and Hysminias

See Macrembolites.

I

I

For Greek names beginning with I (e.g. Iason) see under J (Jason).

Iacchus

A minor deity, perhaps a personification of the ritual cry "iacch o iacche" (cf. Hymenaeus), and associated with the Eleusinian mysteries, where he was regarded as the son of Zeus and Demeter (or Persephone). But, largely owing to the similarity between his name and Bacchus, he was identified with Dionysus.

Iambic Poetry

The word *iambus* was first used by Archilochus, but Aristotle says in the *Poetics* that the *Margites* was the first work in iambics. He says that since iambics are so similar to ordinary speech, the meter was used for satire and invective, which is the way it was used by Archilochus and Hipponax. In Ionian poetry, the iambic meter is typical. But it also became the meter of tragedy and comedy, along with the trochaic (which is, after all, the same meter without the initial upbeat or anacrusis). In Hellenistic times, the iambic meter was again used for satire, as in the case of Callimachus and Menippus, Timon, Sotades, Heraclides Ponticus, and others (qq.v.). In Byzantine poetry, the iambic trimeter, and the political verse, a fifteen-syllable trochaic or iambic line, were the favorite meters.

Iamblichus (1)

Author of a Greek novel, *Babyloniaca* or *Rhodanes and Sinonis,* in the middle of the second century A.D. Only a summary and a few fragments survive.

Iamblichus (2) ca. 250-325 A.D.

Neoplatonist philosopher. Wrote a *Life of Pythagoras,* a *Protrepticus* or exhortation to Philosophy, and three works on mathematics. Other works (lost): *On the Soul, On the Gods, etc.* Iamblichus corrupted the teaching of Plotinus (q.v.) by substituting magic for mysticism.

Iambulus

Author of a travel-adventure story about being captured by pirates, reaching the Blessed Isle (Ceylon?), etc. A sort of ancient Baron Munchausen.

Iapetus

In mythology, son of Earth and Heaven, father of Prometheus. Rose says it is not unlikely that he is to be connected with Japhet, the son of Noah.

Iatrica

Books on medicine, by Marcellus of Side and Aratus (qq.v.).

Ibycus

Lyric poet of the 6th century B.C. Wrote lyrical narratives in the style of Stesichorus. He wrote on the *Funeral Games of Pelias,* the *Sack of Troy,* the *Calydonian Boar Hunt,* and other subjects. According to legend, he was killed by robbers, who were brought to justice by a flock of cranes (the "Cranes of Ibycus") who witnessed the murder. His style is rich and brilliant, his imagination vivid, his love of nature almost Homeric.

Icarus or Icarius

(1) An Athenian who was hospitable to Dionysus, and

received the vine, later killed by his neighbors who thought the wine he gave them was poison.

(2) Penelope's father.

(3) Son of Daedalus (q.v.) who, disregarding his father's advice, flew too near the sun, so that the wax in his wings melted; he fell into the sea (thenceforth the Icarian Sea) and was drowned.

Ichneutae

Title of a satyr-play (q.v.) by Sophocles.

Iconoclastic Controversy

In 726 Leo III published an edict forbidding the worship of images, which was the signal for a general destruction of icons. The movement was a religious one, but political motives were also involved. The controversy continued under the emperor Constantine V, with riots and uprisings. The monks were at the forefront of the Icondules (Image-worshippers), and the controversy raged intermittently for more than a century. Many works were written on both sides: poetry by Ignatius, Sergius, Stephanus, Theodore Studites, polemics by John of Damascus, a work under the name of Constantine Copronymus. The patriarch Nicephorus was one of the chief Icondules.

Idaean Dactyls

Dwarfs or wizards to whom the art of metallurgy (i.e. the discovery and working of iron) was first attributed.

Ideas, Theory of

See Plato.

Idomeneus (1)

A mythical Cretan king, grandson of Minos. In return for a safe voyage, he vowed to sacrifice the first living thing he met. This turned out to be his own son. The story is a familiar folk-tale. Cf. Jephtha.

Idomeneus (2) ca. 315-270

Friend of Epicurus. Wrote on the Socratics, on demagogues, and a history of Samothrace. The works appear to have been full of gossip and scandal and were not much used in antiquity.

Idyll

A short pastoral poem (properly, *eidyllion boukolikon*). See Theocritus.

Ignatius (1)

Bishop of Antiochia, martyred during the reign of Trajan. Wrote letters included among the Apostolic Fathers. If they are genuine, these 7 letters are important documents of early Christianity. They include Epistles to the Ephesians, Magnesians, Trallians, Romans, Philadelphians, Smyrneans, and to Polycarp.

Ignatius (2)

Byzantine poet of the 9th century. Wrote a poem on *Adam's Fall,* and a collection of iambic Sententiae on religious subjects; also, paraphrases of Aesop's Fables.

Ignatius (3)

Byzantine poet and grammarian, about a generation later than Ignatius (2). Wrote elegies and spigrams.

Iketides

See *Suppliants* (Aeschylus and Euripides).

Iliad

Homer's great epic on the Wrath of Achilles. It begins with the quarrel between Agamemnon and Achilles, as a result of which the latter withdraws from the fight. He refuses to return even when the Embassy promises him fabulous rewards (see Achilles), and only when his friend Patroclus is killed does he re-enter the war, using the glorious new armor that Hephaestus has made for him. The *Iliad* ends with the single combat between Achilles and

Hector, and the latter's death and funeral. Memorable scenes are: the quarrel (Bk. I) Hector's farewell (bk. VI), the Embassy (bk. IX) the final battle (bk. XXII), and Priam's ransoming of the body of Hector (bk. XXIV). The noble, dignified, but always moving language, the sharp characterizations, the vivid similes and epithets, the almost Dutch detail, the universality of emotions, the compassion and sympathy, the love of nature—these are some of the reasons for the Iliad's position of pre-eminence in Greek literature. (See Homer)

Ilias Parva

or *Little Iliad.* See Epic Cycle.

Iliou Persis

(or *Iliu Persis*) The Sack of Troy. See Epic Cycle.

Images

See Iconoclastic controversy, John of Damascus, Theodore Studites.

Imberius and Margarona

A Byzantine poem, extant in three versions. A reworking of the popular French story *Pierre de Provence et la Belle Maguelonne.*

Inachus

In mythology, a river god, father of Io (q.v.).

Indica

Works on India. See Megasthenes, Daimachus (2).

Indicopleustes, Cosmas

See Cosmas Indicopleustes.

Infant Heracles

An epyllion by Theocritus (q.v.).

Invulnerability

Many legends deal with this. Common versions are: the

one vulnerable spot (cf. Siegfried, Achilles), the person or animal who can only be wounded by one thing (cf. Balder, by mistletoe; the Nemean Lion, by its own claws, etc.).

Io

In mythology, a priestess of Hera, daughter of Inachus. Loved by Zeus, who turned her into a cow to escape from Hera's jealousy. Hera sent the monster Argus to watch her, and when he was killed, the goddess sent a gadfly to torment Io. After many wanderings (see Prometheus), Io came to Egypt, where she was restored, bore a son, Epaphus. She was identified with the Egyptian Isis.

Ioannes

See John.

***Ion* (1)**

Play by Euripides. The story is not found elsewhere in Greek Drama. Plot deals with Creusa, daughter of Erechtheus, who has borne a son (Ion) to Apollo. The god has taken the exposed infant to Delphi. Creusa has married Xuthus, but they have no children, so they go to Delphi to ask Apollo's aid. Xuthus is told that the first person he meets when going (the word *ion* means "going") from the temple is his son. He meets Ion, whom he supposes to be his *own* son. Just as Creusa is about to kill the lad, the priestess enters with the typical tokens (*gnorismata)* and the happy ending ensues. The play is not a tragedy at all, but almost a New Comedy. In fact, the plot (wronged woman, long-lost child, last-minute reprieve, tokens, etc.) contains the stuff of many Greek (and Roman) comedies.

***Ion* (2)**

Title of a dialogue by Plato. Ion is a rhapsode whose pretense of wisdom is delightfully punctured by Socrates.

Ion of Chios

Greek poet of the 5th century. Wrote tragedy and dithyramb. Titles: *Alcmene, Eurytidae, Agamemnon, Laertes, Teucer, Mega Drama.* The ancients admitted him to the canon or select list of great playwrights, but we cannot judge from the scanty fragments. Ion also wrote epigrams, elegiac poems, hymns, comedies (or a comedy), scolia, history and other works in prose. He was described as faultless but forceless.

Ionian

See Dialects.

Ionians

Greeks on the West Coast of Asia Minor. Many of the early pre-Socratics (e.g. Thales, Anaximander, etc.) were Ionians.

Iophon

Son of Sophocles, who wrote many plays, but was completely eclipsed by his father. There is an apocryphal story to the effect that he tried to get control of Sophocles' property by accusing his father of senility, and that Sophocles refuted the charge by reading from the (newly-composed) *Oedipus at Colonus.*

Iphigenia

Daughter of Agamemnon, sacrificed by him at Aulis. According to a variant legend, she was not killed, but a deer was substituted in her place (cf. Abraham and Isaac); Iphigenia herself being safely transported by Artemis to Tauris. We have two plays of Euripides, one dealing with the first, one with the second version. (See the next two entries)

Iphigenia in Aulis

Play by Euripides, of unknown date. Deals with Agamemnon's sacrifice of his daughter. He induces her to come to Aulis, where she is to be killed, on the pretext of marriage to Achilles. The characterizations of Agamemnon and

Iphigenia, as well as that of Clytemnestra, are well-drawn. The epilogue, which tells of the saving of Iphigenia (and thus conforms to Euripides' other Iphigenia play) is thought to be a later, non-Euripidean addition. The play was produced posthumously.

Iphigenia in Tauris

A romantic melodrama by Euripides. In this play, I. has become a priestess of Artemis in the barbaric land of the Taurians, who sacrifice all new arrivals to the goddess. Orestes, the brother of Iphigenia, is about to be sacrificed by her when the relationship is discovered, and the play ends with a dramatic (melodramatic) rescue.

Irenaeus

One of the early Christian fathers, born at Smyrna (?) ca. 130 A.D. Wrote a *Refutation of the Gnostics* (extant only in a Latin translation). Irenaeus was Bishop of Lyons (Lugdunum) and a leading heresiologist. His work has been called the first systematic exposition of Christian belief.

Irene

Goddess of Peace. Daughter of Zeus and Themis. Title of a play by Aristophanes (*Eirene*). See *Peace*.

Iris

Goddess of the rainbow. In the *Iliad* she is the messenger of the gods, but she does not appear in the *Odyssey*. In Alcaeus, she is the wife of Zephyrus and mother of Eros.

Irus

Beggar in the *Odyssey*. Became proverbial for the type.

Isaac Porphyrogenitus

Probably the same as Isaac Comnenus (Emperor 1057-59), author of works on *Omissions in Homer,* etc.

Isaeus (1) Ca. 420-350 B.C.

One of the Ten Attic Orators. Virtually nothing is

known of his life. He wrote speeches for others, and established a school of rhetoric at Athens. Demosthenes may have been his pupil. He was an authority on the laws of inheritance, and in fact, all eleven of the speeches that are preserved deal with this subject. His language is generally direct and simple.

Isaeus (2)

Assyrian sophist of the second century A.D. Noted for his ability to improvise.

Isaurians

Important family of Byzantine emperors, including Leo III, Constantine V, Irene, etc. The Iconoclastic Controversy arose during the reign of this dynasty.

Isidorus (1)

Author of a work on Parthia, and a general geographical work.

(2) Isidorus of Pelusion. Presbyter and abbot. A collection of about 2000 letters in five books survives.

(3) I. of Alexandria, a Neoplatonic philosopher.

(4) I. Aegeates, Epigrammatist of the 1st cent. A.D. (?)

The list also includes a Gnostic and a writer on mechanics. See Schmid-Stählin.

Isigonus of Nicaea

Paradoxographer of the first century B.C. or the first cent. A.D. Used by Pliny the Elder.

Isis

Egyptian goddess, wife of Osiris, mother of Horus. Originally an earth goddess, later a moon deity. Identified by the Greeks with both Demeter and Io.

Isles of the Blessed

See Fortunate Isles.

Ismene

Daughter of Oedipus, sister of Antigone (qq.v.).

Isocrates 436-338 B.C.

One of the Ten Attic Orators. His teachers were Gorgias, Prodicus and Socrates. An ardent patriot, he desired Greek unity, and wished Athens and Sparta to forget their differences and unite as leaders of all the Greek states. Works: *Against the Sophists, On the Antidosis, Panegyricus, On the Peace, Areopagiticus, Busiris, Encomium of Helen, Archidamus,* and others (21 have survived). His speeches covered all branches of oratory, forensic, epideictic, horatory, political. In addition, a number of letters survive under his name. Isocrates wrote Attic prose in its most elaborate and polished form, avoiding hiatus and dissonance, and paying great attention to rhythm. His periodic sentences are long and elaborate, his vocabulary pure, his moral tone lofty. But one gets the impression that form is more important than content.

Isopsepha

See Leonidas (2).

Ister of Cyrene

Pupil of Callimachus in the third century B.C. Antiquarian and grammarian. Wrote on rituals, cults, games, and Attica (see Atthidographers).

Isthmian Games

Held at Corinth in honor of Poseidon, every second year, beginning in 581 B.C. Pindar wrote odes for the Isthmian victors.

Isyllus of Epidaurus ca. 300 B.C.

Author of a *Hymn to Asclepius,* and a Hymn to the *Idaean Dactyls.*

Italicus, Michael

Teacher of philosophy and rhetoric in the 12th century.

A polymath who wrote on grammar, rhetoric, history, theology, philosophy, astronomy and medicine. Attacked, satirically, the Byzantine propensity for imitation. Also wrote poetry, letters, essays, etc.

Ithaca

The home of Odysseus, an island in the Ionian Sea. It has variously been identified with Thiaki and Leucadia.

Ixeutica

A work on fowling by Oppian. The poem is lost, but a prose paraphrase survives.

Ixion

The first Greek to murder a relative. Purified by Zeus, he attempted to ravish Hera, and was deceived with a phantom resembling her, by which he became father of the Centaurs. He was punished by being chained to a revolving wheel.

Ixionidae

Another name for the Centaurs.

J

J

Most Greek names beginning with I will be found under J.

Jason (1)

In mythology, leader of the expedition of the Argonauts. His uncle Pelias tried to kill him (having ousted his father Aeson) but the child was saved and entrusted to the centaur Chiron. When he grew up, he demanded his patrimony, which Pelias promised him if he brought back the Golden Fleece. Jason set sail in the Argo, collecting the chief heroes of Greece for the expedition. He succeeded with the help of Medea, whom he married, after many adventures. In Euripides (*Medea*) he appears as a supreme egoist, who deserts Medea to contract an advantageous marriage. His death, foretold by Medea, was as follows: as he was sleeping under the Argo, it collapsed and fell on him. The most complete story of the expedition occurs in the *Argonautica* of Apollonius Rhodius.

Jason (2) of Cyrene

A Hellenized Jew, who wrote the history of Judas Maccabaeus in five books. *Maccabees II* is an epitome of his work.

Jeremiah, Letter of

One of the Old Testament Apocrypha.

Jesus Sirach, Wisdom of

The oldest of the O. T. Apocrypha.

Jewish Greek Literature

The Greek language and culture were diffused over Judaea by 200 B.C. Hellenistic-Judaic Literature includes: *The Septuagint,* histories, philosophy, apologetics, prophecies, poetry, etc. See Demetrius (11), Eupolemus, Josephus, Justus, Tiberias, Ezechiel, Philon, Aristeas.

Jewish Kings, Jewish War, Antiquities

See Demetrius 11, Josephus.

Jocasta

Mother and wife of Oedipus (q.v.). In Homer her name is Epicaste.

Joel

Byzantine author of a World-Chronicle in the 13th century. It covers the time from Adam to the conquest of Constantinople by the Crusaders in 1204.

John 1 (A.D. 70?)

Author or authors of the Fourth Gospel, the Epistles, and the Apocalypse. Whether any or all are the same is doubtful. Possibly three or more people are involved: Mark, author of the Gospel according to Mark, John the son of Zebedee, author of the 4th Gospel, and the seer of Revelation. In addition, there are the *Epistles of John* and the *Acts of John.* The date of the Epistles and the Gospel, which most scholars think are by the same author, is ca. 100 B.C. He is probably not the author of the Book of Revelations.

John (2) of Antioch

Several people are known by this name. One was a patriarch and polemicist, ca. 1100 One was a chronicler, mentioned by Tzetzes. Finally, John Chrysostomus is sometimes also called "John of Antioch."

John Beccus
See Beccus.

John Camaterus
See Camaterus.

John Cameniates
See Cameniates.

John VI Cantacuzenus (3)
Emperor 1341-55. Wrote history (4 books on the Byzantine Empire), Apologetics and polemics, and other works. His *apologia* is a well-written work, despite its bias.

John (4) Chrysostomus (347-407)
Author of sermons, speeches, commentaries, treatises, etc. Patriarch of Constantinople. The name Chrysostomus means "golden-mouthed" and is an indication of his rhetorical skill. He died in exile.

John Cinnamus
See Cinnamus.

John (5) "Climax"
Sixth century Byzantine writer of a work called *Climax* (with reference to Jacob's Ladder), which deals with sins and virtues. He was also called Scholasticus and Sinaites.

John Cyparissiotes
See Cyparissiotes.

John Cyriotes
See Cyriotes.

John (6) of Damascus
8th Century theologian. Strong defender of image-worship (Iconodule). Author of a great work *Pege Gnoseos* (the Fountain of Knowledge), a systematization of the doctrine of the Greek Fathers and Church Councils. Wrote

speeches against the Iconoclasts, and religious poetry. Said to have been the author of *Barlaam and Josaphet* (q.v.).

John Doxopatres

See Doxopatres.

John (7) of Epiphania

Byzantine historian of the 6th century.

John Geometrus

See Geometrus.

John (8) Italus

Byzantine philosophical writer of commentaries to Aristotle, on dialectics, rhetoric, *Answers to Questions,* etc. 9th century.

John (9) Lydus

5th century Byzantine author of works *On Omens, On Roman Magistrates, On the Months.*

John Moschus

See Moschus.

John (10) the Sicilian

Under this name a chronicle was written, covering the period from Adam to 1204 A.D. By various hands.

John Xiphilinus

See Xiphilinus.

John

See Krumbacher and Schmid-Stählin for complete list, which includes: J. Argyropolis, a deacon; J. Barbukalos, an epigrammatist; J. Charax, a grammarian; several people called John the Deacon; J. of Gaza, poet; J. of Caesarea, commentator; and numerous others. Nearly 200 in Krumbacher alone.

Joseph (1) of Methone

Byzantine theologian, an outspoken proponent of East-

West harmony; wrote *Apology for the Council of Florence, On the Procession of the Holy Ghost.*

Joseph (2)

Hymnographer. Others of the name include a Patriarch of Constantinople, a Homily-writer, a polemicist, etc. See Krumbacher.

Joseph and Asenath

An apocryphal book, telling the story of Joseph in Egypt.

Josephus, Flavius B. 37 A.D.

Author of *Jewish Antiquities, the Jewish War (De Bello Judaico),* an autobiography, and essays against the Anti-semite Apion. The works were written in Aramaic and translated into Greek. His position was that of a pro-Roman, who had no sympathy with Jewish nationalism, though he stoutly defended the culture and religion of the Jews.

Juba II

King of Mauretania, who wrote a history of Rome, of Libya, and of Arabia, also works on painting and the theater. According to Plutarch, the most cultured of all kings.

Jubilees, Book of

Apocalyptic book found in the O. T. Pseudepigrapha. Also called *Apocalypse of Moses,* and *Little Genesis.* Purports to be a revelation to Moses by an angel.

Judith

Book of the Apocrypha, a Greek translation of the Hebrew original, which tells the famous story of Judith and Holofernes.

Julian (1) "the Apostate"

Nephew of Constantine, Emperor 332-353. He ceased being a Christian and reverted to paganism. Wrote speeches, letters, a symposium, satires, attacks on the Christians, Hymns (to Helios, and to the Mother of the Gods), and other works.

Julian

(2) of Alexandria, a physician.

(3) of Damascus, a sophist.

(4) of Egypt. Writer of epigrams, in Justinian's time.

(5) Commentator on Hermogenes.

(6) of Laodicea, astrologer.

(7) a Lexicographer.

and others. See Schmid-Stählin.

Julius (1) Africanus

Christian author and philosopher, fl. ca. 200 A.D. Wrote *Chronographiai* in 5 books (a world history from the Creation to 221); *Kestoi*, a letter to Origen on Susannah, and other works.

Julius

(2) Tragic poet.

(3) Author of an epic on Dionysus.

(4) Grammarian in Antiochia.

(5) J. Vestinus, author of *Ekloge ek ton Thoukydidou*.

See Schmid-Stählin for the complete list.

Julius Pollux

See Pollux.

Jurisprudence

See Justinian, Leo the Wise, Constantine Porphyrogenitus, Theophilus Antecessor, Xiphilinus.

Justin Martyr

Apologist. Born ca. 100 A.D. Martyred in 165. Wrote four *Apologies for Christianity, a Dialogue with Tryphon* (also a defense of Christianity). Many other works have been wrongly attributed to him.

Justinian I

Emperor 527-565. The Byzantine Age begins with him. Important for his codification of the Roman Law. Built (restored) the great cathedral of Hagia Sophia. Tried without success to reconcile orthodox and Monophysite views. It was Justinian who closed the schools in Athens.

Justinian, History of

See Agathias.

Justo, de

Title of a Pseudo-Platonic work.

Justus (1)

Author of a Jewish History, from Moses to Agrippa II.

(2) Commentator on the Scriptures.

(3) Writer on ophthalmology.

K

K

For Greek names beginning with K, see under C.

Kairos

Opportunity, personified; more frequent in art than literature.

Kings of Judea

See Demetrius (11), Eupolemus, Philon (5).

Kirchoff

One of the leading proponents of the Separatist theory of Homeric composition. See Homeric Question.

Knights (Hippes)

Comedy by Aristophanes. Produced in 424 B.C. An attack on the demagogue Cleon. The hero is Demos (the People), an old man who, at the end, is restored to his youth. The Paphlagonian (Cleon) is deposed, and a black-pudding-seller is appointed to his post. The generals Nicias and Demosthenes also appear in the play.

Koine

The dialect of the Septuagint and the New Testament. With the disappearance of the city-states, and the political unification of Greece, the old dialects are absorbed into the new common (= *Koine*) language. Xenophon is usually regarded as the first writer in this common dialect.

Komos, Kommos

See Comus, Commus.

Kordax

A wild, grotesque and obscene dance, originating in the Peloponnesus.

Kore

Another name for Persephone (q.v.).

Kronos

Son of Uranus, and father, by his sister Rhea, of Zeus, Poseidon, Hades, Hestia, Demeter, and Hera. He swallowed all except Zeus, who was saved by Rhea (she wrapped a stone in swaddling-clothes and Kronos swallowed this instead). Later Kronos vomited up the others, and he was overcome in a long struggle. Probably a pre-Hellenic deity. Identified by the Romans with Saturn.

L

Labyrinth

A maze built by Daedalus for King Minos of Crete, from which no one could escape. The Minotaur lived there, and was killed by Theseus, with the aid of Ariadne, who gave the hero a spool of thread with which to find his way out of the labyrinth.

Lacapenus, George

Byzantine scholar of the first half of the 14th century. Made a collection of the letters of Libanius. His own correspondence is also of importance. Other works: a commentary to the *Enchiridion* of Epictetus; a *Carmen Iambicum,* a work on Homeric figures, and a *Historia.*

Lachares

The last important rhetor of antiquity (end of the 4th century). Wrote on the colon, comma, and period; on Demosthenes; *Dialexeis,* and *Rhetorical Lexicon.*

Laches

Title of a dialogue of Plato (q.v.).

Lachesis

One of the Three Fates (q.v.).

Laestrygones

A race of giant cannibals met by Odysseus in the course of his wanderings.

Lament

See Bion (3).

Lament for Bion

A work on the death of Bion, by an unknown poet. Sometimes ascribed to Moschus, but this is unlikely.

Lamia

A bogey-woman who stole children. Hera destroyed her children because Zeus was her lover. This drove her wild with grief.

Lampoon

Abusive and satirical verse. See Hipponax, Archilochus. The word *iambus* was used for such verse. See also Alcaeus (3), Xenophanes, Aristophanes.

Lamprocles

Athenian musician and composer of dithyrambs in the first half of the 5th century B.C. He favored the Mixo-Lydian mode, and was the author of a famous *Hymn to Athene.*

Laocoön

Trojan priest who warned the people against the Wooden Horse, and then was killed, together with his two sons, by serpents. The story, which appears in Vergil's *Aeneid,* also occurred in the *Iliu Persis,* in Sophocles (in a play called *Laocoön*), and in Bacchylides. The famous sculpture-group, showing the death of the father and sons, is in the Vatican, and was the occasion for Lessing's famous essay on the boundaries of poetry and plastic arts.

Laomedon

A legendary king of Troy, whose grave ensured the safety of the city.

Laonicus Chalcocondyles

See Chalcocondyles.

Lapithes, George

Byzantine ecclesiastical writer of the 14th century. Wrote on theology, and didactic poetry (a long allegorical epic).

Lasus (Born ca. 550 B.C.)

Wrote hymns and dithyrambs, and introduced public performances of the latter. Teacher of Pindar (?); wrote a treatise on music, and lipogrammatic (q.v.) poetry.

Lausiakon

See Palladius.

Laws, the

Last work of Plato, in which he revised some of the ideas of the Republic. Deals with the State, its size (5040 inhabitants), constitution (Assembly and Council), etc. It is perhaps significant that Socrates does not appear at all in the *Laws*.

Leander

See *Hero and Leander*.

Leda

In mythology, mother of the Dioscuri, Helen, and (in some versions) also Clytemnestra. Visited by Zeus in the shape of a swan. In some stories, Nemesis laid an egg which Leda cared for, and Helen came from it.

Leitourgia (or Liturgy)

A state-imposed duty at Athens. Consisted of maintaining a trireme, or producing dramatic performances, missions to Delos, etc.

Lenaea

A Dionysiac festival celebrated in Athens in January or February, at which dramatic performances (originally comedy was preferred) took place.

Leo (or Leon) Diaconus

Byzantine historian, ca. 100 A.D. Wrote a history, in

10 books, of the years 959-975; dealing with the wars against the pirates, the Saracens, the Bulgars, etc. One of the best works of Byzantine historiography.

Leo Grammaticus

Byzantine chronicler. Wrote a history of the world from Adam to the year 948.

Leo III (The Isaurian)

Byzantine emperor 717-741. Wrote on military and naval tactics. "Greek Fire" (i.e. gunpowder?) plays an important part.

Leo VI ("The Wise")

Byzantine emperor 886-911; wrote speeches against the Latins and Jews; Morning Poems, epigrams, palindromes ("O genos emon, en ho meson ego"), etc.

Leon of Pella

Wrote a book on the gods of Egypt, in the form of a letter from Alexander the Great to his mother. In it, the gods are treated as human kings originally (see Euhemerism).

Leonidas (1) of Tarentum

Greek epigrammatist. Fl. ca. 280 B.C. The *Anthology* contains about 100 of his poems, including epitaphs, dedicatory poems, etc. Deals with the life of the poor (including himself). He was greatly admired and imitated.

Leonidas (2) of Alexandria

An astrological poet with many poems in the Anthology. Wrote *Isopsepha* (i.e. poems in which the letters in each couplet, if one assigns numerical values to the letters, are equal in sum).

Leonidas

(3) of Alexandria, a surgeon.
(4) of Byzantium, author of a work on fishes.
(5) reputedly the author of the *Acts of Andrew.*

Leontion

See Hermesianax of Colophon.

Leontius (1) of Byzantium

Author of several theological writings of the 6th century. Probably the first time that Aristotelian concepts and definitions were used in theology.

Leontius (2) "Scholasticus"

Poet in the Anthology; not the same as L (1).

(3) of Neapolis. Popular writer on hagiography.

(4) Sophist and poet of the 4th century.

(5) Wrote a commentary on Aratus.

See Krumbacher; Schmid-Stählin.

Lesbian

The dialect of Sappho and Alcaeus (qq.v.). See also under Dialects.

Lesbonax of Mytilene

Second cent. A.D. Sophist and author of a collection of love-letters, also three declamations.

Leschai

See Heraclides (2).

Lesches of Mytilene

Epic poet of the 7th century B.C. (?) to whom the *Little Iliad* and the *Contest between Homer and Hesiod* were attributed.

Leto

Mother of Apollo and Artemis. According to one legend, she took the form of a wolf to deceive Hera.

Letter of Aristeas

A document written during the time of the Maccabean uprising, which tells the story of the translation of the *Septuagint.*

Letters

There are surviving collections under the names of Demosthenes, Isocrates, and Plato (qq.v.). Some are private, some public. The letters of Epicurus are a means of philosophical exposition. Other important collections are those of the emperor Julian, Libanius, Gregory of Nazianzus, etc. The "letters" of Alciphron are in a different category. See under the authors mentioned above.

Leucippe and Cleitophon

See Achilles Tatius (1).

Leucippus of Miletus

Fl. 440 B.C. Originator of the Atomic Theory. See Democritus.

Leucon

Old Comedy poet of the 5th century B.C. In one play, the *Phrateres,* he attacked the politician Hyperbolus.

Lexica Segueriana

Includes (1) Phrynichus the Atticist; (2) Anonymus Antatticista; (3) *Peri Syntaxeon;* (4) *Dikon Onomata;* (5) *Lexeis Rhetorikai;* (6) *Synagoge Chresimon Lexeon.* (See OCD)

Lexica Vindobonense

Collection of excerpts and quotations from ancient authors. For other lexica, see *Onomasticon,* Hesychius, Suidas, etc.

Libadenus, Andreas

14th century Byzantine author of *Periegetike Historia,* a description of a trip from Constantinople to Egypt and Palestine. Other works include: *Homologia Pisteos,* letters, an encomium, prayers, and religious poetry.

Libanius (314-393 A.D.)

Sophist and rhetorician, teacher of Basil, Chrysostomus,

Gregory of Nazianzus, etc. Sometimes called the "last of the Hellenists." Opened a school in Constantinople in 340. Wrote 64 speeches, 48 declamations, 143 model essays, and over 1600 letters, as well as hypotheses to the speeches of Demosthenes. See Schmid-Stählin for list of speeches.

Libraries

Pisistratus and Polycrates of Samos had the first collections of books, but Aristotle was probably the first systematic collector. The great Library at Alexandria was founded by Ptolemy I, and is said to have contained anywhere from 100,000 to 700,000 volumes. Heads of this library included Zenodotus, Eratosthenes, Aristophanes of Byzantium, and Aristarchus. The Library of Pergamum, containing 200,000 volumes, was also of great importance. The discovery of papyri in Egypt bears witness to private collections of books, but we have little information about this.

Library* of Apollodorus *(Bibliotheke)

One of the most complete summaries of Greek myths and legends. See Apollodorus (5).

Licymnius of Chios

Dithyrambic poet and rhetor; author of a *Techne*.

Life of Apollonius of Tyana

See Philostratus (2).

Life of St. Anthony

See Athanasius.

Limenites, Emmanuel Georgillas

Byzantine poet in the second half of the 14th century. Wrote a *History of Belisarius* (840 political verses); and the *Plague of Rhodes* (644 political verses).

Limenius

Author of a hymn found at Delphi, in the Lydian mode.

"Linear B"

The decipherment of this script by Ventris is of tremendous importance for our knowledge of the Mycenean period. It is an early form of Greek, and has been found on tablets at Knossos, Mycenae, and Pylos. Since Linear B is Greek (and the Myceneans were Greeks, therefore), it has an important bearing on the possibility of early epics having been written down, and consequently on the composition, date, and unity of the Iliad and Odyssey. The date of the earliest Greek inscriptions has been pushed back some 700 years.

Linus

A kind of dirge, containing the word or sound *Ailinon,* which was interpreted as a name. A mythology was invented to fit the supposed name. Actually the expression may well be a Phoenician one: "ai lanu" (woe unto us).

Lipogrammatic verse

A type of verse in which a letter of the alphabet is omitted. For example, a version of the Iliad was written, in each book of which one letter was omitted (i.e. A in Book I, B in Book II, etc.) See Nestor (2), Lasus.

Literary Criticism

In the 6th century (B.C.), Xenophanes and Heraclitus condemned Homer on moral grounds. The Sophists were concerned with literary criticism, as was Aristophanes (cf. *Frogs*). Plato and Aristotle were both critics, the former often criticizing by parody, as well as discussing the forms of literature which should be allowed in the State; the latter submitting poetry to a thorough and rational analysis in the *Poetics,* which may be said to be the first formal work of literary criticism. In the Hellenistic period the interest was more of a scholastic one, Philodemus, Aristarchus and Callimachus being among the chief exponents. Homeric criticism was a frequent and important feature. "Longinus" *On the Sublime* is another landmark, as are Dionysius of

Halicarnassus and, later, Dio Chrysostomus and Plutarch. Lucian criticized by satirizing. After this, lit. crit. falls into the realms of grammar, rhetoric and philology.

Lithica
See Orphica.

Little Iliad
See Epic Cycle.

Liturgy
See Leitourgia.

Lives, Parallel
See Plutarch.

Lives of Eminent Philosophers
See Diogenes Laertius.

Lives of the Sophists
See Philostratus (2).

Lobon of Argos
A literary forger (3rd cent. B.C. ?) who wrote works purporting to be by the Seven sages, Pindar, Semonides, etc.

Lock of Berenice
See Callimachus.

Logic
Some of the Pre-Socratics (e.g. Zeno) and the Sophists (e.g. Protagoras) were the precursors of Socrates, to whom the beginning of general definition and the inductive method may be assigned. Plato, with his use of dialectic, and especially Aristotle, who was the first to regard reasoning as a real science, and therefore the inventor of logic as such, are the first important figures (cf. *Organon: Topica, Prior Analytica,* etc.). The Stoics, Epicureans, and Neoplatonics made further contributions.

Logographers

The first prose-writers, i.e. Hecataeus, Thales, Anaximander, Acusilaus, Hellanicus, Xanthus. Compilers of genealogies, chronologies, descriptions (*periegeseis* or *periodoi*), and so forth. Herodotus was the first to write an all-inclusive history, including Greek and Barbarian deeds. See authors named above.

Logos

"The Word." i.e. thought, the principle of the Universe. In Heraclitus this principle is Change, in Stoicism, it is the dynamic rational principle, and thus it becomes a religious, instead of merely a metaphysical, concept. In Neoplatonism, Logos is subordinate to Nous. The early Apologists (e.g. Justin Martyr) equate the concept of Logos with the incarnate Christ.

Logos Adikos kai Dikaios

Unjust and Just Discourse. See *Clouds.*

Lollianus

Rhetor, probably of the second century A.D. Wrote a *Techne.*

Lollius Bassus of Smyrna

Epigrammatist of the first century A.D. One epigram is on the death of Germanicus.

"Longinus"

The name usually assigned to the (unknown) author of the treatise *On the Sublime.* One of the greatest ancient pieces of literary criticism, the work deals with style, and is important for its interpretation of the classical spirit, its penetrating judgments, insights, and standards, as well as for the fragments it preserves.

Longinus, Cassius

Rhetor of the 3rd century A.D. Wrote a *Techne,* and

works on Homeric problems, on Ends and Beginnings, and other works. The treatise *On the Sublime* was mistakenly attributed to him.

Longus

Probably 3rd cent. A.D. Author of the prose romance *Daphnis and Chloe,* an idyllic love story, with a pastoral setting, but not without the typical incidents of the romantic novels: pirates, war, unwelcome suitors, etc. The pastoral scenes are quite charming, and the work has enjoyed great popularity. (tr. by Hadas)

Lotophagi

The Lotus-eaters, a mythological people. The effect of eating the lotus was to make one forget his own land and wish to remain in the land of the Lotophagi. Odysseus (*Od.* IX) stops there on his way home from Troy.

Lucian (born 120 A.D.)

Author of about 80 works, mostly in dialogue form, dealing with contemporary life and manners, art and literature, and varying in tone from the serious to the ludicrous and satiric. Some are attacks on philosophies and religion, some have no polemic import. Titles include: *Phalaris* (a rhetorical exercise), *Lexiphanes, Dialogues of the Dead, Descent into Hades, Menippus, Charon, Dialogues of Courtesans, of Gods,* the *True History* or *Alethes Historia,* etc. They may roughly be grouped under the following headings: rhetorical, literary, philosophical, satirical, and miscellaneous. Lucian had no real philosophical position, but wrote on all sorts of foibles and other subjects, including mythological burlesques, literary criticism, Oriental religions, and sketches of everyday life.

Lucillius (or Lucilius)

Author of over 100 epigrams in the *Anthology*. Many of them are very funny. He was influenced by Latin satire.

Lucius (or the Ass)

A novel, attributed to Lucian, but the attribution is questioned.

Luke

See Gospels.

Lupercus of Berytus

Philologist and grammarian of the 3rd cent. A.D. Wrote a *Techne Grammatike,* and a work on Genders.

Lybistrus and Rhodamne

A Byzantine romantic verse-novel in 3841 lines. The plot is concerned with love, witchcraft, kidnapping, etc.

Lycanthropy

A man turning into a wolf (werewolf). Plato and others tell of such stories. Cf. Lycaon.

Lycaon

Several people in mythology:

(1) Son of Priam, killed by Achilles.

(2) Father of Pandarus.

(3) King of Arcadia, who founded the cult of Zeus Lycaeus, sacrificed a child, and was turned into a wolf. In some stories, he was responsible for the Flood, by either trying to kill Zeus, or trying to trick him into eating human flesh.

Lyceum

The school of Aristotle and the Peripatetics.

Lycon

A Peripatetic philosopher, and leader of the school for over 40 years.

Lycophron

Grammarian and poet, born ca. 320 B.C. Included in the *Pleiad* (q.v.). Among his works are a satyric drama, the

Menedemus, a prose compilation, and the *Alexandra,* (or *Cassandra*) a dramatic monologue in 1474 tragic iambics. The work has always been proverbial for its obscurity. It touches on the whole Epic Cycle, although it deals primarily with the Fall of Troy. The syntax is difficult, the allusions inconsistent and recondite, and the vocabulary very obscure. The poem contains 518 *hapax legomena* (words occurring nowhere else), and 117 words which appear for the first time.

Lycurgus

One of the Ten Attic Orators. He died in 324 B.C. Only one of his speeches survives: *Against Leocrates.* His style is influenced by that of Isocrates, but much inferior. He included long quotations from the poets.

Lycus of Rhegium

Wrote a History of Sicily, which was one of Timaeus' sources. Also wrote a history of Libya. Lived ca. 300 B.C.

Lyde

Two books of elegiacs on his dead wife by Antimachus (q.v.) of Colophon.

Lydus, John

See John Lydus.

Lynceus

Brother of the tyrant Douris of Samos. Wrote comedies, *bons mots,* on gastronomy, etc.

Lyric Poetry

Songs accompanied by an instrument. Mentioned as early as Homer. Types: Dirge, Maiden-song, Hymenaeus, encomia, Epinician odes, prosodion, Dithyramb. Choral poetry was absorbed by tragedy and dithyramb, and monodic poetry also declined after its heyday ca. 600 B.C. (see Sappho, Alcaeus, Anacreon). Women, e.g. Telesilla, Corinna, Praxilla, etc. also wrote lyric poetry. In the Hellenistic period, paeans, hymns, love-songs and work-songs, etc. were popular. See Theocritus, Mesomedes, and, for fuller treatment, Schmid-Stählin and the OCD.

Lysanias

Alexandrian scholar, fl. 2nd cent. B.C. Wrote on Iambic Poets and on Homer.

Lysias (458-380 B.C.)

One of the Ten Attic Orators. As a metic (resident foreigner) he could not appear in court in person, so he specialized in writing speeches for delivery by others. Works: *Olympiacus, Epitaphios, Against Eratosthenes, For the Cripple, Against Diogiton,* etc. Lysias was known for the purity and simplicity of his style, the felicity of his expression, and the excellence of his characterizations (*ethopoiia*). The speech *Against Andocides* is probably spurious.

Lysimachus

(1) of Alexandria, a paradoxographer.

(2) A historian, pupil of Theodorus.

(3) A poet.

(4) of Cos, author of a Hippocrates-glossary.

Lysippus

Old Comedy Poet. Won prizes in 435 and 410 B.C. *Bacchai* was an attack on Lampon the soothsayer.

Lysis

Dialogue by Plato (q.v.).

Lysis

Originator of *Lysiodia,* or low-class mimes.

***Lysistrata* (or, "Miss Demobilizer")**

Comedy by Aristophanes, produced in 411 B.C. The plot is simple: the women of Greece, tired of the long war, meet and decide to put an end to it by going on a sex-strike. The second part of the play deals with the logical outcome of this situation, and contains many extremely funny scenes, like the one between Myrrhine and her husband, or the one in which the women think of various excuses to break their oath, to the disgust of Lysistrata, or the one with the old men reminiscing about battles 100 years before. In the end, peace is restored, with general rejoicing, and Attic and Spartan songs. Although the play contains a good deal of obscenity, it is such open, natural fun that it is hard to see how people have taken exception to it. Behind the bawdiness and humor, there runs a serious vein: the desire for peace and for Pan-Hellenic union.

M

Macarius

A paroemiographer (q.v.).

Maccabees

Three historical (or quasi-historical) books included in the Apocrypha, O.T. The fourth (Mac. IV) is of a more philosophical nature, and is found in the Jewish pseudepigrapha. The first two books deal with the struggle for religious and political freedom of the Maccabees under the Syrian Empire. The narrative is simple and direct. Mac. II is an epitome of the history of Jason of Cyrene, a Hellenistic Jew, and agrees in large part with Mac. I. The third book was written ca. 100 B.C. and the fourth in the first century A.D.

Macedonius

(1) Author of paeans.

(2) of Thessalonica, writer of epigrams. Possibly identical with (1).

(3) Epigrammatist of the time of Justinian.

Machon

New Comedy poet. Born in Corinth (or Sicyon), lived in Alexandria. Wrote plays and *chreiai,* or iambic *bons mots,* preserved by Athenaeus.

Macrembolites, Eustathius (Eumathius?)

Wrote a prose novel, *Hysmine and Hysminias,* in the

12th century. In eleven books, it contains the usual complications of love, kidnapping, slavery, miraculous escapes, and happy ending. Also made a collection of riddles.

Maenads

Female followers of Dionysus. Dressed in animal skins, and holding the sacred wand (*thyrsus*), they celebrated the power of the god in ecstatic song and dance, roaming through the mountains and forests. They seem to have been inspired with superhuman strength, so that they could tear animals to pieces with their bare hands (cf. *Bacchae*). They represent a complete freedom from ordinary convention, and a union with nature.

Magna Moralia

A work in the Aristotelian corpus, of doubtful authenticity.

Magnes

An early writer of Old Comedy (ca. 500 B.C.) He won 11 victories, the last being in 472. Titles: *Harpers, Birds, Frogs, Flies, Lydians.*

Magnus

(1) C. Julius, tragedian.
(2) of Carrhae, sophist.
(3) of Nisibis, physician.
(See Schmid-Stählin).

Mago

A Carthaginian who wrote a book on agriculture (*Geoponica*) which was translated into Greek in the first century B.C.

Magodia

A kind of sub-literary, low-class mime (cf. *hilarodia, lysiodia, simodia*). The *Alexandrian Erotic Fragment* is an example. The actor would perform to the accompaniment of drum and cymbals.

Maia

Mother of Hermes, daughter of Atlas. Her name means "mother" or "nurse."

Maiden's Lament

See Erotic Fragment.

Malalas, John

6th century author of a World Chronicle, covering the period from Egyptian legend to Justinian. A popular work, it is useful for folk-lore, but not much else. It is full of this sort of error: Cicero and Sallust were Roman poets; Herodotus was a follower of Polybius; etc.

Malchus

See Cleodemus.

Mammas, Gregory

Byzantine theologian and patriarch of the 15th century. A polemicist and strong proponent of East-West unity.

Manasses, Prayer of

A one-chapter book of the Apocrypha, based on the story of the repentance of King Manasseh.

Manasses, Constantine

Byzantine writer of the 12th century. Works: (1) A World-Chronicle from the Creation to the year 1081, in 6733 "political" verses. (2) A novel, *Aristander and Callithea,* in nine books. (3) A small biography of Oppian. (4) Descriptions of mosaics. (5) An elegy on the death of a songbird. Other miscellaneous poetry and prose.

Manetho (fl. 280 B.C.)

High priest at Heliopolis, wrote a history of Egypt from mythical times to 323 B.C. Claimed to have consulted the hieroglyphic records. The threefold division corresponds to the old, middle, and new kingdoms.

Manetho (pseudo)

An astrological compilation, by unknown author(s) has come down to us under this name.

***Manual* (Epictetus)**

See *Enchiridion.*

Manuel Calecas

See Calecas.

Manuel II Paleologus

Byzantine Emperor 1391-1425. Visited Italy, France, England, seeking help against the Turks. Wrote a Political Testament, also speeches, letters, etc.

Marcellus of Side

Poet and physician of the second century A.D. Author of 42 books of *Iatrica* in heroic verse; a work on Werewolves, one on fishes, and epigrams.

Marcus Argentarius

See Argentarius.

Marcus Aurelius, Emperor

See Aurelius, Marcus.

Marcus Eremites

Student of John Chrysostomus. Wrote works on Asceticism for the use of monasteries. Also *To Melchisidek* and *Against Nestorius.*

Marcus Eugenicus

See Eugenicus.

Margites

An early satirical epic (see parody); commonly attributed to Homer.

Marinus

(1) Writer on medical subjects (2nd century A.D.): Anatomy, nerves, muscles, etc.

(2) A Neoplatonic, from Samaria.
(3) A Cartographer from Tyre.

Mark
See Gospels.

Marmor Parium
An inscribed marble stele. Two fragments survive. It contained historical events from the earliest Athenian history to 263 B.C. Seems to have been a medley of literary history, political, military, religious information, etc.

Marriage of Ceyx
A lost poem, attributed to Hesiod.

Marsyas (1)
A satyr, musician and inventor, who challenged Apollo to a contest. The god won, and flayed him alive.

Marsyas (2) of Pella
Wrote a history of Alexander, and one of Macedon.

"Mary the Jewess"
Works on alchemy from the first century A.D. have come down under this name.

Materia Medica
Work by Dioscurides describing the properties of ca. 600 plants.

Mathematics
See Pythagoras, Thales, Hippias, Pappas, Zenodorus, Euclid, Archimedes, Eudoxus, Hipparchus, Ptolemy, Menaechmus, Democritus, Apollonius of Perga, Nicomedes, Heron, Philon, Proclus, Planudes, Theon, Meton, etc. Good article by Heath in OCD.

Matris of Thebes
Rhetor of the 3rd century B.C. Wrote an *Encomium of Heracles.*

Matron of Pitana

Writer of parody (4th century B.C.). His *Attic Banquet* parodies the first line of the Odyssey: "Sing, Muse, of Banquets, nutritious and many."

Matthew

See Gospels.

Mauropus, John

11th century Byzantine author of secular and religious poetry, sermons, letters, etc.

Mausoleum

The tomb of Mausolus, planned by him, and built by his widow Artemisia, ca. 353 B.C. at Halicarnassus. One of the Seven Wonders of the ancient world.

Maxims and proverbs

See Paroemiographers.

Maxims of Chiron (Chironis Hypothekai)

Lost poem of unknown date and author. Attributed to Hesiod.

Maximus (1) ca. 125-85 A.D.

Sophist, author of 41 extant *Dialereis.* Mostly they are exhortations to virtue, full of quotations from Plato, Homer, etc.

Maximus (2)

Second cent. A.D.? author of an extant astrological poem entitled *Peri Katarchon.* (On Beginnings).

Maximus (3) The Confessor

Byzantine writer (born ca. 580 A.D.) on various religious subjects: polemical, exegetical, ascetic, mystic, liturgical, etc.

Maximus Planudes

See Planudes.

Maximus

(4) of Alexandria, a cynic.

(5) of Alexandria, a Sophist.

(6) of Apamia, a poet.

(7) a rhetor.

Also, Stoic and Neoplatonic philosophers, etc. See Schmid-Stählin and Krumbacher.

Mazaris, Maximus

Byzantine monk, author of hymns, sermons, etc.

Mazaris' Journey to the Underworld

A Byzantine imitation of the *Nekyomanteia* of Lucian. Cf. *Timarion.*

Mechanica

A work attributed to Aristotle but not by him.

Mechanics

See Archimedes, Ctesibus, Heron, Philon of Byzantium.

Medea

(Myth) Daughter of the king of Colchis, a sorceress, who falls in love with Jason (q.v.), helps him escape with the Golden Fleece, kills her own brother to delay the pursuing party, and then is abandoned by Jason in Corinth. The *Medea* of Euripides, one of his greatest plays, tells of her hideous vengeance: first she kills the princess of Corinth (together with Creon, the king) whom Jason has married, then, after the most heart-rending wavering, she kills her own two children. Such is the genius of Euripides that we are made to feel sympathy for Medea, in spite of (or because of) her monstrous deeds. Passion is a mighty and destructive force, and Medea goes to great extremes when moved by either love or hate. Jason is pictured as a smug egoist. The play is partly a protest against the double standard that allowed men to divorce women, but not the reverse. At the end, Medea escapes in a chariot sent by the Sun-god, and flees to Athens.

Medicine

See Asclepius, Hippocrates, Galen, Herophilus, Erasistratus, Dioscurides (2), Aretaeus, Soranus, etc. Various schools were: eclectic, empirical, logical, pneumatic. Huge bibliography, large corpus of Hippocratic and Galenic works. See article, with blibliography, by Singer in OCD. Byzantine medicine includes many collections and handbooks (*Iatrica*) as well as works on veterinary medicine, etc.

Meditations

See Aurelius, Marcus.

Medusa

See Gorgon.

Megaera

One of the Furies (Erinyes).

Megale Syntaxis

See Ptolemy (2).

Megara

See Moschus.

Megarian School

Founded by Eucleides of Megara, a contemporary of Plato. It adopted the doctrines of Parmenides and the Eleatics, and stressed skill in dialectics. The nature of the ethical contributions is by no means certain.

Megasthenes

An Ionian who wrote (ca. 300 B.C.) on the history, geography, religion, customs, etc. of India. Became the chief source of the *Indica* of Arrian.

Melampodia

A poem dealing with the adventures of the seer Melampus. Attributed to Hesiod.

Melampus (1)

A prophet, missionary of Dionysus. According to one story, his ears were licked by snakes, with the result that he understood the speech of animals.

Melampus (2)

Author of two works on divination.

(3) Grammarian and commentator.

Melanippides

Dithyrambic poet. Suidas said that there were two of this name, but this is thought unlikely. He changed the structure of the dithyramb by introducing lyric solos (see Bowra in OCD). Works: *Danaides, Marsyas, Persephone.*

Melanthius (1)

Minor tragic poet of the 5th century B.C. Wrote a Medea. Lampooned by comic poets for his gluttony and effeminacy.

Melanthius (2)

An Atthidographer. Also wrote on the Mysteries of Eleusis.

Meleager (1)

In mythology, son of Oeneus. Chief story concerns the famous Hunt of the Calydonian Boar. His life was said to depend on a firebrand; when it was consumed, he would die. His mother Althea quenched the brand and hid it, but, on hearing of the death of her brothers, killed by Meleager, she burned the brand, and Meleager died.

Meleager (2)

Poet and philosopher (ca. 100 B.C.). Made the first great

anthology (see *Anthology*) of epigrams. It was called the *Garland,* and each poet in it was compared to a flower. The anthology contains over 100 poems by Meleager himself, most of them about love. He has been called "the Greek Ovid."

Meletus

Tragic poet of the 5th century. Comic poets attacked him for his immorality and dullness. Wrote a tetralogy on Oedipus. He has been identified with the Meletus who accused Socrates, the *soi-disant* chairman of the Committee to Investigate Unathenian Activities. But this is probably incorrect. Possibly the tragedian was the father of the politician.

Meliambi

See Cercidas.

Melissus of Samos

Middle of the 5th century. Last member of the Eleatic school of philosophy. Wrote a work on Nature, which defended the Eleatics against Empedocles' doctrine of the Four Elements.

Melinno

Poetess of unknown date. Wrote on Rome, in Sapphic stanzas.

Meliteniotes, Theodore

Author of a long allegorical poem, to Sophrosyne. Perhaps written ca. 1300, the work is of little merit.

Melpomene

One of the Muses (q.v.).

Memorabilia

Memoirs by Xenophon, in defense of Socrates. Contain miscellaneous, and sometimes valuable information about Socrates. Greek title: *Apomnemoneumata.*

Memnon (1)

Ethiopian king in the Trojan war, killed by Achilles.

(2) Author of a history of Heraclea Pontica.

Menaechmus (1)

Pupil of Eudoxus (fl. ca. 350 B.C.). Mathematician who discovered three of the conic sections and solved the problem of doubling the cube.

(2) A historian who wrote on Alexander, and was used by Pausanias.

Menander (1) of Athens (342/1-291/90 B.C.)

The greatest of the New Comedy playwrights. Before the 20th century, Menander was known only by reputation and Latin adaptations (Plautus and Terence). Papyri found recently have given us sizable portions of several plays: *Epitrepontes* (the Arbitration), *Perikeiromene* (the Shearing of Glycera), *Samia, Heros,* etc. These, in addition to the more recently discovered *Dyscolus* (Grouch), give us a fairly good idea of the manner and matter of his plays. Predominant characteristics are: simplicity of style, subtlety of characterization, gentle humor and irony, sympathy and tolerance for the foibles of mankind. Menander had great influence on European comedy. See *Epitrepontes, Dyscolus.* Discarding mythological subjects, Menander preferred to mirror his own times. The chief influence on him was not Aristophanes but Euripides.

Menander (2) of Ephesus

Historian of Phoenicia, used by Josephus.

(3) of Laodicea. Rhetor of the 3rd cent. A.D. Wrote treatises and commentaries.

(4) of Capparetia, a Gnostic.

(5) of Tyrrhenion, a grammarian.

(6) Byzantine historian of the 6th century. (Called Menander Protector.)

Menecrates

(1) of Elaia. Periegetic writer.
(2) of Ephesus, a poet.
(3) of Nyssa, a grammarian.
(4) Epigrammatist.
(5) of Xanthus, a historian. Wrote a history of Lycia.

Menedemus

Cynic philosopher of the third century B.C. *Menedemus* is also the title of a satyric drama by Lycophron (q.v.).

Menelaus (Menelaos) (1)

In mythology, the brother of Agamemnon and husband of Helen. In the Iliad he fights a duel with Paris and wounds him, but is prevented by Aphrodite from killing him. After the Trojan War, he takes Helen back to Sparta, where they are living when Telemachus visits them (Odyssey). In later versions, e.g. the *Helen* of Euripides, he goes with the phantom Helen to Egypt, where he is shipwrecked. In the *Trojan Women* he promises Hecuba that he will kill Helen when he gets back to Sparta. Other sources tell of other adventures.

Menelaus (2)

Mathematician of Alexandria. His *Sphaerica* is extant in Arabic. Also wrote six books on Chords in a Circle.

There was also an epic poet by the name of Menelaus, and a tragedian.

Menestor

A botanist who applied the Pythagorean theory of the opposition of warm and cold to plants. Much quoted by Theophrastus.

Menexenus

A dialogue of Plato, consisting mostly of a funeral oration, supposedly by Aspasia. Sometimes considered a satire on funeral speeches and their falsification of history.

Menippus (1) of Gadara (3rd century B.C.)

Originator of the *Spoudogeloion* (serio-comic style). Works included: *Nekuia, Diathekai, Symposium,* etc. He wrote prose interspersed with verses (it is not known, however, whether the verses were original or quoted). Influenced Meleager of Gadara, Varro, Lucian, etc. The Roman *Menippean Satire* was adapted from his works. (Examples, Petronius, Seneca's *Apocolocyntosis,* and ultimately, such works as *Aucassin and Nicolete).*

Menippus (2) of Pergamum. Fl. 20 B.C.

Writer of a *Periplus* (Voyage around the Mediterranean).

Menippus

Also called *Nekuomanteia.* Title of a work by Lucian, in which the philosopher returns from Hades and tells of what he saw there.

Meno

Famous dialogue of Plato, in which the doctrine that all learning is reminiscence is expounded, together with the question whether virtue (*arete*) can be taught.

Meno

Pupil of Aristotle, who wrote *Iatrike Synagoge* (Compendium of Medicine).

Menodotus (1) of Perinthus

Author of a historical work entitled *Hellenikai Pragmateiai* in 15 books.

Menodotus (2)

Perhaps the same as (1). Wrote on Samos and the temple of Samian Hera.

Menodotus (3) of Nicomedia

Leader of the empirical school of medicine (ca. 120 A.D.) Much quoted by Galen, he was a voluminous author.

Mentor

In mythology, the friend of Odysseus. Athena takes his form to advise Telemachus, hence the name Mentor as an advisor.

Mesomedes

Freedman of Hadrian, a lyric poet. Wrote hymns to Nemesis, Helios, Calliopeia, and other poetry.

Metagenes

Old Comedy poet, fl. ca. 400 B.C. Wrote a *Phliothytes*, and *Homer* or *Asketai.*

Merope

(1) A Pleiad, wife of Sisyphus, who "hides her face in shame."

(2) Wife of Polybus of Corinth, supposed mother of Oedipus.

Metamorphoses

Work by Nestor (2) of Laranda.

Metamorphosis

Any kind of magical transformation, much used in etiological myths. In Hellenistic times many such collections were made, e.g. the *Heteroioumena* of Nicander. Ovid's *Metamorphoses* draws almost entirely on Greek sources.

Metaphrastes, Symeon

See Symeon Metaphrastes.

Metaphysics

Aristotle's work on cosmology and ontology, essence, potentiality, activity, unity, etc. Aristotle himself called this *Prote Philosophia* (Primary philosophy) but the title *Meta-*

physics, meaning "that which comes after the *Physics,*" is the familiar one.

Meteorology

Pre-Socratics and Plato considered the phenomena, but the first exact and scientific definition came from Aristotle. Theophrastus and the Epicureans continued his work, as did Posidonius.

Meter

The meter of epic poetry was the dactylic hexameter, consisting of six feet (the first four dactyls or spondees; the fifth nearly always a dactyl; the sixth, a spondee or trochee). The *Elegiac* meter consists of alternating lines of dactylic hexameters and two half-hexameters. The iambic meter, which, as Aristotle remarks, is the closest to ordinary speech, became the meter of satire, invective, and comedy, but also of tragedy, where the normal line is iambic trimeter (we would call it a hexameter, since it has one more iambic foot than the pentameter, but it was considered as three dipodies). Trochaic meters were frequent in comedy but not in tragedy. The lyric meters are far more complex, and consist of various combinations (cretics, dochmiacs, glyconic, pherecratean, anacreontic, as well as the Sapphic and Alcaic stanzas.) Some are extremely complex (e.g. Pindar's), some rather simple, like the Lesbian monodic lyric. For fuller discussion and bibliography see Denniston's article in OCD.

Meter, Byzantine

In general, Byzantine poetry favored the stress-accent. The *Canones,* invented by Andreas of Crete, consisted of lyrics of varying meters strung together into one whole. The religious drama *Christus Patiens* is in iambic meter. Secular poetry was usually in one of the following: epigrams, iambic trimeter, and the so-called "political verse," a fifteen syllable trochaic line, beginning off the stress.

Methodius

Bishop of Olympus, martyred in 311. Works: *Symposium* or *Chastity, Hymn to Christ,* in the form of an alphabetic acrostic (each strophe begins with a succeeding letter of the alphabet).

Metis

The Personification of wise counsel; the consort of Zeus, and wisest of gods and men. Zeus swallowed her, so that he would always have her advice.

Metochites, Theodore

Imperial advisor to the Emperor Andronicus II (1290-1328), died in a monastery in 1332. Chief work: *Hypomnematismoi kai Semeioseis Gnomika*—a philosophic and historical miscellany, dealing with Plato, Socrates, Fate, Fortune, etc. Also wrote on rhetoric, astronomy, poetry, letters, etc.

Meton

Athenian mathematician and astronomer of the 5th century B.C. Proposed a 19-year cycle to correlate the lunar month with the solar year. He is caricatured in the *Birds* of Aristophanes.

Metrodorus (1) of Chios

Pupil of Democritus. Wrote historical works (*Troica, Ionica*) and a work *Peri Physeos* (on Nature).

Metrodorus (2) of Lampsacus

One of the leaders of the Epicurean school. Epicurus addressed letters to him and mentions him often. Wrote many works, mostly polemics against other schools of philosophy.

Metrodorus

(3) An epigrammatist. Wrote on arithmetical problems.

(4) An Academic philosopher. Wrote on Tigranes.

Michael Attaliates, Michael Italicus, etc.

See Attaliates, Italicus, etc.

Michael Syncellus

Patriarch of Jerusalem in the 9th century. Besides his theological works, he wrote on syntax.

Midas

Legendary king of Phrygia. The most familiar story is that of the Golden Touch (an etiological myth: to rid himself of this curse in disguise, he bathed in the Pactolus River, which thenceforth had golden sands). Another story tells of his judging against Apollo in a musical contest, and being given donkey's ears.

Middle Comedy

Unlike Old Comedy, which dealt with personal abuse and political satire, Middle Comedy preferred mythological burlesque and scenes from daily life. The chorus' role was diminished. The *Plutus* of Aristophanes is sometimes considered an example of this genre.

Milesian Tales (Milesiaka)

A popular form of literature. Romantic love-stories, with adventures, kidnapping, hairbreadth escapes, and happy endings. The *Milesiaka* of Aristides were a byword for indecency.

Miltiades

Christian apologist. Wrote works against the Gnostics, and the Montanists, an *Apology on Christian Philosophy; To the Greeks, Jews,* etc.

Mime

An imitative performance or performer. The *Alexandrian Erotic Fragment* is an example, as are the *Mimes of Hero(n)das.*

Mimesis

Imitation, or re-presentation, of life. All literature, (and all art), according to Aristotle is *mimesis.*

Mimnermus of Colophon

Elegiac poet of the 7th century B.C. One book was called Nanno, after a flute-girl. Fragments deal with the pleasures of youth, etc. His language is direct, his images brilliant. He was said to have written a *Smyrneis* (historical poem about Smyrna).

Minos

Legendary king of Crete who became a judge of the dead in the Underworld.

Minos

Title of a pseudo-Platonic work.

Minucianus the Elder (2nd cent. A.D.)

Rhetor, author of a *Techne* and *Progymnasmata,* and a commentary on Demosthenes.

Minyas

Title of a lost poem on Heracles, supposedly by Prodicus the Phocaean.

Mnasalces (or Mnasalcas)

An epigrammatist, fl. ca. 250 B.C. Meleager speaks of the "sharp needles of Mnasalces' pine."

Mnaseas of Patrai

Greek traveller and geographical writer; pupil of Eratosthenes. Wrote descriptions of Europe, Asia, Libya, etc.

Mnesimachus

Middle comedy writer. Titles: *Alcmeon, Busiris, Dyscolus, Philippus.* The titles show he wrote mythological burlesque, comedies of daily life, and political plays.

Moderatus of Gades

Philosophical writer of the first century A.D. Wrote

Pythagorikai Scholai, and played an important part in the formation of the Neoplatonic doctrine.

Modestus

7th century Byzantine author of sermons, etc.

Moeris

An Atticist lexicographer, author of the (extant) *Lexeis Attikon kai Hellenon kata Stoicheion.* The Arrangement was only partly alphabetical, i.e. words beginning with the same letter were grouped together, but no further arrangement within the group was made. The work deals with grammar, diction, meaning.

Moero (or Myro) of Byzantium

Epic poetess, ca. 300 B.C. Wrote *Arai* (Curses).

Moira

See Fate.

Momos

Personification of criticism. Used by Callimachus and Lucian.

Monophysites

Defended the belief in the unity of the human and divine elements in Christ. The Council of Chalcedon, which established the two-fold nature of Christ, was opposed to them. Byzantine polemicists vigorously attacked the Monophysite heresy. The Monothelite doctrine, also upheld by the Monophysites, maintained that Christ had one will. This was also attacked by the orthodox theologians.

Moralia

Collective title of a large number of essays by Plutarch (q.v.). Some are debates, some dialogues, etc. They include anecdotes, antiquarian knowledge, the *Symposiaka Problemata,* essays on love, music, anger, health, etc. Not all of them deal with ethical or moral problems.

Morsimus

Tragic poet ridiculed by Aristophanes.

Moschion

(1) Tragic poet of the 4th cent. B.C. Wrote a *Telephus* and a *Themistocles.*

(2) A paradoxographer.

Moschopulus, Manuel

Byzantine scholar, ca. 1300, friend of Planudes, Wrote on Grammatical questions (*Erotemata Grammatika*) and compiled a lexicon of Attic words.

Moschus of Syracuse

Bucolic poet, ca. 150 B.C. Extant fragments deal with country life, fishermen, love, etc. Other works: *Europa,* an epyllion in 166 hexameters, a graceful narrative of Zeus' Rape of Europa. Moschus has been credited with the *Lament for Bion,* but this is most unlikely; also with a work entitled *Megara,* a duet between the wife and mother of Heracles, which may be by Moschus, but this is not certain. Other works: *Runaway Love, Eros the Plowman.* Moschus has also been called a grammarian, but there is no evidence of this.

Moschus, John

Hagiographical writer, ca. 600 A.D. Wrote on monastic life, and compiled a list of monasteries.

Mouseion

Title of a lost work by Alcidamas.

Mundo, de

Treatise on the universe, in the Aristotelian corpus, but probably written in the first century A.D.

Musa Paedica (or Puerilis)

The 12th Book of the Anthology, devoted to pederasty.

Musaeus (1)

A mythical singer, associated with Orpheus, or with Eleusis.

Musaeus (2) of Ephesus

An epic poet, author of a *Perseid* and other works.

Musaeus (3) Grammaticus 5th or 6th cent. A.D.

Author of the romance *Hero and Leander*. This work was very influential in the Renaissance (e.g. on Marlowe). It was thought that the Musaeus who wrote it was identical with the ancient seer.

Muses

Nine goddesses of poetry, literature, etc. Their home was on Mt. Helicon. Hesiod's account of them became the official one in antiquity, including their names, functions, etc. They were the daughters of Zeus and Mnemosyne (Memory). They are as follows, in the usual (Hesiodic) version: Calliope (heroic poetry), Clio (history), Euterpe (flute-playing), Terpsichore (lyric poetry and dance), Erato (hymns or lyric poetry), Melpomene (tragedy), Thalia (comedy), Polyhymnia (mime), and Urania (astronomy). When Plato says that the studies in the Republic include Music and Gymnastics, he meant, not what we mean today by Music, but all subjects that were the province of the Muses.

Museum

A temple of the Muses at Alexandria, the center of much learning and study.

Music

Of great importance in Greek life, from the earliest times. At the games, at religious festivals, marriages, funerals, agricultural rites, banquets, dramatic performances, music was a vital and integral part. Prizes at the games for musical competitions were as important as the prizes for athletic prowess. In addition, Greek poetry was more usually associated with music than poetry of today. Homeric poems were often chanted to the accompaniment of a lyre, lyric poetry emphasized the tune no less than the words, and the education of a citizen included musical education. The Pythagoreans were the first to study music, which they closely associated with Number, Plato discusses music, as does Aristotle. See Also Aristoxenus, Philodemus, etc. Our knowledge of Greek music is sadly lacking. See the excellent article in OCD on Greek Music, by Mountford and Winnington-Ingram.

Musonius Rufus

Stoic writer of the Roman Empire. (Died ca. 100 A.D.).

Myllus

Old Comedy (?) author.

Myrinus

Epigrammatist of the 1st century A.D.

Myriobyblion

Work by Photius (q.v.) analyzing 280 different books.

Myrsilus or Mrytilus

An Old Comedy Poet, brother of Hermippus.

Myrtis

A Boeotian poetess, teacher of Corinna and of Pindar.

Mysteries

Secret cults, of great importance in Greek life. Among the most important were the Eleusinian Mysteries, associated with Demeter, and the Orphic rites, associated with Dionysus-Zagreus.

Myth

The "telling of tales." There are many sorts of myth. They include etiological myths, folk-tales, etc. and deal with heroes, gods, ritual, worship, natural phenomena, etc. Mythology was the literature, as well as the religious and scientific lore of the early peoples. See Rose in OCD; Rose, *Handbook;* Hamilton, *Greek Mythology;* and Graves, *The Greek Myths.*

Mythiambi Aesopei

Collection of Fables by Babrius.

Mythographers

See Hesiod, Pherecydes, Acusilaus. Hellenistic writers on mythology include Callimachus, Apollodorus, Euhemerus, Palaepatus, etc.

N

Nanno
See Mimnermus.

Narcissus
In mythology, a beautiful youth, who fell in love with his own reflection, pined away, died, and was turned into the flower of the same name. Sometimes associated with Echo.

Nature, On
See Empedocles.

Nature of Animals
See Claudius Aelianus.

Naumachius
2nd century A.D. author of a poem on the duties of a wife. Also, possibly the author of a book of wonders.

Naupactia Epe
A lost poem which dealt with famous women. Possibly by one Carcinus of Naupactus.

Nausicaa
In Homer's *Odyssey,* the daughter of Alcinous. Moved by a dream, she went with her handmaids to the river to wash clothes. A scream from one of the girls woke the sleeping Odysseus. Nausicaa gave him food and drink and pointed out the way to the town. The episode (Od. vi) is an altogether delightful one. Sophocles dealt with it in a

lost play (*Nausicaa*). According to one source, she later married Telemachus.

Neanthes of Cyzicus

Historian, author of a series of biographies, a work on Cyzicus, an *Hellenica*. Was the first to write about the misanthrope Timon of Athens. Also the history of Attalus I has been ascribed to him, but this is probably by a younger Neanthes.

Nearchus

Friend of Alexander the Great, and commander of his fleet. He wrote a chronicle, giving an account of India and of his voyage, which was used by Arrian and Strabo.

Nechepso

Author (together with Petosiris) of a large work on astrology, probably the first to use the signs of the zodiac with their familiar astrological significance. Probably second century B.C.

Neilus Cabasilas

See Cabasilas.

Nekuia

Book xi of the Odyssey; the descent of Odysseus to Hades. Also see Menippus (1).

Nekuomanteia

Title of a work by Lucian (q.v.), also called *Menippus.*

Neleus

In mythology, the father of Nestor. All his other sons were killed by Heracles.

Nemean Odes

See Pindar.

Nemesis

Personification of righteous indignation (i.e. of the gods,

at human presumption or *hybris*). Also possibly a war-goddess. See Rose in OCD.

Nemesius of Emesa

Bishop of the 4th or 5th century, author of a work *On the Nature of Man* which combined the anthropological lore of the Greek philosophers with Christian concepts. A popular textbook, it was also translated into Latin.

Neophron of Sicyon

Wrote a *Medea* which Euripides is said to have used; actually his play was probably later than that of Euripides. Suidas says that he wrote 120 plays, and was put to death by Alexander.

Neophytus

Born ca. 1134. Author of speeches, a letter on the sad state of affairs in Cyprus, and a popular work on the monastic life.

Neoplatonism

The chief philosophy of the pagan world from about the middle of the third century A.D. until 529, when Justinian closed the schools. Actually, a synthesis of Platonic, Aristotelian, Stoic and Pythagorean elements; an attempt to weave them all into one consistent system. The real founder was Ammonius Saccas, but the definitive form was given the movement by Plotinus, whose *Enneads* are the most important product of Neoplatonism. See Porphyry, Iamblichus, "Dionysius the Areopagite," Proclus, Synesius, Ammonius Saccas, Plotinus, Nemenius (1), and Albinus (2).

Neoptolemus (1)

(Mythology) Son of Achilles and Deidameia. After his father's death, the Greeks sent for him, as his presence was necessary for the Sack of Troy. He was one of the party in the Wooden Horse. Sophocles (*Philoctetes*) tells part of the story. According to other versions, he killed Priam (cf.

Aeneid ii); incurred the wrath of Apollo; was killed at Apollo's shrine at Delphi; had a son by Andromache; became the ancestor of the Molossian kings of Epirus (Pyrrhus was the most famous of them, and Pyrrhus was another name for Neoptolemus—in fact, Pyrrhus may have been his original name and Neoptolemus or "young warrior" merely an epithet).

Neoptolemus (2) of Parium

Poet and grammarian of the 3rd century B.C. Wrote a *Dionysias, Trichthonia,* literary criticism, epigrams, an *Art of Poetry* (used by Horace: he said the aim of poetry is "to delight and instruct"), and a treatise on Homer. His nickname was "glossographos."

Neopythagoreanism

Later modifications in the Pythagorean school, plus Platonic and Stoic elements. It merged with Neoplatonism (q.v.).

Nephelai

See *Clouds* (Aristophanes). For Nephelococcygia, see *Birds.*

Nessus

A centaur killed by Heracles for his attempt to violate Deianeira (Heracles' wife) while ferrying her across a river. He gave her his garment steeped in the poison of Hydra, telling her it was a charm to retain the love of Heracles. She later used this, causing the death of the hero. Sophocles tells the story in the *Trachiniae.*

Nestor (1)

Son of Neleus. In the *Iliad* he is pictured as an old man (he has survived two generations and is king among the third), whose advice is respected but not necessarily followed.

Nestor (2) of Laranda fl. ca. 200 A.D.

Author of a lipogrammatic Iliad (in each of whose books,

a different letter of the alphabet does not appear). Also wrote a *Metamorphoses.* His son was the epic poet Peisander of Laranda.

Nestorius

Patriarch of Constantinople 428-31. His doctrine (Nestorianism: stressing the difference between Christ's human and divine natures in such a way that it was impossible to reconcile them) was condemned by the Councils of Ephesus and Chalcedon.

New Comedy

Chief practitioners: Menander, Diphilus, Philemon (qq.v.); others: Apollodorus (2), Baton, Epinicus, Posidippus, Philippides, and many others (see Schmid-Stählin and OCD for the complete list, which includes over 60 names). The characteristics of New Comedy, as seen from the remains of Menander, and the adaptations or translations of Plautus and Terence in Latin, are: a complete lack of personal abuse and political satire, and little mythological burlesque. It is a comedy of manners, with romantic love interest, long-lost children and recognition-scenes, and types portrayed, rather than individuals: the grouchy old man, the clever slave, the scheming parasite, the lovesick youth, braggart soldier, call-girl with the heart of gold, the wicked madam or pimp, etc. New Comedy seems to draw more on Euripides than on Aristophanes, with whom it has almost nothing in common.

New Sophistic (also called Second Sophistic)

A school of rhetoric which began ca. 100 A.D. See Polemon (2), Herodes Atticus, Aelius Aristides.

New Testament

The collection of sacred books added to the Jewish Bible, the latter then being known (by Christians) as the Old Testament. The collection was a gradual process, extending over three or four centuries. The four Gospels

(Matthew, Mark, Luke and John) were regarded as authoritative by the middle of the second century. The Pauline Epistles had probably been gathered even earlier. The language was the vernacular Greek, or *Koine*. See Acts, Gospels, Epistles, Apocalypse, Apocrypha, etc. For a comprehensive discussion, see the article in Ferm's *Encyclopedia of Religion*.

Nicaenetus

Wrote epigrams and a *Catalogue of Women* in the 3rd cent. B.C.

Nicander of Colophon 2nd cent. B.C.

Doctor, poet and grammarian. Wrote two didactic poems in hexameters: the *Theriaca* and *Alexipharmaca.* The first deals with snake-bites and their remedies, and other poisonous creatures; the second with all sorts of poisons and their antidotes. He also wrote a *Thebaica, Oetaica, Sicelia,* and a *Heteroioumena* (Metamorphoses) which was used by Ovid; as well as a *Melissurgica* (on bee-keeping) and *Georgica,* both of which may have influenced Vergil; and works on hunting, farming, on poets and poetry, a collection of Glosses, and a work on Temple Utensils.

Nicanor of Alexandria

Wrote on the punctuation of the *Iliad, Odyssey,* on Callimachus, and a *Peri Stigmes.* Another Nicanor wrote the *Metonomasiai.* There were also a poet, and an Alexander-historian of the same name.

Nicarchus

Author of about 40 poems in the Greek Anthology, mostly rather coarse.

Nicephorus Bryennius, Chumnos, etc.

See Bryennius, Chumnos, etc.

Nicephorus Xanthopulus

See Xanthopulus.

Nicephorus

Patriarch ca. 800, exiled during the Iconoclastic Controversy. Wrote an historical sketch covering the period 602-769; also a popular chronicle from Adam to 829.

Nicetas Acominatus

See Acominatus.

Nicetas (1) of Byzantium

Also called Philosophus and Didascalus. Byzantine apologist and writer of the 9th century. Wrote works against the Armenians, the Moslems, Latins; letters, etc.

Nicetas (2) David

Byzantine author of the late 9th century. Wrote panegyrics, speeches in praise of the Apostles, martyrs, sermons, etc.

Nicetas (3) of Maronaea

Archbishop of Thessalonica in the 12th century. Author of six dialogues on the *Procession of the Holy Ghost.*

Nicetas (4) of Serra

11th century Byzantine bishop and Metropolitan. Wrote theological works, religious poetry, also on grammar (a didactic poem), on mythology, etc.

Nicetas (5) Stethatus

11th century monk, author of several works chiefly dealing with mysticism and asceticism (*on Paradise, on the Soul, Protrepticus*, etc.).

Nicetas

(6) Of Smyrna, a Sophist.

(7) Made a collection of works on surgery.

For others, see Schmid-Stählin and Krumbacher.

Nicholas Cabasilas

See Cabasilas.

Nicholas (1) of Corcyra

12th century Metropolitan; poet and miscellaneous author of such works as: *On Vanity, on the Transience of Earthly Things, On Virtues, on Retirement, etc.*

Nicholas (2) of Methone

One of the chief theological writers of the 12th century. From his works we can see the orthodox and anti-orthodox currents and the theological controversies of his day.

Nicias

(1) N. Curtius, a grammarian.

(2) of Elea, Orphic.

(3) of Miletus, physician and epigrammatist.

(4) of Nicaea, Doxographer.

Nicochares

Old Comedy writer of the 4th century B.C. Ten titles, including *Lacones, Cretes,* and mythological burlesques, are mentioned by Suidas.

Nicocrates

Lyric poet of the Empire (2nd cent. A.D.).

Nicodemus, Gospel of

(or, *Acts of Pilate*) A 4th century work in two parts: 1) an account of the trial, passion, and resurrection of Jesus; 2) an account of the Descent into Hell, appended later.

Nicolaus of Damascus (1st cent. B.C.)

Wrote tragedies, comedies, works on natural science, a biography of Augustus, a universal history, a work on Aristotle, etc.

Nicomachean Ethics

Aristotle's great work on Ethics, so called either because it was edited by Aristotle's son, or because it was dedicated to him. The subject is Happiness, the Summum Bonum for man, virtue, habit, and the Golden Mean. Virtue is defined as the mean between two extremes (excess and defect), and happiness as a virtuous activity of the soul, or mind, i.e. contemplation. At the end of the Ethics, Aristotle says that this happiness can be attained only by the correct education and habit-forming, which means legislation, and forms a bridge to the *Politics*. Important parts: the rejection of Plato's Theory of Ideas, the description of virtue as habit, the final part, about happiness. In spite of the dry, terse style, there are some very fine passages.

Nicomachus

(1) The father of Aristotle.
(2) The son of Aristotle, who edited his father's works.
(3) Tragic poet, of Athens.
(4) Tragic poet, of Alexandria Troas.
(5) N. of Gerasa, Neopythagorean and mathematician.
(6) N. of Tyre, historian.
(7) An epigrammatist.
(8) A New Comedy poet, confused with the tragedian.
(See Schmid-Stählin.)

Nicomedes

Mathematician of the 2nd century B.C. Discoverer of cochloidal or conchoidal curves, by which he solved the problems of trisecting the angle and doubling the cube.

Nicon

(1) Writer of Isopsepha (see Leonidas [2]).
(2) 11th century monk, author of ascetic writings.

Nicophon

Athenian comic poet, contemporary of Aristophanes. Titles: *Pandora, Sirens,* etc.

Nicostratus

(1) Middle comedy poet, said to be the son of Aristophanes.
(2) New Comedy poet.

(3) of Macedonia, a Sophist.
(4) of Trapezus, an historian.

Nilus (Neilos) the Ascetic

Student of Chrysostom. Wrote 1061 letters in 4 books, to many persons, mostly unknown. Also works on monastic life, Christian virtues, on Poverty, Sins, and many other subjects.

Ninus Romance

Papyrus fragments of a romance, probably from the first century, important for proving the early date of this genre.

Niobe

In mythology, the mother of 12 (or 14) children, all of whom were killed by Apollo and Artemis, because of her hybris. She became a stock figure of bereavement. She was turned into a stone or rock, with a waterfall to symbolize her perpetual weeping.

Nisus

Legendary king of Megara, whose life depended on a lock of red hair. His daughter Scylla betrayed him by cutting it off. (cf. Samson and Delilah)

Nome (nomos)

Used for certain types of melody, invented by Terpander as settings for epic texts. Later the word was used for a choral composition such as the *Persae* of Timotheus.

Nonnosus

Byzantine historian of the 6th century. Wrote of his embassy to the Orient. Interesting for geographical and ethnological details.

Nonnus

Epic poet of the 5th century A.D. Wrote an epic *Dionysiaca,* describing the triumphal entry of the god Dionysus into India; as well as a hexameter paraphrase of the Gospel according to St. John.

Nossis

Greek poetess, ca. 500 B.C. of Italy. Her comparison of herself to Sappho is not justified from the extant Doric epigrams in the Anthology.

Nostoi

"The Returns" See Epic Cycle.

Novel

See Ninus Romance, Xenophon (2), Longus, Heliodorus, Achilles Tatius, Chariton. Most of the novels we have are from the second century A.D. or later, but the papyrus fragments of the Ninus Romance point to an earlier date. The novels are prose romances, usually with involved plots (young lovers separated, various wanderings, trials, tribulations, kidnappings, escapes, and other adventures), with the inevitable happy ending. The tales are erotic, but seldom pornographic. The Byzantine novels (more properly romances) are usually in verse, e.g. *Callimachus and Chrysorrhoe, Belthandrus and Chrysantza, Lybistrus and Rhodamne,* etc.

Numenius (1)

of Apamea, ca. 150-200 A.D. Important as a precursor of Neoplatonism. Interested in Judaism and eastern religions. Maintained that there were three Gods, the Father, the Creator, and the Created World.

Numenius (2)

Poet of the 3rd century B.C. Wrote a *Banquet,* a *Halieutica* (on fishing) on drugs (*Theriaka*), etc.

Numenius (3)

A Sophist of the time of Hadrian, who wrote a hypothesis to Thucydides.

Nymphis of Heraclea

Statesman and author of a (lost) history of Alexander, as well as a history of Heracles.

Nymphodorus

A Syracusan Greek of the 4th century B.C. Wrote a *Periplus of Asia, On Marvels in Syracuse* (and in Sardinia?).

Nymphs

Spirits of the mountains (Oreads), trees (Dryads), waters (Naiads), etc. Usually pictured as young and beautiful, and as benevolent.

Nyx

Personification of Night, daughter of Chaos. Important in Orphic literature as a creative force.

O

Oceanus

Son of Uranus (Heaven) and Ge (Earth). In Homer, he is the river encircling the world. Father of the Oceanids. In the *Prometheus Bound* of Aeschylus he has made his peace with Zeus, the new tyrant.

Ocellus

A Neopythagorean, reputed author of a work on nature, which is probably spurious.

Ocypete

One of the Harpies (q.v.).

Odysseus

Son of Laertes, king of Ithaca, hero of the *Odyssey,* he undergoes a progressive deterioration in Greek literature. In Homer, he is a clever hero, a man "of many wiles," a wise counselor, and a brave warrior. In later works (e.g. Sophocles' *Philoctetes*) he is represented as opportunistic, cynical, and cowardly, and strongly contrasted to the young Neoptolemus. For details, see *Odyssey*. His death, at the hands of his son Telegonus, was told in the lost *Telegonia.*

Odyssey

The story of the wanderings, homecoming, and vengeance of Odysseus. Begins in *medias res,* with Telemachus going to look for his father. In Book v, the scene shifts to the island of Calypso, where Odysseus has been for seven years, after the destruction of his ship and comrades. Calypso lets him go (on Zeus' order), he makes a raft and departs, but is shipwrecked, and he swims ashore at Scheria, where he is met by Nausicaa (q.v.). At a banquet given by King Alcinous, he tells the story of his previous adventures and wanderings (Books ix-xii), including the Laestrygonians, Cyclopes, Scylla and Charybdis, the Sirens, the Lotus-Eaters, Circe, the descent to Hades, etc. Alcinous then gives Odysseus a ship to take him home. The second half of the *Odyssey* tells of his homecoming, recognition by Eumaeus, and the tremendous slaughter of the Suitors. The style, language, characterizations, etc. are consistent with the *Iliad*. See Homer, Homeric Question.

Oeconomica

A treatise on the management of the household, attributed (wrongly) to Aristotle.

Oeconomicus

Treatise by Xenophon (q.v. 1).

Oecumenius

Byzantine author of commentaries on the Gospels and the Epistles of Paul, and collector of excerpts from earlier writers, e.g. Clement of Alexandria, Eusebius, etc.

Oedipus

The name means Swellfoot. Subject of two great plays by Sophocles, the *Oedipus Tyrannus,* and the *Oedipus at Colonus.* The former begins with a plague. The oracle says that the murderer of the former king, Laius, must be discovered. Oedipus, the king, who has married the widowed queen Jocasta, after answering the Riddle of the Sphinx, curses the murderer (himself: an unparalleled use of dramatic irony). The rest of the play shows how, step by step, the horrible truth of parricide and incest is revealed. Jocasta hangs herself and Oedipus puts out his eyes. The play is probably the greatest of Greek (if not of *all*) dramas, for the tightly woven plot, the magnificent irony, the great choral odes, the characters of Oedipus, Creon, Jocasta, Tiresias, the balance between the power of Fate and the responsibility of the individual for his own actions. Aristotle thought the *Tyrannus* to be the perfect play.

The *Oedipus of Colonus* takes place when Oedipus (and Sophocles) were both considerably older. The blind old man, led by his faithful daughter Antigone (q.v.) has come to rest at Colonus, in the grove of the Eumenides. The play deals with the attempts of Creon (q.v.) to remove him to Thebes, the refusal of Oedipus (who is aided by the Athenian king, Theseus) to leave, the arrival of O.'s son Polynices, whom the old man curses, and, finally, Oedipus' mysterious death; as with Moses, "no man knoweth his sepulchre." Oedipus' attitude towards his own guilt has changed considerably in the *Colonus:* he says he was not responsible, and that his suffering has been passive, not active. This play, though the plot is episodic and inferior to that of the *Tyrannus,* contains some of the poet's finest lyrics, notably the ode in praise of Colonus (which was Sophocles' own birthplace). Sophocles wrote this play at the age of 90. It was produced posthumously.

Oenoanda, Diogenes of

See Diogenes (5).

Oenomaus of Gadara

Cynic philosopher of the second century A.D. Wrote a *Politeia* and various other works (on oracles, on Homer, etc.).

Oenone

A nymph, beloved by Paris. Jealous over his desertion of her for Helen, she refused to cure him, when he had been wounded by Philoctetes with the arrows of Heracles, until it was too late. She came to Troy, found him already dead, and killed herself.

Oenopides of Chios

Astronomer and mathematician of the 5th century B.C. Said to have been the first to use only the ruler and compass to solve problems.

Oknos

Personification of delay or hesitation. In Hades, he is making a rope which is eaten by a donkey as fast as it is made.

Old Comedy

See Aristophanes. Also Epicharmus, Cratinus, Phrynichus, Eupolis. Characteristic features: Personal abuse, political satire, a fantastic "Happy Idea" in which a chorus either wildly approves or wildly disapproves, a *parabasis* by the leader of the chorus, a set debate or *agon,* puns, slapstick, obscenity, beautiful choral lyrics, and much real wit.

Old Knight, the

A Byzantine poem of the 12th century, in 306 verses.

"Old Oligarch"

A treatise incorrectly ascribed to Xenophon, on the Athenian Constitution, probably written ca. 425 B.C. The work is conservative and bitter in tone; hence the title.

Olen

A mythical epic poet, before Musaeus.

Olive

Important in the economy of the Greeks (for its use as a food, for cooking, soap, fuel, etc.), and therefore in their mythology. The oil was exported by 600 B.C. The olive was sacred to Athena.

Olympian Gods

See Gods, Olympian.

Olympic Games

Celebrated every fourth year since 776 B.C. For poems in honor of the victors, see Pindar, Bacchylides.

Olympiodorus

(1) the Elder, teacher of Proclus (q.v.).

(2) the Younger. Neoplatonic. Wrote a *Life of Plato,* and commentaries on the *Phaedrus,* and on Aristotle.

Olympiodorus (3)

Historian from the Egyptian Thebes.

Olympiodorus (4)

Wrote a commentary to the alchemist Zosimus.

Olympiodorus (5)

Deacon of Alexandria in the 6th century. Wrote various exegetical works, including commentaries on Jeremiah, Ezra, and the New Testament.

Olympus

The highest mountain in Greece (ca. 9600 ft.); thought to be the home of the gods. It is located on the borders of Macedonia and Thessaly.

Olynthiacs

Speeches by Demosthenes (q.v.).

Onasander (Onosander)

A Platonic philosopher, author of a *Strategikos* in the first century A.D.: a treatise on the duties of a commanding officer.

Oneirocritica

See Artemidorus.

Onesicritus

A Cynic and historian of Alexander. Was with Alexander in India, and with Nearchus on the homeward voyage. His history was really more of an historical romance, like the *Cyropaedia* of Xenophon.

Onomacritus

Contemporary of Pisistratus, said to have written Orphic poems. Banished by Hipparchus for adding an oracle of his own to the collection. Possibly edited the Homeric poems.

Onomasticon

See Julius Pollux, Eusebius.

Oppian of Cilicia

Author of hexameter didactic poetry, in the 2nd cent. A.D. Works: *Cynegetica, Halieutica* (which may, however, be by another Oppian).

Oracles

Responses by a god to questions of worshippers; also the shrine or priests in the shrine who administer the oracle. Apollo was the most important of the oracular gods, with oracles at Delphi (q.v.), Didyma and Claros. Zeus had oracles at Dodona and Olympia; and Asclepius had one at Epidaurus.

Orators, Attic

See Antiphon, Andocides, Lysias, Isaeus (1), Isocrates, Demosthenes, Aeschines, Hyperides, Lycurgus, and Dinarchus. The canon of the Ten Orators was mentioned by Caecilius of Calacte, and recognized by Quintilian. Its origin is unknown, but the arbitrary inclusion of a certain number of names was a characteristic of the Alexandrian scholarship.

Orchestra

Derived from the Greek word "to dance." The part of the theater where the chorus stood and danced.

***Oresteia* (Aeschylus)**

The only Greek trilogy that has come down to us. Produced in 458 B.C. It consisted of the *Agamemnon, Choe-*

phori, and *Eumenides* (qq.v.). The first tells of the homecoming of Agamemnon, leader of the Greek forces in the Trojan War, and his murder by his wife Clytemnestra. The chorus of Argive elders know what is happening but cannot do anything about it. Highlights of the play are: the incident of the crimson (purple?) carpet, the ravings of the mad prophetess Cassandra, who is also murdered, and especially, the lyrical forebodings of the chorus. In the *Choephori,* Orestes returns from his exile, is recognized by Electra (by means of his hair, footprints, and a robe—for which Euripides mocks Aeschylus in his *Electra*), and the two plot and carry out the deaths of Clytemnestra and her paramour Aegisthus. At the end Orestes begins to have hallucinations about the Furies. The *Eumenides* tells of the trial and vindication of Orestes, and contains what is probably the first great trial scene in literature. The trilogy is notable, among other things, for the lofty expression of Aeschylus' religious beliefs, for the magnificence of its spectacles, for the language, especially of the choral odes, for the unifying theme of sin and retribution, and for the character of Clytemnestra, who alone appears in all three plays (as a ghost in the *Eumenides;* just as terrible in death as in life). The curse, with its theme of murders begetting more murders, comes to an end in the *Eumenides* with the establishment of public justice, viz. the court of the Areopagus, to replace private vengeance and the old Lex Talionis.

Orestes

Son of Agamemnon and Clytemnestra. He appears in different lights in the plays of the three tragedians. Aeschylus makes him a noble youth who comes by command of the god Apollo, and he is unwilling, or reluctant to kill his mother Clytemnestra. Immediately after the deed he is haunted by the Erinyes. Sophocles eliminates the Furies and the remorse. Euripides makes both Electra and Orestes not only monomaniacs, but Orestes also a coward. Immediately after the murder they are both stricken with feelings of guilt. In the *Orestes* of Euripides, he is insane, and this wild melodrama is full of attempted murder, suicide and arson, all providentially averted by the 11th hour appearance of Apollo, who resolves everything. The play is an interesting study of madness. See also Electra.

Organon

"The Tool" or "Instrument." Aristotle's works on logic, including the *Categories, De Interpretatione, Topics, Sophistici Elenchi,* and, most important, the *Prior* and *Posterior Analytics,* each in two books, dealing respectively with formal logic and epistemology.

Oribasius

Physician of the emperor Julian. Made 70 books of excerpts of medical writings, of which the first ten are extant. They deal with diet, baths, purgations, physiology, pathology, fractures, etc.

Origen (Origenes) Ca. 185-255 A.D.

One of the greatest of the Greek Fathers. Only a small part of his voluminous writings has survived. He was one of the pioneers in Biblical criticism, exegesis, theology, etc. Works include: the *Hexapla* (the Bible in six columns, Hebrew, a Greek transliteration of the Hebrew, and four translations, including the Septuagint). Exegetical: Commentaries on the Scriptures; some are preserved in the original, and some in Latin translations by Jerome and Rufinus. Other works include Apologetic, doctrinal, devotional writings and collections of excerpts.

Origenes

(So called to distinguish him from the Church Father). A Neoplatonist and pupil of Ammonius Saccas. Works: *Peri Daimonon, Oti Monos Poietes Ho Basileus* (That the Supreme Being is also the Creator).

Orion

(1) In mythology, a great hunter, early identified with the constellation.

(2) A 5th century Alexandrian grammarian, compiler of an Attic lexicon.

(3) A grammarian under the Emperor Julian, who made a collection of Gnomes (*Synagoge Gnomon*). There is some confusion between (2) and (3).

Ornithes

See *Birds* (Aristophanes).

Ornithogonia

See Boio.

Orpheus

Legendary Thracian singer, founder of the Orphic religious movement. The most important myths are: the death of Eurydice, his wife, whom he brought back from the underworld. There are two versions, one happy, one unhappy. In the latter, he turns to look at her (cf. Lot) and she is lost; in the former they are happily reunited. The other myth deals with his death at the hands of Thracian women or Maenads.

Orphica, Orphic literature

Under this heading may be listed some pseudepigraphic works: the *Rhapsodic Theogony,* much quoted by Neoplatonics, an *Argonautica,* based on Apollonius of Rhodes, a *Lithica* (on precious stones), and various hymns to the gods. The works have been edited by Abel (*Orphica*) and Kern (*Fragmenta Orphicorum*). Plato was the first to quote Orphic literature, which was also known to Aristotle. Clement of Alexandria, and also Suidas, have preserved lists of Orphic poems and authors.

Orphism

The religious movement founded by Orpheus. Includes

a belief in rewards and punishments after death, and is associated with the worship of Dionysus-Zagreus. Plato was influenced by Orphic doctrine, e.g. the metempsychosis or transmigration of souls, purification, and freedom from the fetters of the body, etc. (*soma,* body and *sema,* tomb were equated by Orphism). For a full discussion, see Nilsson's article in OCD, which also contains a bibliography.

Ossa

A mountain of Thessaly. See Pelion.

Ostrakon

A potsherd, used for voting in the annual Ostracism. This involved banishment for ten years for anyone thought to be dangerous to Athens. The practice was instituted by Cleisthenes in 484-5 B.C. 6000 had to vote for the ostracism to be effective.

Oxyrhynchus

The richest source of Egyptian papyri. Includes the *Hellenica Oxyrhynchia* (q.v.), Biblical fragments, poetry by Ibycus, etc., mimes, and a large selection of fragments of Pindar, Euripides, etc.

P

Pachymeres, George

Byzantine historian and rhetor, ca. 1300. In addition to his historical works, he wrote model declamations, etc. His history goes down to the year 1308. Although his language is stilted, it has also real wit and spontaneity.

Paean

Originally, a hymn of praise to Apollo the Healer; later to other gods (Zeus, Dionysus, Hygieia, Asclepius), and even to important mortals.

Paeanius

See Eutropius.

Paedagogus

See Clement of Alexandria.

Paignion

Literally, "game." A sportive poem. Used of the poems of Crates the Cynic, of Theocritus, Philetas, etc. Gorgias and Isocrates also wrote *Paegnia.*

Palaeography

Study of writing on papyrus (also called papyrology), wax, parchment, etc., as distinguished from epigraphy, which deals with writing on stone and metal.

Palaephatus (4th cent. B.C.?)

Wrote a work entitled *Peri Apiston* (On the Incredible).

Palamas, Gregory

14th century Byzantine polemicist. Wrote on the Hesychastes (Hermits), made collections of the sayings of the Fathers, wrote letters, poetry, etc.

Palamedes

(1) Legendary inventor of the alphabet.

(2) Eleatic grammarian, author of a commentary on Pindar.

Palatine Anthology

Started by Constantine Cephalas, finished by Planudes (qq.v.). Incorporated the *Garland* of Meleager, the *Circle* of Agathias, etc. See *Anthology*.

Paleologus, Manuel

See Manuel.

Palimpsest

A manuscript in which the original text is rubbed or washed away and another text written over it. The original is never, or hardly ever, completely obscured, and thus many valuable texts have been recovered.

Palinode

See Stesichorus.

Palladas of Alexandria (ca. 400 A.D.)

Author of over 150 epigrams in the *Anthology*. They are bitter in tone and have been compared to Juvenal (by Highet) and to Swift (by Wright).

Palladium

Statue of Athena sent from Heaven. Troy's safety depended on its safety. It was stolen by Odysseus and Diomedes. According to another legend, Aeneas rescued it from the burning Troy and brought it with him. It was thought to have saved Rome from the attack by the Gauls in 390 B.C.

Palladius

(1) Bishop of Helenopolis, author of a *Lausiakon,* a partly true, partly fictitious work on Egyptian and Palestinian monks.

(2) Physician, wrote commentaries on Hippocrates.

(3) of Methone, a Sophist.

Pallas

Title of Athena. Also, the name (in a late legend) of a friend of Athena whom the goddess accidentally killed.

Pamphila of Epidaurus

Scholar and historian at Rome under Nero. Her chief work was called *Symmikta Historika Hypomnemata.*

Pamphilus (1) of Alexandria

Lexicographer. Wrote a *Techne Kritike,* a *Peri Botanon,* and a huge (95 books) lexicon, *Peri Glosson etoi Lexeon,* which included many private collections.

Pamphilus

(2) author of epigrams, ca. 200 A.D.

(3) of Berytus, a Church Father.

(4) a Rhetor, author of a *Techne.*

Pamphus

Legendary or mythical figure; writer of pre-Homeric hymns.

Pan

Arcadian god, son of Hermes, represented as human, with a goat's legs, horns and ears. A fertility god, he could induce "panic" terror.

Pan, Hymn to

A Homeric hymn (q.v.) of unknown author and date.

Panaetius (ca. 185-109 B.C.)

Stoic philosopher, of Rhodes. Went to Rome ca. 144.

For the last 20 years of his life, he was head of the Stoic School. His work *Peri tou Kathekontos* was used by Cicero in his *De Officiis.*

Panaretus, Michael

Wrote a chronicle of the Empire of Trebizond 1204-1426.

Panarion

Title of a work by Epiphanius (q.v. 1).

Panathenaicus

Speech by Isocrates (q.v.). Also, see Aelius Aristides.

Pancrates of Arcadia

Author of a didactic poem on fish. There was also an epigrammatist of the same name.

Pandora

In mythology, the wife of Epimetheus. It was she that opened the well-known box or jar containing all the evils in the world, but also hope.

Panegyric

A speech for a general gathering, e.g. the Olympic festival. Gorgias delivered one (called the *Olympiacus*), as did Lysias. The *Panegyricus* of Isocrates is another example.

Panyassis of Halicarnassus

(1) Epic poet of the 5th century B.C., uncle (or cousin) of Herodotus. Wrote a *Heraclea.* Some ranked him second only to Homer.

(2) The author of a work on the interpretation of dreams is a different Panyassis.

Papias of Hierapolis

Author of a lost work: the *Exposition of the Lord's Miracles.* The work was quoted by Eusebius. Some fragments survive.

Pappus of Alexandria (fl. ca. 300 A.D.)

Mathematician who wrote commentaries on Euclid's

Elements, on Ptolemy's *Syntaxis,* etc. His chief work is the *Synagoge* (Collection), which is valuable for the accounts of lost works on geometry, astronomy, problems and solutions, etc. by Euclid, Aristaeus, Archimedes, Aristarchus, et al.

Papyrology

Papyrus was the chief writing material of the ancient world. Because of its arid climate, most of the papyri that we have recovered come from Egypt. Papyrology is the decipherment and study of papyri. Many important and otherwise unknown works have been found on papyri, e.g. Menander, the *Hellenica Oxyrhynchia,* Aristotle's *Constitution of Athens,* fragments of lyric poets, tragedies, etc., as well as many Christian texts. Roberts' article in the OCD gives a full discussion and bibliography.

Parabasis

A feature of Old Comedy, in which the leader of the Chorus interrupts the play and addresses the audience directly, extolling the merits of the play. It has been facetiously, but not without some justification, been compared to the TV Commercial.

Paradoxa

Collections, usually Hellenistic, of wonders, strange animals, etc. The word means "beyond belief." See next article.

Paradoxographers

Collectors of stories of marvels, e.g. the Seven Wonders of the World (the Hanging Gardens of Babylon, the Colossus of Rhodes, the temple of Zeus at Olympia, the Pyramids, the Mausoleum, etc.). Callimachus, Archelaus, Philo of Byzantium, Philostephanus, and Antigonus of Carystus all made collections of wonders. The literary genre does not come into existence until the Alexandrian period, although Herodotus, and even Homer, reveal interest in strange, out-of-the-way sights.

Paraclausithron

A serenade (or lover's complaint) sung at the door of the beloved.

Parallel Lives

The great collection by Plutarch (q.v.) of lives of Greeks and Romans, carefully matched.

Parasite

A stock figure of New Comedy. Appeared in plays of Menander, Plautus, Terence, as well as many others. Lucian wrote on Parasites, as did Alciphron.

Parian Marble

See Marmor Parium.

Paris

In mythology, the son of Priam and Hecuba, whose abduction of Helen was the cause of the Trojan War. He figured in the story of the Judgment of Paris (in the *Cypria).* He was killed by Philoctetes, after himself having slain Achilles. Also called Alexander.

Parmenides (fl. ca. 475 B.C.)

Eleatic philosopher, author of a didactic poem, of which sizable fragments remain. Only Being is important; motion and diversity are illusory. The philosophy is in opposition to that of Heraclitus (q.v.).

Parmenides

Title of a late dialogue of Plato (q.v.).

Parmenion of Byzantium

A lexicographer of the first century B.C.

Parmeniscus

Grammarian, pupil of Aristarchus, whom he defended against Crates of Mallos. Works: *Pros Krateta, On Analogy,* and commentaries.

Parmeno of Byzantium

Author of choliambic poetry, in the 3rd cent. B.C.

Parodos

The word has two meanings: (1) the part of the theater where the chorus makes its entrance, i.e. the wings; (2) the entrance of the chorus in the play itself, together with their first choral ode.

Parody

Used by Aristophanes and Plato, but not originated by them, the *Margites* and *Batrachomyomachia* being of earlier date. Aristophanes frequently parodies the style of Euripides, also Aeschylus. For later parodies, see Lucian. The inventor of parody is said to have been Hipponax.

Paroemiographers

The proverb (paroemia) is a favorite feature of Greek literature. Aristotle was the first systematic paroemiographer, or collector of these proverbs. Others were Chrysippus, Theophrastus, Aristophanes of Byzantium. The extant *Corpus Paroemiographorum* goes back to Zenobius, in the time of Hadrian. Diogenianus made another such collection; later paroemiographers are Gregory of Cyprus, Macarius, and Apostolius.

Parthenion

A poem to be sung by a chorus of girls. See Alcman.

Parthenius of Nicaea

Wrote elegiac poetry in the first century B.C. Teacher of Vergil and Cornelius Gallus. A collection of prose outlines of his love-stories is extant.

Partibus Animalium, de

Work by Aristotle (q.v.) on zoology.

Parva Naturalia

See Aristotle.

Paschal Chronicle

Byzantine chronicle by an unknown author. See *Easter Chronicle.*

Pasiphae

Wife of King Minos of Crete (q.v.).

Passion-Play

See *Christus Patiens.*

Pastoral Epistles

Refers to Timothy I & II, and Titus.

Pastoral poetry

See Theocritus, Moschus, Bion. Supposed to have been invented by Stesichorus.

Patria

An account of the monuments of Constantinople, attributed to Cadinus (q.v.).

Patristic writers

See Athanasius, Synesius, Clement, Origen, Ignatius, Polycarp, Tatian, Basil, Gregory of Nyssa, Gregory of Nazianzus, Cyril, etc.

Patrocles

Explorer and commander at Babylon under Seleucus I. Wrote on geography.

Patroclus

In the *Iliad,* son of Menoetius, friend of Achilles. He puts on the armor of Achilles and fights bravely, but is slain by Hector. It is to avenge his death that Achilles returns to the fight.

Patronage, literary

The tyrants at Athens, Corinth, Syracuse, Samos, etc. made a practice of surrounding themselves with poets and men of letters, such as Arion, Pindar, Bacchylides, Simonides, Aeschylus and Euripides. In Hellenistic times, this was continued under the *Diadochi,* or successors of Alexander, especially the Ptolemies. The same was the case at Rome.

Paul, St.

Important not only as the second founder of Christianity, but as a literary figure. The Pauline Epistles are as follows: Romans I and II, Corinthians, Galatians, Ephesians, Philippians, Colossians, Thessalonians I and II, Timothy I and II, Titus, and Philemon. The authenticity of some has been challenged. The Epistle to the Hebrews, which has come down without any name, has been ascribed to Paul and others.

Paulus (1) Silentarius

Writer of epigrams (about 80 in the Anthology), and descriptions (*Ekphraseis*) of Hagia Sophia, etc.

Paulus

(2) of Aegina, physician and medical writer.
(3) of Alexandria, astrologer.
(4) Athenian rhetor.

And numerous others, including a comic poet, a jurist, a commentator on Lysias, etc. See Schmid-Stählin and Krumbacher.

Pausanias (1) of Lydia (fl. ca. 150 A.D.)

Traveller and geographer. Wrote a *Periegesis tes Hellados* (Description of Greece), including Attica, Megara, Argolis, Laconia, Messenia, Elis, Boeotia, Achaia, Arcadia, Phocis and Delphi. He gives the history and topography of cities, describes the terrain and monuments (the descriptions are quite accurate, as existing remains attest), as well as superstitions, folklore, mythology, etc.

Pausanias

(2) A physician, friend of Empedocles.

(3) Author of an *Erotikos,* mentioned in Plato's *Symposium.*

(4) of Damascus, historian of Antiochia.

(5) of Caesarea, a Sophist.

(6) a Lexicographer, source for scholia on Homer, Thucydides, etc.

Peace, the (Eirene, or Pax)

Comedy by Aristophanes, produced in 421 B.C. after the first ten years of the Peloponnesian War. It tells of the voyage to Heaven of an old farmer named Trygaeus, on a dung-beetle (a reference to an Aesop's Fable). The play contains lampoons on war profiteers and others who do not wish the war to end. The lost goddess of Peace is finally discovered, and the play ends with a merry wedding-procession, Trygaeus marrying Opora (Fruit), an attendant of Peace. The play won second prize.

Pediasimus, John

Byzantine scholar, ca. 1300. Wrote on many subjects, including geometry, commentaries on Hesiod and Aristotle; also on the Labors of Heracles, on the Muses, on Embryology, etc.

Pediasium, Theodore

Byzantine writer, middle of the 14th century. Many works, both sacred and secular: an account of the Deeds of the Martyrs, an *Ekphrasis* (description) of the church of Serra, as well as encomia, biographies, poetry, etc.

Pegasus

The winged horse that sprang from the blood of the dying Medusa (q.v.) and afterwards was tamed by Bellerophontes. Helped B. fight the Chimaera.

Pege Gnoseos

"Fountain of Knowledge." Title of works by John of Damascus and Nilus Diassorinus (qq.v.).

Peisander (1) of Rhodes

Epic poet of the 7th or 6th century B.C. Wrote a *Heracles* which was said to be a plagiarism from Pisinus. The first to represent Heracles with the well-known club.

Peisander (2) of Laranda

Epic poet of the third century A.D. Wrote a long poem on the history of the world: *Heroikai Theogamiai.*

Peisistratos

See Pisistratus.

Peleus

In mythology, son of Aeacus and father of Achilles. As a reward for her virtue, he was given Thetis as his wife. Various accounts tell that he had to wrestle with her to win her, that she left him because he interfered with her attempt to make Achilles immortal, that he was finally made immortal, too. These are post-Homeric. For other legends, see Rose (OCD).

Pelion

A mountain in Thessaly. The giants Otus and Ephialtes tried to "pile Pelion on Ossa" to reach Heaven, but they were thwarted by Apollo.

Peloponnesian War

See Thucydides.

Pelops

In mythology, the son of Tantalus. Various accounts tell how he was killed and cooked by his father, who served the flesh to the gods; how he wooed Hippodameia, etc. See Rose, *Handbook* and OCD.

Penelope

The faithful wife of Odysseus. The most famous story about her is the weaving and unravelling of the shroud, to put off the suitors. Compelled at last to complete the shroud, because of the treachery of one of her maids, she says (prompted by Athena) that she will marry whichever of the suitors can bend Odysseus' bow. In other accounts, she marries Telegonus after the death of Odysseus. Another tradition (perhaps about another Penelope?) says that she was the mother of Pan.

Pentameter

See Elegiac poetry.

Penthesilea

Queen of the Amazons. Came to the aid of Troy after Hector's death, fought bravely, and was finally slain by Achilles. A favorite subject in art.

Pentheus

In mythology, grandson of Cadmus and son of Agave. Because he denied Dionysus, the god caused him to be torn to pieces by his own mother. See *Bacchae* (Euripides).

Pera

A Homeric parody by Crates of Thebes.

Peregrinus

Title of an adventure story by Lucian (q.v.).

Pericles (ca. 495-429)

Athenian statesman, and leader of the city in her greatest period, during which the Parthenon was built, and the greatest dramatic performances took place. He was on friendly terms with such people as Anaxagoras, Sophocles, and Phidias. Thucydides and Plutarch give good accounts of him.

Pericles, Prince of Tyre

A Greek romance, the source for Shakespeare's play.

Perikeiromene

(Or, The *Shearing of Glycera)* Fragmentary play of Menander (q.v.).

Peripatetic School

The name of Aristotle's school has been misunderstood to mean that he taught while "walking around." Actually it comes from the Peripatos, or colonnade, where he taught. See Theophrastus, Straton, Aristoxenus, Praxiphanes, Heracleides, Dicaearchus, Demetrius of Phalerum, Hermippus, etc.

Peripety (peripeteia)

A sudden reversal, or backfiring of a plan, that Aristotle says (*Poetics*) is characteristic of a good play. Examples: the coming of the messenger in the *Oedipus* of Sophocles, and the action of the Nurse in the *Hippolytus* of Euripides.

Periploi

"Circumnavigations." Accounts of various trips around the Mediterranean, Euxine, Red Sea, and other places. See Arrian, Agatharchides.

Periplus Tes Erythraias Thalasses

An anonymous account of a *periplus,* or voyage, around the Red Sea, probably from the first century A.D.

Persae

See *Persians;* Timotheus.

Persaeus of Citium (ca. 305-243 B.C.)

Stoic philosopher, wrote on kingship, on Laconia, dialogues, etc.

Persephone (Lat. Proserpina)

A grain goddess, daughter of Demeter, abducted by Hades. Permitted to return for half the year, at her mother's request, she causes the spring, and the change of seasons. According to another myth, she is the mother, by Zeus, of (Dionysus) Zagreus. Her cult was part of Demeter's. She was also called Kore.

Perses of Thebes (ca. 315 B.C.)

Author of poems in the Anthology. Unlike many of the epigrams, these are real inscriptions.

Perseus

Mythological hero. Warned that his grandson (Perseus) would kill him, Acrisius put his daughter Danae, together with her son Perseus, in a chest which he then set afloat. Perseus' adventures include his rescue and marriage of Andromeda, his killing of Medusa, and finally his accidental killing of his grandfather with a discus. He became king of Tiryns and founded the dynasty of the Perseidae.

Persians, the

Play by Aeschylus (472 B.C.), the only extant historical Greek tragedy. The action takes place at Susa, after the defeat of Xerxes at Salamis. The description of the battle, the appearance of the ghost of Darius, and the sympathetic treatment of the Persians, are noteworthy features of this play.

Persian War, History of

See Herodotus.

Personifications

Typical personifications are: Tyche (Fortune), Ate (Folly), Eris (Discord), Nemesis (Righteous Indignation), Dike (Justice), etc. Hesiod is especially fond of personifications. Some have acquired real personalities, while others remain mere abstractions. Aristophanes uses them frequently (Plutus, Demos, Dikaios Logos, etc.) as do the tragedians. Representations in art are frequent (e.g. Nike, or Victory).

Peter, Acts of

An apocryphal work, probably dating from the third century.

Peter, Apocalypse of

A second century apocryphal work.

Petosiris

See Nechepso.

Petrus

Byzantine historian, born ca. 500. His work deals with Tiberius and other emperors, political institutions, etc.

Others of this name include bishops, hagiographers, exegetical writers, etc. See Schmid-Stählin and Krumbacher.

Phaedimus of Bisanthe

Epigrammatist of the 3rd or 2nd cent. B.C.

Phaedo

One of the greatest of Plato's dialogues, in which the last hours and the death of Socrates are described. The work contains a thorough exposition of the immortality of the soul and the Theory of Ideas. The question of how much of this is actually Socrates' thought has not been resolved, and is still disputed.

Phaedon

Disciple of Socrates (The *Phaedo* is named after him). Wrote dialogues entitled *Zopyrus* and *Simon.*

Phaedra

Wife of Theseus. See *Hippolytus.*

Phaedrus (1)

A character in the *Protagoras* and *Symposium* of Plato, as well as in the dialogue which bears his name. Although not really a pupil of Socrates, Phaedrus was a member of his circle. The *Phaedrus* is famous for the parable of the Charioteer and the winged steeds.

Phaedrus (2)

An Epicurean philosopher, mentioned by Cicero for his work *Peri Theon* (on the Gods).

Phaenias of Eresus

Pupil of Aristotle, who wrote on the tyrants of Sicily.

Phaenomena

See Aratus, Eudoxus (1).

Phaëthon

In mythology, the son of Helios (not of Apollo) and Clymene. He asked his father for permission to drive the chariot of the sun, which proved to be too much of a task. To prevent him from setting the world on fire, Zeus killed him with a thunderbolt.

Phalaecus

Samian poet, ca. 300 B.C. He gave his name to the hendecasyllable meter, a favorite of Catullus.

Phalaris

Tyrant of Acragas in the 6th century B.C. Noted for his cruelty, especially for roasting people alive in a hollow bronze bull. Letters bearing his name have come down to us, but these were written much later, probably in the second century A.D.

Phallus

Model or image of the male generative organ, used in certain rites of fertility, and on images of gods (e.g. Hermes and Priapus).

Phanocles

Poet of unknown place and date. We have six fragments from a work called *Erotes* or *Kaloi,* a catalogue-poem dealing with the love of gods and heroes for beautiful boys. Especially lovely is the fragment which deals with the death of Orpheus.

Phanodemus of Athens

An atthidographer (q.v.) of the 4th cent. B.C. His work on the island of Icus was a source for Callimachus.

Phaon

A (legendary) ferryman with whom Sappho was in love,

and for whose sake she was supposed to have jumped off the Leucadian rock.

Pheidippides

(or Phidippides, or Philippides). The runner who brought the news of Marathon to Athens, and also ran to Sparta, a distance of 150 miles, in two days. He is associated with the introduction of the worship of Pan.

Phemonoe

Legendary inventor of the hexameter.

Pherecrates

Old Comedy writer, fl. 430-410 B.C. Titles include: *Agrioi, Doulodidaskalos, Korianno, Krapataloi, Persai.* He marked a transition to Middle Comedy, with his lack of personal satire.

Pherecydes (1)

One of the earliest writers of prose. Wrote a *Heptamychos* on the origin of the world.

(2) A genealogist who wrote histories, and was confused with (1).

Pherenicus of Heraclea

Author of *Epe* (mythological poems) of uncertain date.

Philaenis

A Samian poetess, ca. 300 B.C. who wrote on the *Pleasures of Love.*

Philammon

A legendary musician, son of Apollo. Invented maiden choruses; the first to institute choruses at Delphi.

Philebus

A late dialogue of Plato, which marks the last appearance of Socrates.

Philemon (1)

In mythology, the husband of Baucis. The two were rewarded by Zeus for their hospitality by being warned about the impending flood. Eventually they were turned into trees.

Philemon (2)

Important New Comedy poet. He wrote nearly 100 comedies, of which considerable fragments, and 64 titles, survive. Plautus made adaptations of his plays, e.g. *Mercator* (from *Emporos*), *Trinummus* (from *Thesauros*), and *Mostellaria* (from *Phasma*).

Philemon

(3) Son of (2), also a New Comedy Poet.
(4) Author of Milesian Tales.
(5) Grammarian of the 2nd cent. B.C.
(6) Grammarian of ca. 200 A.D.

Philemon, Letter to

Letter from Paul to the master of a runaway slave.

Philes, Manuel

Ambassador of the Emperor to Russia, Persia, Arabia and India, in the 14th century. Wrote poetry, dialogues, descriptions of monuments, animals, etc.

Philetaerus

Middle Comedy poet, possibly the son of Aristophanes (so Suidas, but this is disputed). Thirteen titles are preserved, including mythological burlesques.

Philetas of Cos (born ca. 320 B.C.)

Wrote verse: epigrams, elegies to Demeter, etc. epyllia (*Hermes*), and other poetry, Prose: Miscellaneous glosses—a lexical compilation. Supposed to have been abnormally thin, and to have suffered from bad health.

Philicius of Corcyra

Member of the tragic Pleiad. Wrote 42 tragedies, and also lyric poetry, including a *Hymn to Demeter.*

Philinus of Acragas

Historian of the First Punic War, used by Polybius.

Philip of Opus

See *Epinomis.*

Philippica

See Theopompus, Anaximenes (2).

Philippics

Series of speeches by Demosthenes (q.v.) warning the Athenian people of the growing power of Philip of Macedon.

Philippides

New Comedy poet. Won a victory in 311 B.C. Wrote 45 plays, of which we have 15 titles, including mythological burlesques.

Philippus of Opus

See *Epinomis.*

Philippus

Rhetor, edited a *Garland* of epigrams (ca. 40 A.D.)

Philippus (2) of Side, author of a polemic against Julian, and a Christian History.

For others of this name, see Schmid-Stählin and Krumbacher.

Philiscus (1)

Rhetor from Miletus, pupil of Isocrates. Wrote *Milesiakos* and *Amphiktyonos,* as well as a life of the orator Lycurgus.

Philiscus (2)

Middle Comedy poet. Of the six titles mentioned by Suidas, five are mythological burlesques.

Philiscus (3)

Cynic philosopher, said to have taught Alexander the Great, and to have written seven tragedies.

Philistion of Locri

Physician, contemporary of Plato. Assumed, like Empedocles, the existence of four elements. Wrote a famous book on dietetics.

Philistus

(1) of Syracuse, historian. Wrote a *Sikelika,* imitating Thucydides.

(2) of Naucratis, historian.

Philitas of Samos

Epigrammatist of unknown date.

Philo Judaeus

See Philon (3).

Philochorus

An Atthidographer, put to death by Antigonus Gonatas. Wrote an Atthis (q.v.) in 17 books, dealing mostly with contemporary events.

Philocles

(1) Nephew of Aeschylus, who wrote 100 plays, and defeated Sophocles' *Oedipus.* (2) There was also a 4th century poet of the name, possibly the great-grandson of (1).

Philoctetes

Play by Sophocles. The hero has been abandoned on the island of Lemnos by the Greeks on their way to Troy, because of his wounded foot. He has only managed to survive because of the Bow of Heracles in his possession. At the beginning of the play, Odysseus and Neoptolemus arrive on the island, to try to induce or force Philoctetes to accompany them to Troy, since an oracle has informed the Greeks that they cannot win the war without him. The opportunistic Odysseus is nicely contrasted to the noble son of Achilles, who is unwilling to use trickery. After much internal struggle Neoptolemus, who has obtained possession of the magic bow, gives it back to Philoctetes, and the play ends with the appearance of Heracles as a *deus ex machina,* who persuades the old hero to go to Troy to be cured of his wound. The physical and mental sufferings of Philoctetes are admirably described, as is Neoptolemus' wavering. The play, a late one, shows much Euripidean influence.

Philodemus of Gadara

Wrote elegant but indecent love epigrams, which were imitated by the Roman poets Ovid and Horace. Also devoted himself to the task of popularizing Greek philosophy, writing a *Syntaxis* of the Philosophers, including theology, rhetoric, logic, esthetics, psychology, etc.

Philodamus of Scarpheia

Wrote a paean to Dionysus, ca. 335 B.C. It was discovered at Delphi, and deals with the childhood, travels, and cult of the god.

Philolaus of Croton

Pythagorean philosopher, contemporary of Socrates.

Philology

See Zenodotus, Aristarchus, Rhianus, Didymus, Dionysius Thrax, Apollonius Dyscolus, Photius, Psellus, Tzetzes, etc. In Alexandrian times, this was a favorite subject for study, and continued to be so in the Byzantine period.

Philomela

In mythology, daughter of Pandion, turned into a swallow (or a nightingale). The former fits the story better, as her tongue had been cut out by Tereus to prevent her telling what he had done to her. She did, however, manage to communicate by embroidering the story of his violation and mutilation on a piece of cloth. Procne, her sister, avenged her by serving to Tereus the flesh of their son Itys. Tereus was turned by the gods into a hoopoe, and the sisters into the birds mentioned above.

Philon (1) of Byzantium

Wrote on mechanics in the 2nd cent. B.C. Used by Heron. Wrote on *Pneumatica, Automatica,* and on the Seven Wonders of the World.

Philon (2) of Larissa (160-80 B.C.)

Founder of the Fourth Academy, teacher of Cicero.

Philon (3) ca. 30 B.C.-45 A.D.

Usually known as *Philo Judaeus.* Lived in Alexandria, where he was the leader of the Jewish community. A bridge between the Jewish and Hellenistic traditions, he tried to demonstrate similarities between Jewish and Greek doctrines. Indebted to Plato, Aristotle, and the Stoics; an important forerunner of Christianity and Neoplatonism. He explained God's relation to the world through the intervention of the *logos.* Works: *Embassy to Gaius, On the Eternity of the World, Hypothetica, Every Good Man is Free, On Providence;* numerous exegetical works, e.g. commentaries on Genesis, biographies of Abraham, Joseph, and Moses, *On the Decalogue, On Sobriety, On Drunkenness,* and other works. See Schmid-Stählin for complete list. Like the Christians (of whom he had no knowledge), Philon relied on revelation; like the Neoplatonists, he had his basis in rationalism.

Philon (4) of Byblos

Author of a euhemeristic work, based on the Phoenician Sanchuniathon. Eusebius has preserved fragments. Much of the dispute about the validity of the alleged translation has been removed by recent discoveries at Ras Shamra (Ugarit). Philon also wrote a *Rhematikon,* on verb inflexions, and a dictionary of synonyms.

Philon (5) the Elder

Epic poet who wrote on the Jewish Kings, ca. 200 B.C.

Philon

For others of this name, including writers on architecture, etc. see Schmid-Stählin.

Philonides

Comic poet, contemporary of Aristophanes. His *Kothornoi* was an attack on Theramenes. Other titles: *Philotaerus, Apene.*

Philopatris

A dialogue, in imitation of Lucian, concerning which a long dispute has raged. At first it was thought to be by Lucian himself, then it was dated in the 4th century. More recent authorities put the work in the 7th century. It is a debate between Christianity and Heathendom, the last in a long line of anti-pagan polemics.

Philoponus, John

Sixth century Byzantine grammarian, philosopher and theologian.

Philosophy

See Plato, Aristotle, Stoics, Epicureans, Diogenes Laertius, Pre-Socratics, Neo-platonism, etc. Until Justinian closed the schools in Athens, they were still flourishing after a life of nearly one thousand years. In general, the pre-Socratics were interested in problems of the world and cosmos. Socrates introduced the study of ethics, while Plato and Aristotle gave the first systematic approaches to the subject; the former laying the foundations, the latter classifying, defining, and codifying the various areas. The Alexandrians began the philosophical biography, and Diogenes Laertius combined biography and doxography in the only complete ancient history of philosophy.

Philostephanus of Cyrene

Pupil and friend of Callimachus. Wrote geographical works, about marvels, rivers, etc., an antiquarian treatise; *On Discoveries.*

Philostratus (1)

A sophistic writer of the second century. Wrote tragedies.

Philostratus (2)

Son of (1). Wrote the *Life of Apollonius of Tyana, Heroikos,* and *Lives of the Sophists,* as well as other works.

Philostratus (3)

Great-nephew of Phil. (1) and son-in-law of (2). Author of *Eikones* (descriptions of pictures in a Neapolitan collection), and *Dialexeis.*

(4) Grandson of (3), wrote a later *Eikones.*

Philotheus Coccinus

Patriarch of Constantinople, died 1379. A follower of Palamas, he wrote polemics (vs. Latins, Nicephorus Gregoras, etc.), exegetical and liturgical works, on Canon Law, speeches, letters, etc.

Philoxenus (1) of Cythera

Dithyrambic poet. Fl. ca. 400 B.C. Lived at the court of Dionysius of Syracuse, and wrote a *Cyclops,* parodied by Aristophanes in the *Plutus.*

Philoxenus (2)

Author of a poem: *The Banquet.*

Philoxenus (3) of Alexandria

Wrote on Homeric text, accents, meter, verbs, and compiled a lexicon of Homeric and other dialects.

Philumenus of Alexandria (2nd cent. A.D.)

Medical writer, member of the eclectic school of medicine. Wrote on poisons, diseases of the bowels, and a work on gynecology.

Philyllius

Comic poet. Fl. 400 B.C. Titles are mostly mythological burlesques: *Aegeus, Atalante, Helen, Heracles, Nausicaa,* etc.

Phineus

In mythology, a Thracian king who was plagued by the Harpies (q.v.), who stole or befouled his food. Rescued by the Argonauts. Accounts of the offense for which he was so punished differ.

Phlegon of Tralles

Freedman of Hadrian. Wrote *Olympiades,* from the first Olympics to 140 A.D. Also wrote on Marvels, and on longevity.

Phlorius and Platziaphlora

A Byzantine verse-novel: a love story from the 12th century, in 1874 verses. Actually, an adaptation of the French Romance called *Flore et Blanche-Fleur.*

Phlyakes

Farces performed in Italy and Alexandria in the 4th and 3rd centuries B.C. Also called *Hilarotragodiai.* Authors were Rhinthon, Sciras, and Sopater of Paphos.

Phocas, Nicephoras, Wars of

A fulsome description in verse, by Theodosius the Deacon.

Phocylides

Elegiac poet who flourished ca. 540 B.C. His work was mostly gnomic. He often began lines with the formula: "Thus says Phocylides:"

Phoebe

A Titaness, mother of Leto. Her name means "shining" and is sometimes also used for Artemis (identified with the moon in later authors).

Phoenicides

New Comedy poet. One fragment refers to a peace made in 287 B.C.

Phoenissae

Play by Euripides, ca. 409 B.C. The chorus who give the play its name have very little to do with the action, which is concerned with the Theban cycle. The play contains some good scenes, but is over-long, and almost certainly contains some later additions, e.g. a reference to *Oedipus at Colonus* which was written later. The play is about the deaths of Polynices and Eteocles, and their burial. Oedipus himself appears, as do Creon, Antigone, and even Jocasta, as well as the ubiquitous Teiresias.

Phoenix (1)

In the *Iliad,* the old tutor and friend of Achilles. He is one of the three who try, in Book ix, to persuade the hero to return to the fight. Euripides wrote a *Phoenix* (lost) in which Amyntor blinded Phoenix, who was cured by Chiron the centaur.

Phoenix (2) of Colophon

Iambic poet of the 3rd cent. B.C. Wrote choliambics, and a poem entitled *Coronistae,* based on a Rhodian beggars' song. There are 22 lines in a Heidelberg papyrus, and 5 quotations in Athenaeus.

Phorcyads

Graeae and Gorgons, daughters of Phorcys.

Phormis

(or Phormus) Writer of comedies. All of the titles mentioned by Suidas have historical or mythological titles. Said to have introduced long cloaks, and curtains for the stage.

Photius (ca. 820-891)

Patriarch of Constantinople in the 9th century. Great scholar and polymath. His chief work was the *Bibliotheca* or *Myriobiblion,* an account of 280 works read by him, (all prose, unfortunately,) containing valuable evidence about lost works, criticism, theology, history, oratory, romance, philosophy, science, medicine, philology. He also compiled a *Lexicon.* His letters are also worth mention.

Phrantzes, George. b. 1401

Secretary to the emperor Manuel II. Imprisoned by the Turks, later freed, went to Venice and Rome, then to a monastery in Corfu. Here he wrote his history of the period 1258-1476, with a strong anti-Latin and anti-Turk bias.

Phrynichus (1)

Athenian tragic poet; one of the originators of tragedy. His first victory was in 511 B.C. Wrote *Phoenissae* (historical; dealing with the Persian War). Other titles: *Pleuroniae, Aegyptii, Danaides, Antaeus, Alcestis, Actaeon.* Famous for the beauty of his lyrics, and for being the first to use a feminine mask. Aristophanes admired him.

Phrynichus (2)

Comic playwright. Fl. 430-400 B.C. He was frequently confused with the tragedian (1), also with an actor and a politician of the same name. Titles: *Ephialtes, Komastai, Monotropos,* and *Mousai* (containing an *agon,* or debate, between Sophocles and Euripides).

Phrynichus (3) Arabius

A rhetor and lexicographer of the 2nd cent. A.D. Compiled a *Sophistike Proparaskeue,* a lexicon of Attic words, of which fragments are preserved; and *Attikistes.* His models are Plato, the Ten Attic Orators, Thucydides, and the tragedians.

Phylarchus of Athens

Historian of the "pathetic" school, an important source for Plutarch. His History was in 28 books, and was known for its moralizing tendencies.

Physics

Part of philosophy, until Plato and Aristotle. The Presocratics were much occupied with various physical problems (e.g. Pythagoras, Empedocles, Heraclitus, Democritus, Anaxagoras, qq.v.). Empedocles actually performed experiments to demonstrate the nature of air. Aristotle wrote several works dealing with aspects of physics: *De Caelo, De Generatione et Corruptione, Meteorologica,* and the *Physics.* See also: Archimedes, Heron, Ctesibus, Philon (1) (mechanics), Euclid and Theon (Optics), Aristoxenus, Ptolemy, Archytus, etc.

Physiognomica

A work, probably of the 2nd or 3rd cent. B.C., attributed to Aristotle.

Physiognomonici

Authors who make assumptions about people by comparing them to animals, or by making inferences based on gestures, color, hair, skin, etc. In early writers, poets, philosophers, medical writers.

Physiologus

A Byzantine collection of fabulous tales, mostly about animals and birds (e.g. the Phoenix). Of unknown author, place, and date. It became extremely popular and was translated into all the chief languages of Europe and the Near East, and the medieval Bestiaries are based on it.

Pierius

Presbyter of Alexandria, ca. 300. Wrote sermons, works on asceticism, etc.

Pigres of Halicarnassus

Brother of Artemisia, the wife of Mausolus. He is said to have inserted pentameters in the *Iliad,* and to have written the *Margites.* The *Batrachomyomachia* was also attributed to him.

Pilgrimages

Many accounts of pilgrimages are useful for topographical and other information, e.g. Epiphanius, Phocas, Perdicas, Daniel of Smyrna, etc.

Pinakes

Work by Callimachus, in 120 Books. A monumental literary history and catalogue. Classifying authors by genre, he included biographies and lists of works.

Pindar (518-438 B.C.)

Boeotian lyric poet. Wroe Epinician Odes, for the victors in the Olympian, Pythian, Nemean, and Isthmian Games. Also hymns, paeans, dithyrambs, maiden-songs, dirges, etc. Known for the brilliance of his style and the sublimity of the myths, he wrote in elaborate, sometimes difficult language. The victory in the games is treated as a religious occasion, hence the introduction of myth, usually with a moral. With one exception, no two poems have the same metrical pattern. We have only fragments of the other works, but the Epinicians have survived intact. He is usually, and not unjustly, referred to as the greatest of the Greek lyric poets.

Pisander

See Peisander.

Pisides, George (7th century A.D.)

Called the best secular Byzantine poet. Wrote historical poetry, on the Persian campaign of Heraclius, on the attack of the Avars on Byzantium in 626, a poem on the Creation (*Hexaemeron*); epigrams, theological poetry (e.g. On the Vanity of Life; against the heretic Severus, etc.), panegyrics, and other works.

Pisistratus (Peisistratos)

The "Good Tyrant" of Athens. During his reign (560-527 B.C.) the drama was introduced at Athens, pottery and coinage took on new importance, commerce and building were encouraged. He remained to the last a benevolent despot.

Pittacus of Mytilene

Statesman and sage. Fl. ca. 600 B.C. One of the Seven Sages. Introduced a law doubling the penalty for offenses committed under the influence of drink.

Plagiarism

Must have been fairly frequent in antiquity. Aristophanes accused Eupolis of it, as did Isocrates with his rivals. Plato was said to have taken the idea of the *Republic* from Protagoras. In the period of Alexandrian scholarship, the investigation of plagiarism was a frequent activity.

Plants, on

A treatise attributed to Aristotle, who did write one, but this is not it.

Planudes, Maximus (ca. 1260-1310)

Left a collection of 121 letters, a work on grammar, philological writings, as well as the *Anthology* on which his fame rests. See *Anthology*.

Plato (1) 429-347

Pupil of Socrates. Left Athens after the trial, visiting Megara, Egypt, Italy, and Sicily. Returned to Athens and founded his school, the Academy, which occupied him for the last 40 years of his life. The tremendous influence of Socrates upon him is shown by the fact that in only one dialogue (the *Laws*) is Socrates absent. Works: *Hippias Minor, Laches, Charmides, Ion, Protagoras, Euthyphro, Apology, Crito, Gorgias, Meno, Lysis, Menexenus, Euthydemus, Cratylus, Symposium, Phaedo, Republic, Parmenides, Theaetetus, Phaedrus, Sophist, Statesman, Philebus, Timaeus, Critias, Laws.* Doubtfully genuine: *Hippias Major, Clitophon, Epinomis, Letters* 2-13. Probably spurious: *Letter I, Alcibiades I & II, Hipparchus, Amatores, Theages,*

Minos, De Justo, De Virtute, Demodocus, Sisyphus, Eryxias, Axiochus, Definitions. Best books (in English): Shorey: *What Plato Said,* Burnet: *Greek Philosophy,* Taylor; *Plato, the Man and his Work.* The usual translation, that of Jowett, of all the standard works, is delightful but not very accurate.

Plato may be said to be the man who laid the foundation upon which all subsequent philosophy had to build. His powers of synthesis are an important feature of his work: he shows the influence of Homer, the tragedians, the historians, the pre-Socratics, and most of all, of Socrates himself, all fused and bearing the stamp of Plato's own genius. Socrates stands out in the dialogues, impressive for his moral earnestness, and it is impossible to determine the degree to which Socrates was responsible for the ideas Plato puts into his mouth. Cardinal in Plato's philosophy is the Theory of Ideas, a dualistic concept which maintained the existence of a more real world of essences or Forms, than the tangible, spatial-temporal world around us. Another important concept in Plato's teaching is the immortality of the soul, best expounded in the *Phaedo.* The *Republic* deals with the Ideal State, but touches on ethics, political science, education, psychology, esthetics, economics, and metaphysics, etc. In other works, he deals with epistemology, etymology, piety, friendship, rhetoric, courage, love, virtue, prudence, natural science, cosmology, and constitutions (in the *Laws,* he revises some of the ideas of the *Republic*). Plato's style is graceful, charming, capable of great pathos and religious fervor. His language is poetical and metaphorical. He is unrivalled as the master of Greek prose style, as well as being the greatest synthesizer in the field of philosophy. It is this wedding of form and content that has given Plato the supreme place in the history of literature and thought that he unquestionably occupies. Whitehead said that all subsequent philosophy is merely "footnotes to Plato." See the individual works. Plato also wrote poetry; some lovely epigrams are attributed to him.

Plato (2) Fl. ca. 400 B.C.

Athenian comic poet. Wrote mythological burlesques, political plays, etc. The fragments have a prevalence of erotic material. Titles: *Zeus, Kakoumenos, Peisander, Cleophon, Presbeis, Nikai, Kercopes, Adonis, Daidalos, Laius, Meneleos, Sophistai,* etc.

Platonius

Date unknown. Wrote on the *Differences Between Comedies.*

Pleiad

A group of seven tragic poets of the Alexandrian period. The usual list includes: Lycophron, Sositheus, Alexander of Aetolia, Sosiphanes, Dionysiades, Homer of Byzantium. There is some doubt about the seventh. Philicus of Corcyra is the one most frequently mentioned.

Plotinus (205-270 A.D.)

The series of philosophical essays arose out of discussions in his seminars, which were collected by Porphyry, who classified them and arranged them according to subject, into six *Enneads* (groups of nine). They deal with: ethics, esthetics, physics, cosmology, psychology, metaphysics, logic, epistemology, etc. With the exception of Aristotle, it is the most complete philosophical corpus that we have. He has been called the most powerful philosophical mind between Aristotle and Aquinas. Among his doctrines are that of a single, impersonal force (= Plato's Idea of the Good), the World-Mind (*nous*) the World-Soul (*psyche*), and Nature (*physis*). He was not the founder of Neoplatonism (q.v.) but gave it its definitive form. He makes no real reference to Christianity.

Plutarch (1) (ca. 46-120 A.D.) of Chaeronea

Philosopher and biographer. Studied physics, natural science, rhetoric and ethics, but the emphasis was on the latter. Works: 277 works, not all authentic, having been ascribed to Plutarch: *Moralia,* including a host of works, all, dealing in one way or another, with ethics. They include debating questions, problems, Greek and Roman Questions, etc. The most important work is the *Parallel Lives,* a series of fifty biographies, of which 46 are in pairs, a Greek matched with a Roman, and four have no counterparts. His chief interest was in the characters themselves, in the moral lessons to be drawn from them, and in telling a good story well. At this he was almost the equal of Herodotus. His style is pleasant, his philosophy eclectic, his influence was enormous. See OCD and Schmid-Stählin for complete list of works.

Plutarch (2)

A Neoplatonic philosopher. Wrote commentaries on Aristotle.

Plutarch (3) Grandson of the above. Professor of grammar; also a Neoplatonic.

Pluto

(Pluton) i.e. the Giver of Wealth, another name for Hades (q.v.).

Plutus

God of wealth, associated with Demeter. The play of this name by Aristophanes is a Middle Comedy, and appeared in 388 B.C. Chremylus goes to the oracle of Delphi for advice on the rearing of his son. Apollo tells him to bring home with him the first person he meets. This turns out to be a blind old man, viz. Plutus, the god of wealth. He is taken to the temple of Asclepius, where his sight is restored, despite the protests of Poverty and the other gods —Hermes, arriving with threats from the gods, remains to take service under Plutus, who, being no longer blind, can distinguish honest men from thieves. The chorus in this play is unimportant, and marks the transition to New

Comedy. This is the last play Aristophanes produced under his own name, and the last that survives.

Pneumatica

Work by Heron of Alexandria (q.v.) describing various ingenious inventions, such as puppet theaters, slot machines, water organs, and the like.

Poetesses

See Sappho, Hipparchia, Corinna, Erinna, Anyte, Moero, Nossis, Philaenis, Praxilla, Telesilla, Cleobuline, Melinno, Myrtis, Archelais, Casia, Eudocia.

Poetics

Aristotle's treatise: the first to be devoted entirely to literary criticism. It originally dealt with Epic, Comedy and Tragedy, but the only part which survives in full is the one on Tragedy. He deals with the theory of art as *Mimesis* (imitation, or representation), with the function of tragedy (to produce a *catharsis,* or purging, of pity and fear), with the criteria for the ideal tragic plot (complex, containing reversals and discoveries, unified—the only unity he insists on being the unity of action—logical but unexpected in its sequence of events), and with the hero (a basically, but not completely good man, of noble birth, who falls from happiness to misery because of a *hamartia*—variously interpreted as an "error in judgment" or a "tragic flaw"). The work has had enormous influence—plays are still being reviewed in the newspapers in terms of Aristotle's *Poetics.*

Poetry

Characteristically, the Greek word *Poiesis* means Creation, from *poieo* (to make), and the Greeks thought, not in terms of Poetry, but of Lyric, Epic, Tragic, etc. See under these headings, or under separate authors.

Poikile Historia

See Aelian (1).

Poimandres

A collection of 18 treatises on Hermetica. See Hermes Trismegistus.

Poimen

See *Hermas, shepherd of*

Polemics

An important aspect of Byzantine writings, testimony to the constant struggle to defend the orthodox belief against the numerous heresies, e.g. Monophysitism, Monothelitism, Iconoclasm; and against the Latins, pagans, Jews, Islam, etc. See Leontius, Maximus the Confessor, Theodore Studites, Photius, Psellus, Zigabenus, Nicholas of Methone, Acominatus, etc. Krumbacher deals with the subject in every aspect.

Polemon (1)

Geographer, fl. ca. 150 B.C. Wrote various works on the Acropolis of Athens, on Eleusis, on Delphi, describing inscriptions, monuments, etc. Also wrote epigrams and letters. Used by Pausanias.

Polemon (2) ca. 88-145 A.D.

A sophist, two of whose declamations survive, in the Asian style.

Politeia

See *Republic* (Plato).

Political Verse

A fifteen-syllable, trochaic line, with or without rhyme. One of the most popular of Byzantine meters.

Politics

Aristotle's great treatise on political science, closely allied to the field of ethics. Contains a picture of Aristotle's ideal state, classification of constitutions, a section on education, and the statement that man is by nature a "political animal," that is, one whose characteristic it is that he lives in a "polis" or city-state. In keeping with Aristotle's emphasis on the Golden Mean (it has been remarked that he carries moderation to the point of excess!), the state should be of intermediate size, with a powerful middle class. This work has been widely read and studied, and has had a great influence on later political theory.

Polity of the Lacedaemonians

A laudatory account, by Xenophon (q.v.1) of Spartan institutions.

Pollux

See Castor, Dioscuri.

Pollux, Julius

Rhetor and scholar of the second century A.D. His *Onomasticon* is a sort of rhetorical handbook, arranged topically, not alphabetically, and treats of such subjects as: law, religion, theater, anatomy, ethics, war, arts and crafts, games, cooking, ships, and numerous other subjects.

Polus of Agrigentum

A sophist, pupil of Gorgias, and a younger contemporary of Socrates. Mentioned by Plato and Aristotle. Wrote a *Techne* on Rhetoric.

Polyaenus (1)

Disciple of Epicurus. Wrote on philosophy.

Polyaenus (2) Macedonian rhetor, made a collection of *Stratagems* (ca. 162 A.D.)

Polyaenus (3) Julius—Writer of epigrams (1st cent. A.D.)

Polybius (1) (ca. 203-ca. 120 B.C.)

Brought to Rome as a prisoner in 168 B.C. Works: A Panegyric on Philopoemen, a book on military tactics, and the *Universal History* in 40 books. Only the first five are intact; the rest survive in excerpts, and were used by Livy, Diodorus, Plutarch, and Appian. He modelled his work on that of Thucydides, and was inspired by the rise of Rome.

In spite of his political bias, and his moralizing reflections, the work is an extremely valuable one. Like Herodotus, he visited countries he described in his history. The history covered the period from 220-145 B.C.

Polybius (2)

Freedman and secretary of the emperor Claudius. Translated Homer into Latin and Vergil into Greek.

Polybus

(1) Son-in-law of Hippocrates, and author of a work on anatomy, containing the doctrine of the four humors (blood, phlegm, black bile and yellow bile) which has persisted until recently. Indeed, traces of it are still to be found in such words as "sanguine," "phlegmatic," "melancholy," and "bilious."

(2) Supposed father of Oedipus (q.v.).

Polycarp (ca. 69-ca. 159 A.D.)

Bishop of Smyrna. His only surviving work is a letter to the Philippians, which included the Epistles of Ignatius (q.v.). He was martyred during a popular anti-Christian uprising at Smyrna.

Polycleitus of Larisa

Wrote a work on geography, which was used by Eratosthenes.

Polycrates

Athenian rhetor of the 4th century B.C. Censured by Isocrates for his triviality. His works include: *Busiris, Kategoria Sokratous, Helen,* and other writings.

Polydeuces

See Pollux, Julius, and Dioscuri.

"Polydeuces"

Under this name, we have a Byzantine chronicle entitled *Historia Physike.* It covers the Creation, the Jews,

Babylonians, Persians, Alexander and the Ptolemies, Roman emperors, etc.

Polyeidus

Sophist and poet, mentioned by Aristotle for the recognition-scene (*anagnorisis*) in his *Iphigenia.*

Polyglot Bibles

Editions in more than one language, e.g. the *Hexapla* of Origen, which was the first and most famous. The *Complutensian Polyglot* (1514-1517) contained the N. T. in Greek and Latin; and the O. T. in Hebrew, Vulgate, Septuagint, and Chaldaic.

"Polyhistor"

See Alexander (4).

Polyhymnia

See Muses.

Polynices

Son of Oedipus (q.v.). Appears in the *Oedipus at Colonus,* where he is cursed by the aged Oedipus, in the *Phoenissae* of Euripides, where he and Etocles kill each other. He does not appear, but is mentioned, and is an important part of the story, in the *Seven Against Thebes* and the *Antigone.*

Polyphemus

Son of Poseidon, one of the Cyclopes. Odysseus blinds him (*Odyssey,* IX, and Euripides: *Cyclops*). He falls in love with the nymph Galatea (q.v.) and kills her lover Acis. The story is told by various pastoral writers, and is the theme of Handel's delightful *Acis and Galatea.*

Polyphrasmon

Son of the tragedian Phrynichus. Wrote a tetralogy on Lycurgus, presented in 467 B.C. and defeated by Aeschylus.

Polystratus (1)

Disciple of Epicurus, writer on philosophy.

(2) A writer of epigrams.

Polyxena

Daughter of Priam and Hecuba. Not mentioned in Homer. In the *Iliu Persis* she was sacrificed as an offering on the tomb of Achilles (cf. Euripides, *Hecuba* and *Troades*).

Polyzelus

Comic playwright. Titles (*Niptra, Aphrodites Gonai,* etc.) suggest Middle Comedy, although other plays mention 5th century figures, e.g. Theramenes and Hyperbolus.

Pompeius of Mytilene

Epigrammatist of the Age of Augustus.

Porikologos

A Byzantine book about fruits, for children: King Quince, Lord High Pomegranate, etc.

Porphyrogenitus

See Constantine VII.

Porphyry (232-305 A.D.)

Scholar and philosopher. In addition to his editing Plotinus' *Enneads,* he wrote numerous other works: *History of Philosophy, Life of Pythagoras, Pros Markellan,* on astronomy, history, religion, philosophy, letters, commentaries on Homer, Plato, Aristotle, etc., on grammar, embryology, rhetoric, and the history of scholarship. He was a remarkable polymath, and is valuable for his preservation of many important fragments of older learning, although as a thinker, he is not particularly original.

Poseidon

God of the sea, and of earthquakes. One of the three sons of Kronos. Associated with horses (the reason is not certain, but see Rose). Hostile to Odysseus in the *Odyssey.*

Posidippus (1)

New Comedy poet, imitated by the Romans. Fl. 285 B.C.

(2) Author of some 20 poems in the Anthology, on love, feasting, etc.

Posidonius (1) of Apameia (ca. 135-50 B.C.)

A polymath who can only be compared to Aristotle for the variety and breadth of his interests and achievements, which included the fields of philosophy, astronomy, meteorology, mathematics, moral philosophy, natural science, geography, history, poetry, anthropology, lexicography, rhetoric, etc. In history he influenced Sallust, Caesar, Plutarch and Tacitus; in philosophy, Cicero and others. As Aristotle had summed up the achievements of the classical world, so Posidonius summed up the Hellenistic or Greco-Roman heritage, and transmitted it to the Renaissance. Unfortunately, only the scantiest fragments remain. He was not a mere collector of information, but made important contributions (in the field of tides, primitive cultures, geography and map-making, etc.). In philosophy he was a Stoic.

Posidonius

There were also a sophist, a physician, and a didactic poet of this name. See Schmid-Stählin.

Posterior Analytics

See Aristotle.

Post-Homerica

See Quintus Smyrnaeus.

Potamon of Alexandria

Founder of the Eclectic School, which attempted to combine Platonic, Peripatetic, and Stoic elements.

Pratinas of Phlius

Said to have been the first to compose satyr-plays. 32 of his 50 plays were of this type.

Praxagoras (1)

Physician and anatomist of the 4th century B.C.

Praxagoras (2) Athenian historian of the 4th cent. A.D. Wrote a history of Alexander, one of Constantine, and one on the Kings of Athens.

Praxilla of Sicyon

Poetess of the 5th century B.C. Wrote Dithyrambs, drinking songs, and a *Hymn to Adonis.*

Praxiphanes of Mitylene

Peripatetic writer, and pupil of Theophrastus. Wrote on Poets, on Poems, on History, ethical dialogues, etc.

Preaching of Peter

A second-century work in defence of Christianity; perhaps the first of the apologetic writings. Mostly lost; only short quotations in patristic writings survive.

Pre-Socratics

The term does not refer to any school of philosophy, although most of the Pre-Socratics were interested in problems of physical causation. See Thales, Anaximander, Anaximenes, Heraclitus, Empedocles, Parmenides, Zeno (1), Pythagoras, Anaxagoras, Leucippus and Democritus.

Priam

King of Troy at the time of the *Iliad.* His death was described in the *Iliu Persis* (cf. Vergil, *Aeneid* II). His name was proverbial for a man who, having had a long and prosperous life, experienced extreme reverses in old age (so Aristotle, Juvenal, etc.).

Priapeia

Poems addressed to the fertility god Priapus. Only Latin examples are extant, although Greek ones existed as well.

Prior Analytics

Aristotle's (q.v.) work on logic.

Priscus

(1) A Neoplatonic of the time of the emperor Julian.

(2) A sophist of the 5th century A.D. Wrote about an embassy to Attila the Hun.

Proagon

A parade in costume, before the Dionysia and Lenaea, in which the titles and subjects of the plays were announced.

Problems

A work attributed to Aristotle, consisting of questions and answers on scientific and literary topics. Actually it may be as late as the 5th or 6th cent. A.D.

Proclus (1)

Compiler of the *Chrestomathia;* Probably from the first or second century, but almost certainly not identical with the Neoplatonic (2) Proclus. See Epic Cycle.

Proclus (2) (410-485)

Neoplatonist, one of the chief instruments in the transmission of this philosophy to the West. Also one of the final supporters of paganism in its struggle against Christianity. Wrote hymns, commentaries on Hesiod, Euclid, and especially Plato; various anti-Christian works, manuals of theology and physics.

Proclus (3)

Patriarch of Constantinople in the 5th century. Wrote 25 sermons and 7 letters; *Against Nestorius, On the Virgin Mary,* etc.

Procopius

Byzantine historian of the 6th century. Died in 565 A.D. Wrote a history of his times, devoted chiefly to the Vandal and Gothic Wars, based on accurate first-hand information, as he had accompanied the general Belisarius on these campaigns. Also wrote *Ctismata,* orations, and the *Anecdota,* or

Secret History, famous for its malicious revelations about the Empress Theodora and the Emperor Justinian.

Procrustes

Owner of the famous "Bed" on which he would force travellers to lie down, and then he either stretched them or cut off part of their limbs to make them fit the bed. He was also called Damastes or Polypemon or Procoptas. He was killed by Theseus.

Prodicus (1) of Ceos

Sophist of the 5th century. Best known for his myth on the "Choice of Heracles," told by Xenophon in the *Memorabilia.*

Prodicus (2) of Phocas

Early poet, reputed author of *Minyas,* a lost poem on Heracles.

Prodromus, Theodore

An extremely versatile and prolific Byzantine author of the first half of the 12th century. He wrote a verse-novel, *Rodanthe and Dosicles,* a *Battle of Cats and Mice (Galeomyomachia),* various satires (the *Lustful Old Man, Old Longbeard,* etc.), an astrological poem, hymns, other religious poetry, the *Twelve Months,* epigrams, occasional verse, works on hunting, diet, weather, letters, speeches, rhetorical exercises, philosophical works, grammatical works, etc.

Progymnasmata

Preliminary exercises, designed to introduce students to the art of rhetoric. See Hermogenes, Theon (3), Aphthonius.

Prologomena ad Homerum

See Wolf; Homeric Question.

Prologue

The opening portion of a play. In the tragedies of Sophocles and Aeschylus, this usually consisted of dialogue, giving the necessary expository material; in the plays of Euripides, the prologue was usually spoken by one character, frequently a god. Aristophanes' *Frogs* contains a section on the prologues of Euripides and Aeschylus.

Prometheus

("the Forethinker") A Titan who stole fire from the gods and gave it to men. Tricked Zeus into taking the inferior parts of the sacrificial meat. He was punished by being chained to a rock and having an eagle daily eat his liver (which grew back at night), until he was released by Heracles.

Aeschylus' play, the *Prometheus Bound,* introduces a further complication, namely, that Zeus is intending to marry Thetis; that if he does, he will be destroyed by the offspring, since she is fated to bear a son mightier than his father; and that only Prometheus is aware of this. The play, of unknown date, is the first of a trilogy. It begins with Hephaestus, accompanied by Power and Force, chaining Prometheus to a rock in the Caucasus. Oceanus, his daughters, Io, and finally Hermes appear, and during the course of the play, the secret is hinted at (see above), and we learn that Prometheus is champion of the downtrodden human race, having not only given them fire, but numbers, metallurgy, ships, reading, divination—"All human arts are from Prometheus." We know the titles of the other two plays: *Prometheus Unbound,* and *P. the Fire-Bearer,* and much speculation has taken place as to the content of these plays.

Proemium

Standard opening for a speech, or other work. Collections were made by Cephalas, Antiphon, and others.

Propemptikon

A work wishing someone a good voyage. Examples by Sappho, Erinna, Callimachus, Theocritus, etc.

Prose

See under various categories (history, philosophy, oratory, etc.) and authors. For works on prose, Aristotle's *Rhetoric* is the best extant one; others were by Theophrastus, Ephorus, etc. See the long and excellent article and bibliography by Shewring in the OCD.

Prosuch, Nicephorus

Byzantine author, in the 12th century, of iambic poems, answers to riddles, hymns, and epigrams.

Protagoras

One of the first, and most successful of the Sophists. He professed to teach excellence *(arete)*, and was a much-respected man. His chief saying had to do with relativity: "Man is the measure of all things." The *Protagoras* of Plato is a dialogue in which the famous sophist gets the worst of an argument with Socrates.

"Protector," Menander

See Menander (6).

Protrepticus

An exhortation to philosophy. Aristotle wrote one, based partly on the sophistic *protrepticus* given by Plato in the Euthydemus. For other examples, see Iamblichus (2), Clement of Alexandria, Chamaeleon, Nicetas Stethatus.

Psalms of Solomon

A pseudepigraphic work patterned after the Biblical Psalms. Probably written in the first century B.C.

Psaon of Plataea

A Hellenistic historian (ca. 200 B.C.) who continued the work of Diyllus (q.v.).

Psappho

See Sappho.

Psellus, Michael (1018-78)
Byzantine polymath. Wrote on science, mathematics, music, astronomy, physics, metaphysics, ethics, alchemy, demonology, law, geography, medicine, topography; paraphrases of the *Iliad* and *Odyssey,* commentaries on Plato and Aristotle, an allegorical study of Homer, poems on Greek dialects, rhetoric, grammar, *Chronographia,* funeral orations, panegyrics, letters (ca. 500 survive), rhetorical essays and exercises, satirical and epigrammatic verse.

Pseudepigrapha
Non canonical, non-apocryphal works, including the *Book of Jubilees, Letter of Aristeas, Psalms of Solomon, Sibylline Books, Testaments of the Twelve Patriarchs,* etc.

Pseudepigraphic Literature
Works attributed to authors who did not write them. Sometimes accidental, owing to the general tendency to ascribe works to authors of a similar genre, as for example, other poems in the Epic Cycle have been ascribed to Homer; works by followers of a philosopher, which tended to be attributed to him; rhetorical exercises attributed to real people; and forgeries. Examples: Neopythagorean treatises, imitations of Demosthenes, the Sibylline oracles, various works in the Aristotelian corpus, Christian pseudepigrapha, etc.

Pseudo-Aristotle
De Mundo, Magna Moralia, Mechanica, De Coloribus, De Plantis, etc. See Aristotle, and the OCD.

Pseudo-Callisthenes
The "Alexander-Romance," a late work on the exploits of Alexander was attributed to Callisthenes.

Pseudo-Codinus
A work on the Officers of the Court in the 14th century was wrongly attributed to Codinus (q.v.).

Pseudo-Democritus

Physica & Mystica: four books on alchemy (gold, silver, stones).

Pseudo-Eupolemus

Fragments attributed to Eupolemus (q.v.) but not by him, as E. was a Jew, and this "Eupolemus" was a Samaritan.

Pseudo-Longinus

See "Longinus."

Pseudo-Phocylides

A didactic poem in 230 hexameters, probably by an unknown Alexandrian Jew (or Christian), ca. 100 A.D. Allegedly by Phocylides.

Pseudo-platonic works

See Plato.

Pseudo-Plutarch

See Aetius (1).

Pseudo-Polydeuces

See "polydeuces."

Psyche

The soul (or a butterfly). Different ideas held at different times. See article by Hanfmann in OCD; Rohde's *Psyche.* The story of Cupid and Psyche in Apuleius is a late telling of an old folk-tale.

Ptocholeon

Byzantine story, in vulgar Greek, of a wise old man. See Krumbacher.

Ptolemaeus (1) of Ascalon

Pupil of Aristarchus; wrote on metrics and orthography, and on Homer.

Ptolemaeus (2) Chennos, of Alexandria

Fl. ca. 100 A.D. Author of the *Sphinx,* rhapsodies, and other works.

Ptolemaeus (3) "Epithetes"

Grammarian, opponent of Aristarchus. Wrote on Homer, Bacchylides, etc.

Ptolemaeus, Claudius

See Ptolemy.

Ptolemaeus

(4) Wrote on the Egyptian kings.

(5) Rhetor, from Egypt.

(6) Wrote commentaries on Pindar and Homer. Also sophists, Gnostics, peripatetics, etc. See Schmid-Stählin.

Ptolemy (Claudius Ptolemaeus)

Astronomer and mathematician of the second century A.D. His great work was the *Megale Syntaxis;* in Arabic, Al-Majisti, whence Almagest. The definitive work on Greek astronomy. Other works include: *Geography, Optics, Planispherium, Analemna, On Scales, On Mechanics,* etc. His geography was the most authoritative and the most accurate of the ancient works on the subject, and was standard until modern times, despite its faults. (See Heath in OCD)

Ptolemy I Soter

Founder of the dynasty which bears his name. Wrote a history of Alexander the Great.

Pulologos

Byzantine work (in vulgar Greek) on Birds. Like the Children's Animal stories. In 650 political verses. King Eagle, the Stork and Swan, Gull and Goose, Sandpiper and Pheasant, etc. appear.

Pygmalion

(1) King of Tyre, brother of Dido.

(2) Creator of the famous statue which was brought to life by Aphrodite. No ancient author gives a name to this statue.

Pylades

Companion of Orestes (q.v.). Appears in the Choephori, where he bolsters up Orestes' failing resolve, and elsewhere.

Pyrrha

Wife of Deucalion (q.v.).

Pyrrho (360-270 B.C.)

Founder of the Sceptic school. He wrote nothing.

Pythagoras

Fl. ca. 530 B.C. Mathematician and philosopher. In addition to the well-known Theorem which bears his name, he applied mathematics to acoustics, music, and the theory of weights and measures. He believed in the transmigration of souls. He founded a religious society in Croton. His followers devoted themselves to arithmetic, which tended to take on a mystical interpretation of Number (Heaven, the First unit), and to explain everything in the universe by Number.

Pytheas

Greek navigator, ca. 300 B.C. Circumnavigated Britain, reported an island Thule (Iceland?), noted the influence of the moon on tides; wrote *Ocean*.

Pythermus

(1) Lyric poet, wrote drinking songs.
(2) Author of a *Hellenistic History* in 8 books.

Pythian Baths

Poem by Paulus Silentarius (q.v.).

Pythian Odes

See Pindar.

Pythius of Priene (4th cent. B.C.)
Architect who described the Mausoleum of Halicarnassus and wrote on other temples, etc.

Python
Author of a satyric play called *Agen* (324 B.C.).

Q

Quadratus (1)

Wrote a chronicle of Roman history from the beginnings to Severus.

Quadratus (2)

Christian apologist of the second century. Mentioned by Eusebius. Nothing survives.

Quintus Smyrnaeus

4th cent. A.D. author of an epic poem: *Posthomerica,* which continued the story of the Iliad, including such episodes as the deaths of Penthesilea, Memnon, Achilles and Ajax, the Wooden Horse, the sack of Troy, etc. It is not without merit, although it naturally falls far short of Homer.

Quirinus (1) of Nicomedia

Second century sophist.

Quirinus (2) Fourth century sophist.

R

Rape of Helen

See Colluthus.

"Rape of the Lock"

See Berenice.

Religion

See gods, mythology, Mysteries, Orphism, Theology, Apologists, etc.

Religious Poetry, Byzantine

See Romanus, *Acathistus,* John of Damascus, Andreas (Andrew) of Crete, *Canones,* Cosmas, Theodore Metochites, Mauropus, *Christus Patiens.* In general, it may be said that the religious poetry of the Byzantine Empire was greater and had more feeling than the secular poetry.

Republic

Plato's greatest work, and one of the great books, not only of Greek civilization, but of all literature, owing to the perfect wedding of style (see article on Plato) and content. Socrates is the chief speaker, and after a brief verbal tussle with the sophist Thrasymachus on the nature of Justice, he says that before it can be found in the individual, it should be sought in the State (note the close connection between ethics and politics, a typical feature of Greek thought). There begins the creation of the State, beginning with two or three occupations (the doctrine of specialization is swiftly introduced), and gradually taking shape as a full-blown society. In the process, Plato deals with economics, education (music and gymnastics; mathematics, harmonics, dialectics, etc., literature to be censored for moral purposes), ethics, psychology (anticipating Freud in some ways), literary criticism, political science, metaphysics and epistemology, esthetics and semantics. There is scarcely a single area of life that is not touched upon, and yet the transitions are smooth and effortless. The doctrine of the three classes (workers, soldiers, and philosopher-kings, who will have neither property nor families); the equality of women; and others are also introduced, together with a classification of governments. Democracy is at the very bottom nearly, with only tyranny represented as being worse. The central portion of the *Republic* deals with the Theory of Ideas, which is explained in several ways, by the analogy of the opposites, the Divided Line, and the famous Allegory of the Cave, picturing humanity imprisoned by their senses, until they can be released by the study of mathematics and philosophy to the perception of the realm of Ideas, and the beatific vision of the Idea of the Good. The work ends with a majestic myth, the Vision of Er, who returns from the funeral pyre to tell of the after-life, the judgment of the dead, the choice of future lives, and the transmigration of souls. During the course of the discussion, Socrates returns to the idea of Justice, with which the work began, and concludes that it is the harmonious functioning of the various classes of society, each doing its proper job; and from this he turns to Justice in the individual, which means that each part of the soul (the rational, irrational and spirited elements) does *its* job properly. The work is full of charming metaphors (e.g. the Guardians as watchdogs; the search for Justice as if one were hunting an elusive animal; the Cave, etc.) and the basic seriousness is lightened by fine moments of humor. In the end, the doctrine of Thrasymachus that the tyrant is happy, and that Justice is the advantage of the stronger party, is thoroughly refuted.

***Republic* (2)**
Title of a lost work by Zeno of Citium.

Respiratione, de
See Aristotle.

Returns, the
See Epic Cycle.

Revelations
See Apocalypse, Apocalyptic Literature.

Rhadamanthus
Son of Zeus and Europa, brother of King Minos, one of the Judges of the Dead.

Rhapsodes
Reciters (literally, "stitchers") of epic poetry, either their own or others'. Later the class of rhapsodes became a distinct one from the poets themselves.

Rhapsodic Theogony
See Orphic Literature.

Rhea
Ancient goddess of the earth, daughter of Uranus and Ge, wife of Kronos, mother of Zeus, Poseidon, Hades, Hera, Demeter, and Hestia. Identified with the Great Mother or Magna Mater (Cybele, Dindymene), whose priests were called Corybantes.

Rhesus
A play in the Euripidean corpus. Its authenticity is much doubted. Some have thought it to be a consciously archaizing play from a much later period; others assign it to an unknown playwright of the fourth century; still others to Euripides himself. For discussions, see Rose, Hadas, OCD, and Schmid-Stählin. Hadas calls the work a "cento of faults with no apparent explanation, no redeeming excel-

lence of story, characterization, or dramatic idea . . ." The play is a dramatization of *Iliad,* Book X. Dolon is spying on the Greeks, while Odysseus and Siomedes are spying on the camp of Rhesus, a Trojan ally. They kill Rhesus (after getting the password from Dolon), and he is promised a sort of immortality by his mother, a goddess. According to one tradition, if his horses had tasted Trojan grass and drunk the water of the Scamander, Troy could never be taken.

Rhetoric

See Orators (Demosthenes, Isocrates, etc.); Aristotle's work on *Rhetoric* has come down to us; it deals with style, arrangement, arguments, etc. In the Aristotelian corpus there is another work called *Rhetorica ad Alexandrum* (now usually attributed to Anaximenes of Lampsacus), which is a handbook of rhetorical tricks. Books on rhetoric (*techne* is the word for such a book) were written by many of the later authors (e.g. Aristides, Menander, Theon, etc.). See also Hermogenes, Hermagoras, Gorgias, Sophists, and in general, for discussion and bibliography, see article by J. W. H. Atkins in OCD.

Rhetorica ad Alexandrum

See Anaximenes (2).

Rhianus

Lyric poet, Born in 276 B.C. Wrote epic poetry *(Heracleias, Thessalica, Achaeica, Messeniaca, Eliaca),* epigrams with a pederastic element; also edited the *Iliad* and *Odyssey.*

Rhinthon of Tarentum

Wrote phlyax-plays in the third century B.C. Nine titles are known to us, out of 38 works attributed to him. Nearly all of them are burlesques of Euripides. Only meager fragments have come down to us.

Rhizotomikon

See Amerias, Crateuas, Cassius Dionysius.

Rhodanes and Sinonis

See Iamblichus (1).

Rhodian Love-Songs

A fourteenth or fifteenth-century MS containing some rather artificial erotic poetry, although some of the poems have charm and spontaneity.

Rhyme

A feature of Byzantine poetry, religious and secular. Both internal and end-rhymes were frequent.

Rhythm

See Meter.

Riddles

Early examples in Hesiod. Oracles were generally expressed in enigmatic form. The riddle of the Sphinx is well-known. Collections were made by Cleobulus and his daughter Cleobuline, by Clearchus, and by Athenaeus. Examples: The Riddle of the Sphinx: "What creature walks on four legs, then two, then three." Answer: Man. Another example: "A man and not a man, with a stone and not a stone, hit a bird and not a bird, sitting on a tree and not a tree." Answer: Eunuch, pumice-stone, bat, fennel-stalk. Other examples: "What is the strongest thing in the world?" Answer: Love: Iron is strong, the blacksmith bends iron, but love conquers the blacksmith. "A man went fishing. What he caught he threw away, what he did not catch, he took home with him. What was he fishing for?" Answer: Fleas.

Rodanthe and Dosicles

Verse novel by Prodromus (12th century). It is a romantic love-story, with kidnappings, meetings and partings, escapes, and the inevitable "lived happily ever after" ending.

Romaic

The Greek vernacular: The language of (New) Rome.

Romaica

See Appian.

Roman Antiquities

Historical work by Dionysius (q.v. 5) of Halicarnassus, in 20 books.

Roman History

See Dio Cassius.

Romance

From the *Odyssey* onwards, this has been a favorite form of Greek literature, even when it went under the heading of history (as in Herodotus) or biography (e.g. Xenophon's *Cyropaedia*). Examples: Milesan Tales of Aristides (q.v. 1), Euhemerus *(Hiera Anagraphe), Daphnis and Chloe,* and the novels of Chariton, Achilles Tatius, Heliodorus, and Xenophon of Ephesus. Romance is also a feature of the plays of New Comedy. In Byzantine times, the romance was also popular. See *Callimachus and Chrysorrhoë, Belthandrus and Chrysantza, Phlorius and Platziaphlora,* etc.

Romance, Alexander

See Alexander Romance.

Romanus

Great Byzantine hymnographer. Fl. ca. 500 A.D. He wrote about 1000 hymns, in varying rhythms, based on stress, often with acrostics, and frequently using a sort of antiphonal dialogue, Romanus "achieves a combination of simplicity of language and magnificence of imagination unequalled in religious poetry." (Runciman)

Rufinus (2nd cent. A.D.)

Author of some 40 poems in the Anthology varying from the obscene to the charming.

Others of the name include a Peripatetic and a Sophist.

Rufus of Ephesus

Physician, ca. 100 A.D., who wrote works on dietetics

and pathology. He was opposed to general theory, and believed in studying single diseases.

Rufus

Others of this name include: a writer on music, a sophist, a historian, a rhetor and author of a *techne*.

Rustic Epigrams

Epistolai Agroikikai. See Aelian (1).

S

Sabinus

(1) Author of a commentary on Thucydides.

(2) S. of Heraclea, author of a collection *(Synagoge ton Synodikon).*

(3) A sophist.

Sacadas

Poet and musician of Argos. Composed tunes and elegiac poems in the 7th century B.C. Nothing at all survives.

Saccas, Ammonius

See Ammonius Saccas.

Sachlikis, Stephanus of Crete

Poet of the second half of the 15th century. Wrote on morals, and an autobiographical poem, in the vernacular Greek.

Sacred Literature

See Bible, Septuagint, Gospels, Patristic writers, Apocrypha, theology, etc.

Sallustius

(1) Grammarian, wrote commentaries on comedy, Herodotus, etc.

(2) Cynic of the 5th-6th cent.

(3) Friend of the Emperor Julian. Wrote on gods and the universe.

Samian Girl, the

Play of Menander. Enough survives to give an idea of the plot, which deals with the consequences of a lovers' intrigue. Chrysis, a freeborn Samian woman, is the concubine of an Athenian Demeas, whose son Moschion is in love with the girl next door. The latter has a child, which Chrysis agrees to adopt. Demeas discovers that his son is the child's father and thinks Chrysis is the mother, etc. The play ends with the lovers reconciled and married. (Much of this is conjectural)

Sanchuniathon

See Philon (4).

Sannyrion

Athenian comic poet, ca. 400 B.C. Fragments survive from three mythological burlesques: *Io, Danae,* and *Gelos.*

Santa Sophia

See Paulus (1) Silentarius, Hagia Sophia.

Sappho (born ca. 612 B.C.) of Lesbos

(Psappho, in her own dialect) Greatest of Greek poetesses, and one of the great lyric poets of all time. Only fragments remain of her work, which was collected in seven books. Included in the fragments are: an address to Aphrodite, a poem to another girl, a *propemptikon* to her brother, and other poems of great beauty, directness, power of imagery, and personal feeling. Most of her poetry is highly personal, for herself and her friends. She wrote in the Lesbian (Aeolic) dialect, and invented the Sapphic stanza, three long lines and one short one, imitated by Catullus (Ille mi par esse deo videtur) and Horace (Integer vitae, scelerisque purus).

Sarpedon

In the *Iliad,* an ally of the Trojans, who takes an important part in the fighting until he is killed by Patroclus.

Satire

Probably began with old comedy and the iambic lampoons of Archilochus and Hipponax. Plato, in his dialogues, is often satirical, as were the Cynics, Phoenix of Colophon, Menippus, and especially Lucian. In the Byzantine period, examples are: Prodromus, various animal-stories (*Physiologus, Pulologus,* etc.) Satire as a separate form, however, was invented and developed by the Romans.

Satyr-play

The fourth play in a tragic tetralogy was often a satyr-play, a light treatment of a tragic or semi-tragic theme, with satyrs, wine, Sileni, etc. The *Cyclops* of Euripides and the *Ichneutae* of Sophocles are examples. The *Alcestis* also seems to have satyric elements, e.g. the drunken Heracles and the almost-comic ending.

Satyrs

Wild spirits of the woods, with either horse's tails or goats' legs. Appear in the satyr-plays (e.g *Cyclops*), and in art. They are associated with Dionysus. See article by Hanfmann in OCD, and Rose, *Handbook.*

Satyrus (1)

Peripatetic biographer. Wrote *Lives* of Sophocles, Demosthenes, etc. *Characters,* etc. Fragments were found at Oxyrhynchus, and others appear in Athenaeus, and Diogenes Laertius. Satyrus delighted in anecdotes.

Satyrus

(2) "Zeta" Author of a collection of myths.
(3) Architect.
(4) Physician.
(5) Actor. For details see Schmid-Stählin.

Scazons

See *Choliambics.*

Sceptics (or Skeptics)

Philosophers who criticize but give no positive solutions. Examples: Pyrrhon, Timon, Arcesilaus, Philon of Larissa (the last two actually belonged to the Academy, but may be classified as Sceptics also).

Schedographia

A textbook on parsing forms. Popular in Byzantine times. Moschopulus wrote one, and others were anonymous. See Krumbacher.

Scheria

The island home of the Phaeacians in Homer's *Odyssey*. The first picture in literature of an ideal society, or Utopia. Attempts to identify it (e.g. Corfu) have not been entirely successful.

Scholarship (in Antiquity)

Aristotle may be said to have begun the tradition of literary history and scholarship with his *Didascaliae*. Later Peripatetics followed in his footsteps. Ptolemy Soter founded the Library at Alexandria, which was the chief center of scholarship and its real beginning. The chief librarians (e.g. Zenodotus, Aristophanes, etc.) were learned scholars, who adopted the practice of comparing manuscripts and tried to establish original texts, especially of Homer. Grammar, philology, lexicography, and metrics continued to be fruitful areas of research and scholarship. In the 4th and 5th centuries, manuscripts were copied on vellum, with marginal notes or *scholia*. After a period of "Dark Ages" there was a revival in scholarship, with such people as Photius and Arethas (qq.v.) and the lexicon of Suidas. Tzetzes and Eustathius (2) annotated Homer. Under the Paleologi many editions of classical authors were produced, as well as handbooks, lexica, and commentaries.

Scholarship, Classical, in modern times

Sandys made a division into four main periods: Italian,

French, English-Dutch, and German. In the Italian period, which may be said to extend from the death of Dante to the death of Leo X (1321-1521), Petrarch, Valla, Politian, and Ficino are outstanding examples of classical scholarship. During this period, Greek scholars began to appear in Italy, manuscripts were discovered, and texts began to be printed. In the French period, which begins in the 16th century, important names are: Budé, Scaliger, Casaubon, Lipsius, etc. In the 18th century in England, Bentley and Porson and others were pre-eminent in the field; and travel, archaeology, epigraphy and comparative linguistics became significant. German scholars in the 19th century include Lachmann, Dindorf, Hermann, Boekh, Müller, etc.; and more recently, Christ, Wilamowitz-Moellendorff, Schmid, Stählin. Pauly-Wissowa is the greatest monument of German scholarship. (See Duff in OCD, and Sandys, *Hist. of Class. Scholarship*)

Scholia

Marginal notes, including the *lemma* (a word or phrase together with a commentary) the *gloss* (an interpretation of the meaning of a separate word), and *commentary* (a more continuous explanation of a text).

Sciras

Third century B.C. author of phlyax plays. The *Meleager* contained a parody of Euripides' *Hippolytus.*

Scolia

Drinking-songs. Some are preserved by Athenaeus. The singer held a myrtle branch while he sang, and upon finishing, passed it to another, whose turn it then was to sing. Choral scolia also existed.

Scopelianus

Sophist of Smyrna in the 2nd cent. A.D. Wrote an epic entitled *Gigantia.*

Scylax

An explorer, quoted by Strabo, Aristotle, etc. There is an extant *Periplous* under his name, but that is a fourth-century compilation.

Scylitzes, John

Byzantine chronicler of the 11th century. His work covers the period from 811 to 1079, and was used by Cedrenus.

Scylla

(1) Daughter of king Nisus of Megara (q.v.).

(2) A sea-monster, living opposite Charybdis, in a cave. She had six heads, and when a ship passed, she would seize six men and eat them. Sometimes confused with (1).

Scymnus of Chios

Alleged author of a *Periegesis,* but probably not the author of the one attributed to him, i.e. an iambic summary of ancient geography.

Scythinus of Teos

Contemporary of Plato. Wrote Iambics on the doctrine of Heraclitus, a prose work on Nature, and a History dealing with the deeds of Heracles.

Secret History

See Procopius.

Seguerianus

See *Lexica Segueriana.*

Selene

Moon goddess, identified, among others, with Artemis.

Seleucus (1)

A supporter of Aristarchus' heliocentric theory. Wrote a work on Tides, ca. 150 B.C.

Seleucus (2) Homericus

Wrote commentaries on nearly all the Greek poets, as well as works on philosophy, biography, theology, etc.

Seleucus (3)

Poet and grammarian. Author of *Aspalieutica* (on fishing), *Parthica.*

Semele

In mythology, daughter of Cadmus of Thebes. Loved by Zeus, she insisted on seeing him in his full Olympian splendor (on the advice of the jealous Hera), and was consumed by lightning. Her unborn child was rescued by Zeus, who put the baby in his own thigh, whence he was born in due time as the god Dionysus.

Semonides of Amorgos

Iambic and elegiac poet of the 7th cent. B.C. The best-known fragment discusses ten types of women by comparing them to various unprepossessing animals (dog, pig, fox, etc.). Only the tenth type (the bee) is worth anything. He wrote in the Ionic dialect, with humor and satire.

Semos of Delos (ca. 200 B.C.)

Made various compilations: on geography, antiquities, on Delos, Paros, Pergamum, on Islands, Paeans, etc.

Separatists

Those who believe that the Homeric poems are the work of two or more authors. See Wolf, Homeric Question.

Septuagint

The Greek version of the Old Testament. According to the *Letter of Aristeas,* it was so called because 72 men (six from each of the twelve tribes) worked on it for 72 days. It consists mostly of translations from the Hebrew, but contains some books (e.g. *Maccabees, Wisdom of Solomon,* etc.)

which were not in the original. The Septuagint is not the only Greek translation of the Bible; see Hexapla.

Serapion (1) of Alexandria

Medical writer, ca. 200-150 B.C.

Serapion (2) Mathematician, geographer and author of an astrological work.

Serapion (3) Bishop of Antiochia in the 4th cent. friend of Athanasius.

Serapion (4) Bishop of Thmuis.

Serenus

Mathematician of the 4th century B.C. Wrote on conics and cylinders, and made a commentary on Apollonius of Perga.

Sergius

(1) Grammarian of Ephesus.

(2) Jurist, ca. 400 A.D.

(3) Byzantine hymnographer and patriarch, ca. 600 A.D.

(4) Iconoclast. See Krumbacher for others of this name.

Seth, Symeon

See *Stephanites and Ichnelates*

Seven Against Thebes

Play by Aeschylus (467 B.C.) The last play of a trilogy, the first two plays being the *Laius* and the *Oedipus.* It tells the story of the attack on Thebes by Polynices and his allies; and of the deaths of Eteocles and Polynices, the sons of Oedipus, at each other's hands. The play contains very little action.

Seven Sages

Thales, Solon, Chilon, Pittacus, Bias, Cleobulus, and Myson are the usual names (Periander and Anacharsis are sometimes included). To them were attributed many of the maxims and gnomes of popular Greek wisdom (e.g. Know thyself, Nothing in excess, etc.)

Severus

(1) of Antiochia. Theological writer.

(2) Sophist in Rome.

(3) Platonic philosopher.

(4) Writer on medicine.

Sextius Niger

Physician and writer on medicine, used by Pliny and Dioscurides. He may be identical with the Sextius Quintus who founded an eclectic school of philosophy.

Sextus (1)

Of Chaeronea, nephew of Plutarch, teacher of Marcus Aurelius.

Sextus (2)

S. Empiricus. Physician at Rome in the 2nd century A.D. As his epithet testifies, he belonged to the "empirical" school of medicine. Wrote on Pyrrhonism, Dogmatics, and Mathematics, as well as on medicine.

Sextus (3)

Made a collection of gnomes, probably in the 2nd cent. A.D. to which later Christian additions were made. The collection was used by Origen, and translated into Latin by Rufinus.

Shearing of Glycera

Perikeiromene, title of a fragmentary play of Menander, q.v.

Shepherd of Hermas

See Hermas.

Shield of Heracles (Aspis)

A surviving epic ballad, a description of the Shield of Heracles, in 480 lines, attributed to Hesiod (q.v.).

Sibylline Books

Collections of prophecies, of an ecstatic nature, usually,

in fourteen books—a patent Judaeo-Christian forgery, much used by later authors. The Sibyls had a respected place in Christian literature and art (cf. the Sistine Chapel ceiling by Michelangelo), almost like that of the O. T. prophets.

Sicelidas

See Asclepiades (2).

Sicily

Always an important colony; many writers (e.g. Pindar, Bacchylides, Simonides, Aeschylus, Plato) went there, at the invitation of Hieron and Dionysius.

Sileni

Wood-spirits, like the satyrs (q.v.). Appeared in satyr-plays (e.g. Euripides' *Cyclops*). Generally represented with horses' tails or some other bestial feature.

Silentarius, Paulus

See Paulus.

Silloi

Lampoons by Timon (q.v. 2).

Simmias (or Simias) of Rhodes

Alexandrian grammarian and poet, inventor of shape or figure-poems, called *Technopaegnia* (poems in the shape of an ax, egg, wings, etc.), also epigrams, glosses, lyric poems, etc.

Simmias

A friend of Socrates, one of those who were with him on the day of his death. Diogenes Laertius ascribed 23 dialogues to him.

Simocattes

See Theophylactus (2).

Simon of Athens

A shoemaker and friend of Socrates. Diogenes Laertius

says he was the first to write Socratic dialogues, but there is no other evidence of this, and Plato and Xenophon never so much as mention him.

Simodia

A type of mime, by Simos. See Magodia, mime, *Alexandrian Erotic Fragment.*

Simon Magus

Magician who offered money to the Apostles for the gift of the Holy Spirit (whence the word *simony*). Supposed to have been the founder of Gnosticism.

Simonides (ca. 556-468 B.C.)

Lyric and elegiac poet. Among the fragments are: the famous lines on Danae, dirges, hymns, elegies, inscriptional epigrams, such as the famous one to the dead at Thermopylae (which may not be genuine), Scolia, encomia, etc.

Simplicius

(1) Poet of the 5th cent. A.D.

(2) S. of Emona, a grammarian.

(3) A Neoplatonist who wrote commentaries on Aristotle, Epictetus and Euclid.

Simylus

(1) Greek iambographer of unknown date.

(2) A comic poet, who may or may not be identical with the above.

(3) Author of an epigram on Tarpeia. Augustan Age or earlier.

Sirens

Fabulous creatures, half birds, half women, whose song lured sailors to their destruction. Odysseus, on the advice of Circe, stops his sailors' ears with wax, and has himself tied to the mast. Thus he hears the song and avoids shipwreck.

Sisyphus

In mythology, the son of Aeolus. He is punished (Homer does not say why; others give a reason associated with an offense against Zeus) by eternally rolling a rock uphill in Hades; the rock always rolls down again. Poet-Homeric accounts make him the father of Odysseus, and his name becomes a nickname for clever people. The *Sisyphus* is a pseudo-Platonic work.

Skeptics

See Sceptics.

Smyrnaeus, Quintus

See Quintus Smyrnaeus.

Socrates (1)

The problem of the historical Socrates is a difficult one, as he wrote nothing himself (except some poetry, in prison), so that we have to rely on the accounts of him in Plato and Xenophon (qq.v.). He figures as the chief character in all the Platonic dialogues except the *Laws*. The question, then, is: how much of what Socrates says in these dialogues may be taken to be the philosophy and ideas of Plato, and how much comes from the historical Socrates himself? Burnet and Taylor maintain that the contents of the Crito, Phaedo, and Apology may be fairly assigned to the historical Socrates, which would give him a far larger place in the history of philosophy than is accorded him by most others. This much at least seems certain: that Socrates was the first to insist on systematic definitions; that he was the first, or one of the first, to apply critical thought to the examination of ethical problems; and that he was one of the great teachers (with characteristic irony, Socrates claimed to be not a teacher, but a midwife). The story about the Delphic oracle, which told Chaerephon that Socrates was the wisest of men (or rather, that there was no one wiser); the little voice or "daimonion" which warned him against doing anything he ought not to do; the trial for atheism and corrupting the youth, his speech (see *Apology*), his refusal to escape, and his death—these are well-known, as is Socrates' physical appearance, his genial personality, his power of endurance, his keen sense of humor, his great sense of duty, his love of the truth, and the devotion of the circle of his friends. His religious views are less clear. He was known for his irony and his use of the dialectical method. He may be said to be the inspiration, if not the actual founder, of moral philosophy and logic.

Socrates (2) of Argos, a historian

(3) of Constantinople, wrote a church history (345-439) continuing that of Eusebius.

(4) of Rhodes, a historian.

Solomon, Odes of

A pseudonymous collection of 42 hymns, attributed to Solomon but probably written 75-150 A.D. Christian, but containing Jewish, Oriental and Gnostic elements.

Solomon, Psalms of

See *Psalms of Solomon*.

Solon (ca. 640-560 B.C.)

Athenian lawgiver, poet, and statesman. Reformed the constitution and put an end to serfdom, encouraged industry, stabilized the coinage and system of weights and measures. His poems were on the following subjects: the capture of Salamis, the dangers of *hybris,* the ages of man, the Muses, tyranny, etc. See article by Bowra in OCD. His meeting wih Croesus, described by Herodotus, with the famous saying: "Call no man happy while he lives." is most unlikely.

Sopater

Greek writer of parodies and *phlyakes* Fl. ca. 300 B.C. Fourteen titles: *Bacchis, Hippolytus, Nekuia, Orestes,*

Galatai, etc. Some of the fragments have the flavor of Attic Comedy.

Sophaenetus of Stymphalus (fl. ca. 400 B.C.)
Wrote an *Anabasis* of Cyrus. Probably a source for Ephorus and Diodorus, where their accounts differed from Xenophon's.

Sophilus
Middle Comedy author. Titles: *Androcles, Tyndareos* or *Leda.*

Sophist
A dialogue by Plato (q.v.), dealing with metaphysics, truth and falsehood, being and not-being.

Sophistic, Second
See New Sophistic.

Sophistici Elenchi
See Aristotle.

Sophists
Originally the term meant a wise man, but it acquired a pejorative connotation (cf. "wise guy"). The sophists were itinerant teachers, who professed to teach *arete* (excellence, or virtue), rhetoric, successful living, memory-training, etc. They were, on the whole, successful and some became quite wealthy. They did not have any one set of philosophical beliefs (the word is for a profession, not a school). Some, like Protagoras, had definite philosophical teachings, others, like Thrasymachus, encouraged a cynical disbelief in everything and a life based on the selfish pursuit of personal ambitions. Later the term came to have a more specialized meaning (i.e. rhetorician, as in the Second Sophistic). See Protagoras, Hippias, Gorgias, Prodicus, Thrasymachus, etc. Also *New Sophistic.*

Sophocles (1) of Athens (496-406 B.C.)

Sophocles' life completely spanned the Fifth Century, of which he is perhaps the best representative. He had a long, happy, prosperous and extremely productive life, producing plays right up to his death (the *Oedipus at Colonus* was written in his ninetieth year; he thus ranks with Verdi, Titian, Goethe, etc. as one of the best examples of a productive longevity). He composed 123 plays, and won 24 victories. His plays never were ranked third in the dramatic contest. He discontinued the practice of composing trilogies, added the third actor, enlarged the chorus from 12 to 15, and introduced scene-painting. He was supreme in the fields of character-delineation and especially plot-construction. His use of dramatic irony, of secondary characters as foils for the main ones (cf. Ismene and Chrysothemis), his skill in creating suspense, his mastery of dialogue, his beautiful choral lyrics, the balance he always managed to achieve between the religious emphasis of Aeschylus and the psychological probing of Euripides (although his latest plays seem to show some influence of the younger playwright), and the dignity and stature of his characters—these are some of the reasons for the pre-eminence of Sophocles among Greek (and therefore all) dramatists. He has been held to be Shakespeare's equal in character and language, and his superior in the construction of plots. Although his works indicate a certain sadness that man, for all his goodness and intelligence, falls so short of really achieving perfection, Sophocles was not a pessimist. Suffering is not in vain. Even if his characters are sometimes in the grip of powers beyond their control or even comprehension, Sophocles believed in man's free-will and ultimate responsibility for his actions. To Aristotle, and to many others, he was the supreme playwright. Perhaps this is why Aristophanes did not choose to parody him in the *Frogs*.

The extant plays are: *Ajax, Antigone, Oedipus Tyrannus,*

Electra, Trachiniae, Philoctetes, Oedipus at Colonus. Large fragments survive of his satyr-play the *Ichneutae* (Trackers). Other plays include: *Aegeus, Aegisthus, Aleadae, Alcmeon, Amphiareos, Andromeda, Antenoridae, Daedalus, Dolopes, Epigonoi, Eris, Hermione, Eumelus, Euryalus, Heracles, Iberians, Inachus, Ixion, Iobates, Hipponus, Iphigenia, Camicoi, Colchides, Crisis, Laocoön, Meleager,* and others. See Rose, *Handbook of Greek Literature,* for list and discussion of lost plays. See also OCD article by Pickard-Cambridge for further discussion and bibliography.

Sophocles (2) "the Younger"

Grandson of Sophocles (1). Wrote plays of his own.

Sophocles (3) Hellenistic tragedian.

Sophocles (4) son of (3), ca. 100 B.C. Wrote tragedies and satyr-plays.

Sophocles (5) Commentator on Apollonius.

Sophron (Ca. 470-400 B.C.)

Writer of mimes. From Syracuse. Titles include: *Thynotheras* (the Tunny-Fisher), *Holieus, Akestriai, Synaristosai* (Ladies at Breakfast), and others. The subjects were mostly drawn from every-day life, and the mimes were written in rhythmical prose. Sophron was greatly admired by Plato. He was the first literary mime-writer.

Sophronius

Seventh-century patriarch of Jerusalem, born in Damascus. Distinguished as a writer of poetry, homiletics, and hagiography.

Sophrosyne

The most important of all Greek virtues: right-mindedness, moderation and sanity—The antidote to *hybris* (overweening pride).

Soranus of Ephesus

One of the great physicians of antiquity. Flourished

under Trajan and Hadrian. Works on gynecology, midwife, conception, child-care, pathology, etc. are preserved.

Sosibius of Lacedaemon

Grammarian, who wrote a history of Sparta.

Sosicrates (1)

Rhodian biographer, of unknown date. Wrote lives of philosophers. May be identical with the Sosicrates mentioned in Timachidas; if so, his floruit is ca. 150 B.C.

Sosicrates

(2) Comic playwright.

(3) Author of a *Catalogue of Women.*

Sosipater

Comic poet; one of the earliest of the New Comedy authors.

Sosiphanes of Syracuse

Flourished about the last third of the 4th century B.C. Supposed to have written 73 tragedies and won 7 victories. Sometimes included in the Pleiad (q.v.). There may have been two poets of the name.

Sositheus

Alexandrian poet of the 3rd century B.C. A member of the Tragic "Pleiad" (q.v.). Wrote tragedies and satyr-plays.

Sostratus

Zoologist and physician. Second only to Aristotle among the writers on zoology. Works: *Peri Zoon* (or *peri Physeos Zoon*), *peri Bleton kai Daketon;* works on gynecology, etc.

Sosylus of Lacedaemon

Freedman of Hannibal, whose history he wrote. An important source for Polybius.

Sotades (1)

Middle Comedy poet of the 4th cent. B.C.

Sotades (2) Iambic poet, of Maronea, inventor of the *Versus Sotadeus,* into which he transcribed the *Iliad.*

Soterichus

Epic poet (ca. 300 A.D.) who wrote on Dionysus, Alexander, etc.

Sotion (1)

Alexandrian Peripatetic, ca. 200 B.C. Wrote a *Diadoche ton Philosophon* in 13 books, and a book on the *Silloi* of Timon. A source for Diogenes Laertius.

Sotion (2)

Peripatetic philosopher of the first cent. A.D. Wrote *Strange Stories,* on rivers, springs, and pools, Dioclean Disputations, and a commentary on Aristotle's *Topics.*

Sozomenus of Gaza (fl. 450 A.D.)

Author of a Church History continuing that of Eusebius, something like the history of Socrates (q.v. 2) but better. It covered the period 324-439 in nine books.

Spaneas

Title of a didactic poem in Vulgar Greek, which exists in several versions. Written for the nephew of Alexius (d. 1142).

Spendon

Early Spartan poet. Not even a single line survives.

Speusippus

Nephew of Plato, whom he succeeded as head of the Academy. Wrote on biology, ethics and mathematics. A prolific writer, but hardly anything survives.

Sphaerus of Borysthenes

Pupil of Zeno and Cleanthes, fl. 240 B.C. Wrote on various philosophical subjects, chiefly ethics and politics.

Sphekes

See *Wasps* (Aristophanes).

Sphinx

A mythological monster which originated in Egypt. Asked the Thebans the famous riddle (see Riddles) which Oedipus answered. See article by Hanfmann in OCD.

Spoudogeloion

A type of satirical writing (e.g. Menippus'), combining jest with a moral or point. See Blaesus.

Staphylus (1)

Personification of the grape-cluster; attached to Dionysus.

Staphylus (2) An Alexandrian who wrote histories of Athens and Thessaly.

Stasimon

The choral ode which comes between the episodes of a tragedy.

Stasinus of Cyprus (8th cent. B.C.?)

Epic poet, perhaps the author of the *Cypria* (See Epic Cycle).

Statesman

Title of a dialogue by Plato (q.v.).

Stentor

In the *Iliad,* a man with a very powerful voice (as loud as the voices of 50 other people).

Stephanites and Ichnelates

A Byzantine story, also called *Mirror of Princes,* in which animals talk and act like people. Original was a Sanskrit work by Buddhists; translated into Persian, Arabic, Hebrew, Latin, and Greek (11th century), and thence into other European languages. Originally called *Kalilah and Dimnah.* The Greek translation was by Symeon Seth.

Stephanus (1) of Alexandria

A Neoplatonic writer of a commentary on Aristotle, and supposedly of a book on alchemy.

(2) Sophist of Antiochia.

(3) S. of Byzantium. Lexicographer. Wrote a work called *Ethnica.*

(4) a comic poet.

Krumbacher lists over 20 authors of this name, including mathematical, grammatical, hagiographical, polemical, writers, bishops, martyrs, iconoclasts, church poets, etc.

Stesichorus (ca. 630-555 B.C.)

Lyric poet. His works were collected in 26 books. Only meager fragments remain. They deal with the Argonauts, the Calydonian boar-hunt, the Wooden Horse, and Helen of Troy. The legend is that after a poem telling the usual story of Helen, he was stricken blind, and did not recover until he wrote the famous *Palinode,* recanting and saying that Helen never went to Troy at all.

Stesimbrotus

Biographer of the 5th cent. B.C. Wrote on Homer, Themistocles, Pericles, Thucydides.

Stethatus, Nicetas

See Nicetas Stethatus.

Sthenelus

Tragic poet of the 5th cent. Mentioned for his insipidity by Aristotle, and ridiculed by Aristophanes. Plato accused him of plagiarism.

Stibles, Constantine

Wrote a poem on the fire of Constantinople (1198) and other poems.

Stichometry

The measuring of texts by the number of lines. The equivalent of a line of hexameter was taken as a unit for measuring prose works (i.e. approximately 16 syllables or 36 letters).

Stichomythia

Rapid dialogue in the plays in which each character speaks a line at a time.

Stilpon (ca. 380-300 B.C.)

Philosopher, head of the Megarian school, which reached its greatest popularity under him. He wrote dialogues, but nothing is preserved.

Stoa

The school founded by Zeno. The Early Stoa is represented by Zeno, Cleanthes, Chrysippus; the Middle Stoa, by Panaetius and Posidonius, and Hecaton. The Stoics taught that Virtue is Knowledge, that a man should live at harmony with nature, not seeking things that are beyond his power. To be virtuous is the only good; evil does not exist unless we think so. The ideal of the Stoics was a complete self-sufficiency for the individual, who would not be moved either by fear of pain and death (which are not evil) or by pleasure (which is not good). See *Enchiridion,* Epictetus.

Stobaeus, Joannes

Compiled an anthology of excerpts, probably in the 5th century A.D. The range of subject-matter is wide (metaphysics, ethics, household economy, etc.). It is useful for the many quotations from earlier literature.

Stoicism

See Stoa, *Enchiridion,* Epictetus.

Strabo (64/63 B.C.-21? A.D.)

Geographer and historian. His *Historical Sketches* in 47 books are lost; his *Geography* in 17 books is extant. Although his knowledge of mathematics and astronomy were not up-to-date, his work is useful and readable. He includes mythological and historical data and comments on earlier authors. He deals with the whole known world: the Mediterranean, Spain, Gaul, Britain, Italy, the Roman Empire, Greece, the Euxine, Caspian, Asia Minor, India, Persia, Mesopotamia, etc.

Stratagemata

A military work, largely a collection of tricks and ruses, by Polyaenus (2). For other works on stratagems and tactics, see Aelian (2), Asclepiodotus, Aeneas Tacticus, Onasander, Arrian.

Straton

(1) Peripatetic philosopher and physicist. D. ca. 270 B.C.

(2) New Comedy Poet, ca. 300 B.C.

(3) Epigrammatist, author of ca. 100 poems (mostly erotic) in the Anthology.

Stratonicus (fl. ca. 410-360 B.C.)

Famous wit, whose bons mots were collected and excerpted. He was also known as a musician.

Strattis

Comic playwright, ca. 400 B.C. His plays included mythological burlesques *(Atalanta),* parodies *(Medea, Philostetes)* and personal satires *(Cinesias).*

Stromateis

See Clement of Alexandria.

Studites, Theodore

See Theodore Studites.

Style, on

Work by Demetrius of Tarsus, based on Aristotle's *Rhetoric.*

Styx

A river of Arcadia, thought to be one of the rivers of the underworld. Oaths sworn by the Styx were especially sacred.

Sublime, On the

See "Longinus."

Suidas

Under this name, we possess a great lexicon, very useful for grammatical, lexical, historical and literary information, which was compiled in the 10th century A.D. Texts and scholia were consulted in some cases, in other cases, the work is based on later abridgements and excerpts. In spite of the errors, inconsistencies, and interpolations, it is extremely valuable for the early learning and scholarship that it preserves.

Suppliants (Aeschylus)

The first extant European play. Largely a lyrical drama, it contains very little action. The chorus (the daughters of Danaus, fleeing from Egypt) are the Suppliants, and the chief characters in the play.

Suppliants (Euripides)

A play from the Theban saga, whose action takes place after the people of the city have repulsed the Seven Against Thebes; the play deals with the burial of the dead, which is finally allowed to take place, after the intercession of Theseus. The Suppliants of the title are the mothers of the slain champions.

Symeon (1)

Archbishop of Thessalonica 1410-25. His chief work was a statement of church dogma in the form of a dialogue on the mystic and liturgical rites of the Church.

Symeon (2) Metaphrastes

The greatest of the Byzantine hagiographers. For others of this name, including a church poet, an ascetic, a grammarian, a writer of speeches and hymns, and several others, see Krumbacher.

Symmachus

Symeon (3) Seth

See *Stephanites and Ichnelates.*

(1) Fl. ca. 100 A.D. Author of a commentary on Aristophanes.

(2) Translated the Bible into Greek. His translation is included in the *Hexapla* of Origen.

Symposium

Plato's great dialogue on the subject of Eros, or Love. In this the Platonic doctrine of love is elaborated (not what is meant today by this term). It is a passion at first aroused by a beautiful body, which rises until it becomes a passion for Beauty itself, i.e. the Idea of beauty, perceptible only to the intellect. The scene is a banquet or drinking party.

Symposium Literature

Other examples of the type to be found in the works of Xenophon, the *Deipnosophistai* of Athenaeus, Plutarch; lost works by Aristotle and Epicurus. Lucian's *Symposium* is satirical.

Syncellus, George

See George Syncellus.

Syncretism

The process by which different gods, from different cultures, become identified (e.g. Osiris with Asclepius, or Zeus or Pluto). See Rose in the OCD.

Synesius of Cyrene (370-ca. 412 A.D.)

A prolific and versatile author. Most important are his 156 Letters. Other works: *On Monarchy, Egyptian Tales, Praise of Baldness, Dion, On Providence, Hymns,* etc. He blends the Greek and the Christian tradition in his works.

Synopsis Sathas

Chronicle, by an unknown author, from the Creation to the recovery of Constantinople in 1261.

Synoptic Gospels

This name is usually given to the Gospels according to Matthew, Mark, and Luke.

Syntipas the Philosopher

A Byzantine version of an Oriental tale of Sinbad (also known as the *Seven Wise Masters, Dolopathos,* and *Erasto).* The story is about a king and his son, and a stepmother who falsely accuses the latter (cf. Hippolytus, Bellerophon, etc.). The son is condemned to death, and the seven (or ten, or forty) Wise Men each tell stories about the deceitfulness of women. The book is thus a framework (like the *Decameron* or the *Arabian Nights)* for a whole series of tales. Translated from the Syrian by Michael Andreopulus.

T

Tachygraphy

Xenophon was the first to use any kind of shorthand. Specimens from a later period can be seen on papyri found in Egypt.

Tactics

See Aeneas Tacticus, Asclepiodotus, Aelian, Onasander, Polyaenus, Arrian.

Talthybius

A herald in Homer's *Iliad,* who also appears in later works (e.g. Euripides, *Troades*).

Tantalus

For a crime variously explained (most common: that he stole food from the gods) he is punished in Hades with eternal hunger and thirst; he stands in water which recedes when he tries to drink, and the fruit above his head is blown away by the wind when he reaches for it. Hence the word "tantalize."

Tartarus

The place in Hades where Tantalus, Sisyphus, et al. are punished.

Tatian

Christian author in the middle of the 2nd century. Became a follower of Justin Martyr (q.v.), and wrote an apologetic work: *Address to the Greeks.* Became a heretic towards the end of his life. His most famous work is the *Diatessaron* or *Harmony of the Gospels,* which for a time displaced the Gospels themselves.

Tatius, Achilles

See Achilles Tatius.

Tauriscus

A grammarian and anomalist, pupil of Crates of Mallos (q.v.).

Technopaegnia

Poems in various shapes, e.g. Simmias' *Ax, Wings, Egg;* Theocritus' *Pipe,* and Dosiadas' *Altar.* Cf. the Mouse's Tale in *Alice in Wonderland.* Popular in Latin, as well, with Ausonius and others writing them.

Teiresias

See Tiresias.

Telamon

In mythology, the brother of Peleus, father of Ajax and Teucer.

Teleclides (fl. 450-420 B.C.)

Comic writer who won eight victories. Depicted a Golden Age in his *Amphictyones* and *Prytanes;* and attacked Pericles.

Telegonia

Poem in the Epic Cycle (q.v.) which told of the death of Odysseus by the hand of his son Telegonus (whose mother was Circe).

Telemachus

The young son of Odysseus who sets out to look for his father in the beginning of the *Odyssey.* He grows up during the course of the events in the poem, showing a good deal of character, determination and courage.

Telephus (1)

In mythology, the son of Heracles. Exposed like Oedipus, he almost married his mother Auge. He was wounded by Achilles, and cured by the use of the rust on his spear.

Telephus (2) of Pergamum

Stoic grammarian. Wrote on Homer, the history of literature and scholarship, bibliography, antiquities, and compiled an alphabetical lexicon, and an *Ocytocion* of adjectives.

Teles (fl. 235 B.C.)

Cynic philosopher. Wrote *Diatribes* or ethical discussions.

Telesilla

Poetess of Argos, of the 5th cent. B.C. The surviving fragments are from hymns (especially to Artemis and Apollo).

Telestes

Dithyrambic poet of Selinus, ca. 400 B.C. Titles of his dithyrambs: *Argo, Asclepius, Hymenaeus.*

Ten Attic Orators

See Orators.

Terpander

Poet and musician of Sparta in the 7th cent. B.C. Said to have written Nomes, Prooemia (preludes), and Scolia, and to have invented the seven-stringed lyre. Fragments are attributed to him, but of doubtful authenticity.

Terpsichore

See Muses.

Testament of Abraham

A Jewish apocryphal book, probably written in the second century A.D., telling of the death and ascension to heaven of the patriarch Abraham.

Testament of the Twelve Patriarchs

An apocryphal and apocalyptic (qq.v.) work.

Testament, Old (New)
See Old (New) Testament, Bible, etc.

Tetrabiblios
An astrological treatise in four books by Ptolemy (q.v.).

Tetralogies
See Antiphon (1).

Tetralogy
A group of three plays (first a trilogy, later three unrelated plays), followed by a fourth (usually a satyr-play).

Teucer
(1) Ancestor of the Trojan kings.
(2) Brother of Ajax (1).
(3) Author of works on the Arabs, Jews, Mithridatic Wars, etc. (1st cent. B.C.)
(4) T. of Babylon, astrologer who united Greek, Egyptian, and Oriental elements, and thus had much influence on medieval astrology.

Thales of Miletus
One of the Seven Sages. Believed water to be the prime element, of which the world consists. Using his knowledge of the Babylonian calendar, he predicted the solar eclipse of 585 B.C. (within a year).

Thalatus of Gortyn (Crete)
Lived in Sparta in the 7th cent. B.C. and wrote songs and paeans. No fragments.

Thalia
See Muses.

Thallus (1)
A Hellenized Jew or Samaritan who wrote a chronological, euhemeristic work, covering the period from the Trojan War to 109 B.C.

Thallus (2) Minor poet of the Augustan Age.

Thanatos

Personification of Death. Heracles wrestles with him for the life of Alcestis (Euripides, *Alc.*).

Theaetetus

Mathematician and friend of Plato. The dialogue *Theaetetus* is a refutation of the pragmatism of Protagoras, and an inquiry into *episteme,* or knowledge.

Theagenes

The first person to attempt (ca. 525 B.C.) an allegorical interpretation of Homer.

Theagenes and Charicles

See Heliodorus (4).

Theages

A pseudo-Platonic work. Theages was a pupil of Socrates. The dialogue deals with philosophy and politics and the relation between them.

Theano

Wife (or pupil) of Pythagoras, to whom several books and letters were ascribed in antiquity.

Theater

See Tragedy, Comedy, authors (Sophocles, Aristophanes, etc.).

Thebais

Poem on the Theban cycle. See Antimachus of Colophon, Antagoras of Rhodes, Epic Cycle.

Themis

Goddess personifying Law or Justice. Consort of Zeus, mother of the Horae and Moirae, as well as of Prometheus.

Themison

Physician, pupil of Asclepiades. Lived in Rome in the

Age of Augustus. The first to study the problem of chronic diseases.

Themistius (ca. 317-388)

Rhetor and Sophist. Made paraphrases of Aristotle and Plato, and wrote 33 speeches.

Themistogenes of Syracuse

Author of an Anabasis (?), unless this was the name under which Xenophon himself wrote his *Anabasis.*

Theocritus (1) (fl. ca. 280 B.C.)

Pastoral poet, a native of Syracuse. His *Idylls* are dramatic and represent the daily life of the common people of Sicily. He is the creator of bucolic poetry in Greek (and, through imitators, in Latin as well). Also wrote epyllia, epigrams, and a work entitled *Berenice.* The combination of realism and romanticism gives his work a great deal of charm, and makes him perhaps the best of the later poets.

Theocritus (2) of Chios

Rhetor and historian, compiler of *Chreiae* (q.v.).

Theodectes (ca. 375-334 B.C.)

Rhetorical writer and tragedian. Also wrote popular riddles in verse. His plays included a *Lynceus, Mausolus,* and a *Philoctetes.*

Theodore (1) of Cyzicus

Wrote a World Chronicle from the Creation to 1261.

Theodore (2) of Edessa. Wrote on asceticism.

Theodore (3) Emperor Th. II (1254-58). Wrote on the Trinity, the Procession of the Holy Ghost, homilies, speeches, etc.

Theodore Metochites. See Metochites.

Theodore (4) of Mopsuestia (died 428). Wrote commentaries on Genesis, Psalms, the Prophets, Samuel, Job, the Gospels, etc. Also wrote on dogma; letters, etc.

Theodore (5) Studites (759-826)

Prolific Byzantine writer on theology. Banished three times in the Iconoclastic Controversy. Works cover the fields of theology, asceticism, poetry (hymns, epigrams) etc.

For the many other writers of this name see Krumbacher and Schmid-Stählin. Also see Theodorus.

Theodoretus of Antiochia (ca. 390-458)

Pupil of John Chrysostomus. Wrote a Church History in five books, covering the period 324-498; also speeches (e.g. *On Providence*).

Theodoridas of Syracuse

Epigrammatic poet of the third cent. B.C.

Theodorus (1)

Mathematician, pupil of Protagoras, teacher of Plato.

Theodorus (2) of Gadara, rhetor. Fl. 33 B.C. Teacher of Tiberius; wrote on grammar, rhetoric, history, politics.

Theodorus (3) Tragic poet of the first cent. B.C.

Theodorus (4) Author of *Metamorphoses*.

Theodorus (5) Physician and medical writer.

Theodorus (6) Compiler of a lexicon of the Attic dialect.

Many others of this name; see Schmid-Stählin and Krumbacher.

Theodosius (1) of Bithynia (ca. 100 B.C.)

Mathematician and astronomer; invented a sun-dial, wrote on spheres, on days and nights, made astronomical tables, wrote a commentary on Archimedes, etc.

Theodosius (2)

Byzantine monk of the 9th century. Wrote a letter in prison, on the capture of Syracuse by the Saracens.

Theodosius (3) Melitenus

Byzantine chronicler (Creation—948).

Theodosius (4) Byzantine poet of the 10th cent. Wrote on the capture of Crete.

Theodosius (5) Grammarian.

Theodosius (6) Epic poet.

Theodosius (7) Neoplatonist.

For others of this name, see Schmid-Stählin and Krumbacher.

Theodotion

Translator of the Bible. See *Hexapla*.

Theodotus

(1) Wrote an epic on the Jews. 47 lines survive.

(2) of Chicos, a rhetor.

(3) Julius, a Sophist.

(4) Writer of Satyr-plays.

See Schmid-Stählin and Krumbacher for others.

Theognetus

One of the later New Comedy poets.

Theognis (1) of Megara (Fl. ca. 540 B.C.)

Elegiac poet. 1389 lines survive, including some interpolations, repetitions, etc. which make the whole problem of the lines a vexed one. He speaks of a "seal" on his work which can be neither stolen nor replaced. The name "Cyrnus" occurs often. The poems to Cyrnus show a strong aristocratic bias, world wisdom, and traditional ideas of Greek morality. Also some love poems, sympotic elegies, etc.

Theognis (2)

Tragic poet, mentioned contemptuously by Aristophanes. Possibly identical with the Theognis who was one of the Thirty Tyrants.

Theognostus

Byzantine grammarian of the 9th century, author of a book on orthography, consisting of 1003 rules; also wrote on Euphemius' insurrection in Sicily.

Theogony

See Hesiod, Epic Cycle.

Theology, writers on

See John of Damascus, Maximus the Confessor, Photius, Psellus, Nicetas Acominatus, Zigabenus, Origen, Clement, Basil, Gregory of Nyssa, Gregory of Nazianzus, etc. The list is too long to give here. Krumbacher (q.v.) lists hundreds. See also Diehl *(Byzantium: Greatness and Decline)*, Runciman *(Byzantine Civilization)*, and Puech *(Histoire de la lit. grecque chrétienne jusqu'à la fin du IVe siècle)*.

Theon (1) of Alexandria

First century A.D. Compiled a lexicon of Tragedy and Comedy; wrote commentaries on the Alexandrian poets (Aratus), Ptolemy, and Euclid, wrote a treatise on syntax.

Theon (2) of Smyrna (fl. ca. 115-40 A.D.)

Platonist, wrote on mathematics, on the *Republic,* and on the order of Plato's dialogues.

Theon (3) Aelius, of Alexandria (2nd cent. A.D.)

Wrote commentaries on Xenophon, Isocrates, and Demosthenes, also a *Techne, Progymnasmata,* etc.

Theophanes (1) of Byzantium

Byzantine historian of the period 566-581 (in ten books).

Theophanes (2) of Mytilene, historian of Pompey's campaigns.

Theophanes (3) Cerameus. Under this name there exists a large collection of Sunday and feast-day sermons; probably by several different people. See Krumbacher.

Theophanes (4) Confessor 8th cent. A.D.

Completed the *Chronicle* of his friend Syncellus (q.v.).

Theophanes Continuatus

Hist. Compilation edited by Constantine VII (Porphyrogenitus).

Theophilus (1)

Middle Comedy poet. Won a victory in 330/229 B.C.

The titles indicate mythological burlesques and comedies from daily life.

Theophilus (2)

Apologist, bishop of Antiochia.

Others of this name include a physician, an astrologer, a grammarian, etc. See Schmid-Stählin and Krumbacher.

Theophrastus (ca. 370-285 B.C.)

Peripatetic philosopher, pupil of Aristotle. After the latter's death, T. became the leader of the school. Works: *On Plants (Peri Phyton Historias, peri phyton Aition);* Characters, a collection of 30 short character-sketches of typical people, e.g. the mean, talkative, etc. Also several treatises (*On Stones, On Fire, On Winds, Odors, Sweat, Fainting, Paralysis,* etc.). Many other works are lost. He was a man of prodigious energy (he also wrote on history, physics, sense-perception, metaphysics, etc.).

Theophylactus (1) of Achrida

11th century Byzantine theological and exegetical writer. Wrote on the Four Gospels, on the Epistles of Paul, Polemics against the Latins, letters and other secular works.

Theophylactus (2) Simocattes

Byzantine author of the 7th century. Wrote a series of Natural Problems (e.g. Why does Goats' Blood soften Diamonds? Why Don't Ravens Drink in Summer? etc.). Also wrote history, letters. The latter were translated into Latin by Copernicus.

Theopompus (1)

Comic poet, fl. ca. 400 B.C. The 24 titles include mythological burlesques *(Admetus, Penelope),* Political plays *(Peace),* and comedies of manners (the *Dwarf*).

Theopompus (2)

Historian, author of a *Hellenica* and a *Philippica.* The former is a continuation of the history of Thucydides, dealing mainly with the Spartan hegemony. Only fragments remain. Some have thought him to be the author of the *Hellenica Oxyrhynchia* (q.v.).

Theorianus

12th century Byzantine theologian, who wrote on the religious controversy between Byzantium and the Armenians in the 12th cent.

Theriaca

See Nicander, Numenius (2).

Thersites

An ugly, foul-mouthed person in the *Iliad.* He is beaten by Odysseus, and (in the *Aethiopis*) slain by Achilles.

Theseus

In mythology, the son of Aegeus (or Poseidon), the national Athenian hero. He figures in many different cycles of myth: the Oedipus (cf. Sophocles, *Oed. Col*), Heracles (in the expedition against the Amazons), Helen (he carried her off when she was very young), Meleager, the Argonauts, etc. In addition he took part in the Medea story, went to Crete, slew the Monotaur, with the aid of Ariadne, whom he abandoned on the island of Naxos, later marrying her sister Phaedra (see *Hippolytus*). He is shown variously in the tragedies as a good and wise king (Eur. *Suppl.*, Soph. *Oed. Col.*) and as a tragic hero *(Hippolytus*).

Thesmophoriazusae

Comedy by Aristophanes, produced in 411 B.C. A lampoon on Euripides, based on the popular misconception that the dramatist was a misogynist. One Mnesilochus is admitted to the women's festival of the *Thesmophoria,* dressed as a woman. He is discovered, after making a speech in which he says that women are even worse than in Euripides' plays. He is pilloried, and Euripides himself, using several devices from his own tragedies, tries to set him free.

In the end, he succeeds, amid general pandemonium, and the broken Greek of the Scythian policeman.

Thespis (fl. ca. 535 B.C.)

Semi-legendary inventor of the drama; i.e. the first to have an actor (*hypokrites*) as separate from the chorus. The word means "the answerer"; the pejorative connotation came later. Thespis is not mentioned by Aristotle.

Thessalus

(1) Son of Hippocrates; also a physician.

(2) Physician under Nero.

Thetis

A Nereid, fated to bear a son mightier than his father (cf. Aeschylus, *Prometheus*). The gods, when they finally learned this fact, married her off to Peleus, and she became the mother of Achilles (Lycophron says she had seven children, but the others were burned to death when she tried to make them immortal).

Theudas of Laodicea

Sceptic and physician of the 2nd century A.D. Wrote an *Eisagoge* and a *Kephalaia*.

Thomas Magister

Secretary of Andronicus II (1282-1328). Chief work: *Eklogai* (an alphabetized, but only as far as the first letter, collection of words and expressions). Also scholia to the tragedians and Aristophanes; declamations, letters, etc.

Thrasyllus of Mendes (died 36 A.D.)

Platonist, astronomer, and (especially) astrologer. In addition to his work on astrology, he divided the works of Plato into tetralogies.

Thrasymachus of Chalcedon (fl. ca. 430-400 B.C.)

Sophist who appears in the beginning of Plato's *Republic,* where he cynically argues that justice is the interest of the stronger. An important figure in the development of oratory, for his appeal to the emotions, his interest in rhythm and periodic sentences, etc.

Three Children, Song of the

An Apocryphal fragment, which appears in the Septuagint, but not in the Hebrew or Aramaic Bible.

Thrasymedes

(1) Son of Nestor, one of the men in the Wooden Horse.
(2) An epic poet.

Threnos

Greek word for Dirge (q.v.).

Thucydides (ca. 460-400 B.C.)

The greatest of ancient historians. He planned to write his history of the Peloponnesian War at its outset, realizing its magnitude and significance, with a profound didactic purpose (i.e. to be a *ktema eis aei* or everlasting treasure). He regarded human nature as a constant; therefore, people would always act in what they believed to be their own best interest; therefore, certain patterns in history were likely to recur. He is the most objective and critical of all historians. He never tries to whitewash the Athenian policy; on the contrary, he does not conceal his dissatisfaction with the War Party's machinations. His style is difficult, rhetorical, and somewhat involved. His concept of history is a dramatic one, with the speeches, contrasts (e.g. the Funeral Oration of Pericles, which lauds the idealized Athenian citizen as a public-spirited, law-abiding man, followed by a horrendous description of the Great Plague, in which we are shown the complete demoralization and disintegration of this citizen when he is in the grip of a catastrophe); there are also other parallels to the drama: the unities of time, place, and action are well kept, the elements of discovery and peripety (reversal) are seen in the final Sicilian disaster; the error (hamartia) consists in the failure to follow the wise policy of Pericles, and the recall of Alcibiades. Particularly note-worthy parts of the History are: the first section, in which he gives a closely-reasoned analysis of previous hisory, including that of the Trojan War, which he says was greatly exaggerated; the Speech of the Corinthians, a brilliant means of contrasting the Spartan and Athenian characters; the Funeral Oration and Plague; the description of Pericles, his character and policy; the picture of Cleon (the one instance in which Thucydides allows his personal feeling of loathing to appear); the gloomy analysis of the revolutionary spirit (at the moment of writing this article, there are head-lines in the newspapers about Cuba; the timeliness of Thucydides is almost frightening); the Melian Dialogue; the stark picture of the end of the disastrous Sicilian Expedition; these are but a few of the brilliant and timely sections of this great work. He tells, in the introduction, about his own historical method: of reporting only what he had either seen himself, or else what he had checked and cross-checked. Of the speeches, he says that he tried to put into speakers' mouths the proper sentiments in the proper language, while endeavoring, at the same time, to reconstruct what was actually said. Some people, he continues, may be disap-pointed by the "historical" nature of this work. His truthful-ness and objectivity, as well as his feeling for the historical process, have given him a universality above all other his-torians. General Marshall once said that no one can under-stand the present world situation without reading Thucydi-des. (See Article by Denniston in OCD; also J. H. Finley's *Thucydides).*

Thule

A remote land, described by Pytheas (q.v.). Possibly Iceland or Norway.

Thyestes

Brother of Atreus (q.v.) and father of Aegisthus. He was

served his own children by Atreus, and as a result, cursed the whole family.

Thyillus

Epigrammatist of the 1st cent. B.C. A lovely epigram for Aristion, a dead dancer, is from his pen.

Thymocles

Epigrammatist of the 3rd-2nd cent. B.C.

Tiberius

(1) The Emperor of this name wrote Greek verses.

(2) A rhetor who wrote commentaries on Herodotus, Thucydides, Demosthenes and Xenophon.

Timachidas of Lindos (Rhodes), ca. 100 B.C.

Wrote several commentaries, a miscellaneous glossary, and a *Deipnon* (Banquet) in at least 11 books.

Timaeus (1) of Locri

Chief speaker in Plato's dialogue of the same name; nothing else is known about him. There is a bad paraphrase (probably of the first century) of Plato's *Timaeus,* which goes under the name of one "Timaeus Locrus."

Timaeus (2) of Sicily (ca. 356-260 B.C.)

Author of a history, in 38 books, chiefly on Sicily, down to the year 272 B.C. He introduced the practice of dating by Olympiads.

Timaeus (3)

A Neoplatonist of the 4th (?) cent. A.D. who compiled a lexicon of Plato.

Timagenes of Alexandria

Teacher of rhetoric at Rome; wrote a *History of Kings,* used by Pompeius Trogus.

Timarchus, against

See Aeschines.

Timarion

A Byzantine imitation of Lucian: a journey to the Underworld, by an unknown author of the 12th century. Based on Lucian's *Nekyomanteia;* in dialogue-form.

Timocles

(1) Wrote a travel-book under the name of Konchlakonchlas.

(2) Comic poet of the 4th century. Most fragments have personal ridicule.

(3) Stoic philosopher. (Schmid-Stählin).

(4) One of the first of the Byzantine hymnographers (Krumbacher).

Timocreon (first half of the 5th cent. B.C.)

Lyric and elegiac poet, known as a great athlete and glutton. Wrote scolia and epigrams (Bowra in OCD).

Timon (1) of Athens

The famous misanthrope of Shakespeare. Mentioned by Lucian, Aristophanes, and Plutarch.

Timon (2) (ca. 320-230 B.C.)

Sceptic philosopher, author of *Silloi,* ridiculing dogmatic philosophers in mock-Homeric language, also of tragedies, comedies. *Opinions,* prose works, etc. Only fragments remain.

Timostratus

Comic poet of the 2nd century B.C. One of the latest of whom we have fragments.

Timotheus (1) Fl. ca. 410 B.C.

Dithyrambic poet; wrote a *Persae,* a lyric nome, with prologue by Euripides. Parts of this are preserved in a 4th century papyrus. It deals with the battle of Salamis, and is said to have influenced Euripides. Timotheus claimed to have revolutionized music.

Tiresias (Teiresias)

The famous blind Theban soothsayer. Appears in many plays (e.g. *Antigone, Oedipus, Bacchae, Phoenissae*). Even his ghost is consulted by Odysseus (*Od.* xi). According to one tradition, he was blinded because he saw Athena bathing; according to another, he saw snakes coupling, hit them with a stick, and turned into a woman; the same thing happened again and he turned back into a man; according to still another, he was asked by Zeus and Hera which sex enjoyed love more; he said the female; whereat Hera blinded him and Zeus gave him the gift of prophecy, as a compensation. (See Rose)

Tisias of Syracuse (5th cent. B.C.)

Pupil of Corax, and teacher of Gorgias, Isocrates, and Lysias. Wrote a *Techne,* based on that of Corax.

Tisiphone

One of the Furies (Erinyes).

Titanomachia

Poem on the battle of gods and Titans; see Epic Cycle. Attributed to Arctinus or Eumelus.

Titans

Pre-Olympian deities, children of Heaven and Earth. The following are listed by Hesiod: Oceanus, Coeus, Crius, Hyperion, Iapetus, Theia, Rhea, Themis, Mnemosyne, Phoebe, Tethys, and Cronus.

Titus of Bostra

Christian author of the late 4th century. Wrote two works against the Manicheans, and sermons on Luke.

Tityus

Son of Earth. As a punishment for assaulting Leto, he was chained to the ground in Tartarus (cf. *Od.* xi) while vultures ate his liver.

Tobit

See Apocrypha, O. T.

Topica

See Aristotle.

Trachiniae

Play by Sophocles, of unknown date. Deianira, the wife of Heracles, begins the play with an almost Euripidean prologue; and she is the main character of the play, which revolves around her attempt to win back the love of Heracles; to do this she uses the Cloak of Nessus (q.v.) and thus she unwittingly brings about the death of the hero. She then commits suicide, and the play ends with Heracles, in dreadful agony, instructing his son Hyllus about his own funeral pyre on Mt. Oeta.

Tractatus Coislinianus

A brief treatise (date and author unknown) on dramatic imitation or representation *(mimesis)*.

Tragedy

Means "goat-song." Part of the festival of Dionysus. The first actor was introduced by Thespis (q.v.), Aeschylus added the second; Sophocles the third. The chorus, which is of the greatest importance in the plays of Aeschylus, gradually loses its significance, so that, in the plays of Euripides, one feels that it is almost an embarrassment (except in the *Troades* and *Bacchae,* where the choruses are almost Aeschylean). The meter for speeches is the iambic trimeter. Characters either speak in the rapid dialogue (see *Stichomythia*) or in set speeches. The leader of the chorus acts to elicit information, and give the reaction of the average spectator. Masks were worn, and elevated shoes, to give the players greater stature. The plays are religious in origin, but not part of the active worship; in this respect they might be compared to a work like Beethoven's *Missa Solemnis* whose text comes out of the regular service of the Roman Catholic Church, but whose spirit is rather far removed from this. Except for the *Persae* of Aeschylus, all the plays that have come down to us are on mythological subjects (e.g. the Trojan War, Theban Cycle, Argonauts, Heracles story, etc.) with considerable variation in the handling of the legend, but usually an adherence to the basic plot. In all three playwrights' handling of the Electra myth for example, Orestes comes home, is recognized by Electra (although Euripides makes fun of the *anagnorisis* of the other two dramatists), and they (or he) kill Clytemnestra and Aegisthus. Variations occur in the character of (e.g.) Electra and Clytemnestra, in the order of the deaths, in the amount of participation by Electra, the consequences of the deed of vengeance, the minor characters, the timing of the recognition (Sophocles puts it very late in the play, so as to gain the maximum dramatic irony), and the choruses. The plays were at first presented in trilogies and followed by a satyr-play. Later, the practice of producing trilogies was discontinued (by Sophocles) and unrelated plays were presented. The lyric element, out of which tragedy originally sprang, never entirely disappeared. Violent deeds were always performed offstage, and related by a messenger. The "Unities" of time, place, and action are more accidental than essential (Kitto), except for the last; when the chorus can logically be moved (as in the *Eumenides*) the reason for the unities of time and place is gone, and we have both a change of scene and a lapse of time. Aristotle says, in his *Poetics* (q.v.) that the function of tragedy is to produce a *catharsis* of pity and fear, and that the best plays have the elements of reversal (peripety) and discovery (anagnorisis). See under the individual authors and plays; see also Pickard-Cambridge's article in the OCD, as well as his book *(Dithyramb, Tragedy and Comedy),* and the books *(Greek Tragedy)* of Norwood and Kitto.

Tragicocomoedia

A play containing both tragic and comic elements. The *Alcestis* of Euripides has been so called.

Tralles, Alexander of

See Alexander of Tralles.

Transmigration of Souls

Part of the belief of the Orphics and Pythagoreans, thence it passes to Plato and his followers. Caesar mentioned the Druids' belief in transmigration of souls.

Trichas

Author of a 12th century Byzantine work on *Metrics.*

Triclinius, Demetrius

Byzantine scholar of the early 14th century. Wrote on philology, metrics, made editions of Pindar, Hesiod, the tragedians, etc.

Trilogy

A group of three tragedies on a related subject. See *Oresteia,* tragedy.

Triton

Pre-Greek sea deity or merman. Frequently represented as playing on conch shells (cf. Vergil, *Aen.* vi).

Troades

See *Trojan Women.*

Troilus (1)

A son of Priam, mentioned in the *Iliad, Cypria,* etc. The story of Troilus and Cressida (Chrysis) has no ancient precedent, but is medieval fiction.

Troilus (2) of Side, a Sophist, who made a commentary on Hermogenes. Also wrote *Logoi Politikoi,* and letters. (5th century A.D.).

Trojan War

See *Iliad, Epic Cycle,* Quintus Smyrnaeus, etc. Thucydides, in his introduction, says that it really was only a small-scale expedition, and the only reason it lasted so long was the difficulty of getting a food supply: i.e. logistics.

***Trojan Women (Troades)* Produced in 415 B.C.**

Euripides' great anti-war play. The plot is more a pageant of harrowing scenes than a tragedy in the Aristotelian sense. The characters are Hecuba, Andromache, Cassandra, Helen, Menelaus, Talthybius, and the young son of Hector, Astyanax. Troy has fallen, and the women are waiting to learn what their fate will be. The prologue, spoken by Poseidon and Athena, tells of the destruction of Troy and hints of the coming woes of the Greeks. The episodes tell of the apportionment of the women to the Greek leaders, the death of Polyxena, the madness and foreknowledge of Cassandra, the meeting of Helen and Menelaus, the Greeks' putting to death of Astyanax (the scenes when Andromache and Hecuba lament the child's death are among the most pathetic in Greek literature), and the final burning of Troy and departure of the captives. The courage and heroism of the women, especially Hecuba, is magnificent.

True History

Work by Lucian (q.v.).

Tryphiodorus

Epic poet of the 5th century A.D. His *Iliu Halosis* is extant, and deals with the sack of Troy, containing the episodes of the Wooden Horse, etc. but not of Laocoön.

Tryphon

Greek grammarian under Augustus. His works included glossaries of music, botany, dialects, zoology; he wrote on orthography, breathings, etc. His works are all lost.

Tyche

Fortune, personified; more an abstraction than a deity. Not in Homer, but in the Homeric Hymns, lyric poets, tragedians, etc. In Thucydides, the word is used, not for a divine power, but merely for chance.

Tyndareos

In mythology, husband of Leda and father (?) of Helen, Clytemnestra, Castor and Pollux.

Tynnichus

Poet of the 6th cent. B.C. who wrote a famous paean to Apollo, admired by Aeschylus and Plato.

Typhon, Typhoeus

A monster with 100 heads, destroyed by Zeus, and (according to one account) buried under Mt. Aetna; hence the eruptions.

Typica

Formulae for ritual, precepts, etc. of a monastery or cloister. Many examples of these: Attaliates, Christodulus, John Comnenus, Gregory Pacurianus, Empress Irene, etc. See Krumbacher for details.

Tyrannio (1)

The "Elder"—1st cent. B.C. Theophrastus by name, nicknamed Tyrannio. Wrote on meter, Homer, grammar, etc.

Tyrannio (2) "The Younger," often confused with (1); also wrote on grammatical subjects. Teacher of Strabo.

Tyrtaeus

Elegiac poet of the 7th century B.C. Probably a Spartan, since he was a general in the Second Messenian War. Fragments deal with *arete,* with tactical arrangements, the glory of dying for one's country, etc.

Tyrtamos

Apparently the real name of Theophrastus, who was given this nickname by Aristotle.

Tzetzes, Isaac

Brother of John (q.v.). A grammarian and philologist. Wrote on Pindar's meters, scholia to Lycophron, etc.

Tzetzes, Johannes (John)

Byzantine scholar and polymath of the 12th century. Wrote a commentary on the *Iliad, Allegories,* scholia on Hesiod, Aristophanes, etc., and his chief work was *Biblos Historike,* or *Chiliades,* a review of Greek literature and scholarship in 12,674 lines, with quotations from more than 400 authors. In spite of his inaccuracy, he is extremely valuable for the information he preserves on ancient scholarship.

U

Ulysses

See Odysseus, *Odyssey*.

Unitarians

Those who believe that the *Iliad* and *Odyssey* are the work of a single author. See Homeric Question.

Unities

Aristotle really only insists on the unity of plot. However, most tragedies have no change of scene, and take place within the span of one day. The *Eumenides* is an exception to both of these.

Urania

See Muses.

V

Valentinus
Gnostic of the 2nd century A.D.

Various History
See Aelian (1), *Poikile Historia.*

Ventris, Michael
See Linear B.

Vestricius Spurinna
Wrote lyrics in Greek and Latin.

Virtute, de
Title of a Pseudo-Platonic work.

"Vision of Er"
The last portion of Plato's Republic (q.v.), a vision of the afterlife, judgment of the dead, and transmigration of souls.

Visit of Mazaris to Hell
See *Mazaris' Journey to the Underworld.*

Vulgar Greek literature
Not really within the scope of this volume. Many of the chronicles were in the vulgar (vernacular) Greek, as were the *Rhodian Love-Songs, Digenis Akritas,* the *Belisarius-romance,* proverbs, *Syntipas, Poricologus, Pulologus, Physiologus,* etc. See Krumbacher for complete list and bibliography.

W

Wasps (Sphekes)

Comedy by Aristophanes (422 B.C.) It is a satire on the law-courts and litigation of Athens. Racine's *Les Plaideurs* is derived from it. Philocleon and Bdelycleon (Love-Cleon and Hate-Cleon) are the main characters, and a dog is brought to trial for stealing a Sicilian cheese. The dog's name is Labes, an obvious reference to the politician Laches (whose alleged malfeasance in Sicily was a topic of public discussion of the day). The play ends with a drunken, hilarious climax.

Werewolf

See Lycanthropy.

"Wisdom-Literature"

A general term describing books of the Bible not based on prophets or the Torah, but on human experience. Much of the "wisdom-literature" was ascribed to Solomon: *Proverbs,* etc. Other examples: *Ecclesiastes, Job,* the apocryphal *Testament of the Twelve Patriarchs, Wisdom of Solomon,* etc.

Wisdom of Jesus (Joshua), son of Sirach

One of the oldest of the Apocryphal books.

Wisdom of Solomon

Appears in the Septuagint but not the original Hebrew Bible. A warning to the Hellenized Jews against idolatry. See Apocrypha, O. T.

Wolf, F. A.

Author of the *Prologomena ad Homerum;* one of the chief exponents of the Separatist theory of Homeric composition. See Homeric Question.

Works and Days

See Hesiod.

X

Xanthippe

The wife of Socrates. She had the reputation of being a shrew.

Xanthopulus, Nicephorus Callistus (14th century)

Author of a Church History in 18 books; commentaries, lists of emperors, patriarchs, apostles and saints, in iambic verse.

Xanthus (1)

Poet of the 7th century B.C. Who wrote an *Oresteia.* He is responsible for the story that Electra's name was originally Laodice, but it was changed because she was unmarried.

Xanthus (2)

A Lydian, the first "barbarian" to write in Greek; wrote a *Lydiaca* (history of Lydia), *Magiaca,* and *Life of Empedocles.*

Xanthus (3)

The talking horse of Achilles, who foretold his master's death.

Xenagoras

Historian who fl. ca. 90 B.C. Wrote on Italian cities, and Islands.

Xenarchus

(1) Sicilian writer of mimes; son of Sophron.

(2) Middle Comedy poet.
(3) of Seleucia, a Peripatetic philosopher.

Xenocles (1)
Wrote tragedies *(Oedipus, Lycaeon, Bacchae, Athamas).* Parodied by Aristophanes. Son of the elder Carcinus.
(2) Wrote tragedies in the 4th century B.C. Son of the younger Carcinus.

Xenocrates
(1) of Aphrodisias. Physician, a source for Galen.
(2) of Chalcedon. Head of the Academy 339-314 B.C.
(3) of Ephesus, wrote on Natural Science.
(4) Kydantides, a tragic poet.

Xenomedes
Prose chronicler, used by Callimachus.

Xenophanes of Colophon (fl. 545 B.C.)
Poet and satirist. Extant fragments are from elegiac pieces or from the satires *(Silloi).* Criticizes Homer and Hesiod; believes in a single deity. Rejects traditional mythology; denounces the accepted canon of *arete.* May be called the first philosophic theologian.

Xenophilus
Wrote a history of Lydia. Nothing is known of him.

Xenophon (1) (ca. 430-354 B.C.)
Disciple of Socrates. Took part in Cyrus the Younger's expedition against his brother Artaxerxes, and led the army back to the Black Sea (this is narrated in his *Anabasis*). Other works: *Hellenica,* A history continuing Thucydides down to the battle of Mantinea (362 B.C.); *Cyropaedia,* an idealized biography of the elder Cyrus; *Lacedaemonian Constitution* (a laudatory account of Spartan laws); *Agesilaus* (an encomium of the king of that name); *Memorabilia* (memoirs of Socrates in four books—greatly inferior to Plato's dialogues); *Apology* (about the defense of Socrates);

Oeconomicus (on the management of estates); *Symposium* (a drinking party); *Hieron* (the tyrant of Syracuse); *Hipparchicus* (on cavalry commanders and their duties); *On Horsemanship; Ways and Means; Cynegeticus* (on hunting). The *Athenaion Politeia* is not by Xenophon. See Old Oligarch. Xenophon is a versatile but second-rate author. His prose style is simple; his philosophy derivative. See under the individual works.

Xenophon (2) of Ephesus

Wrote the novel *Anthea and Abrocomes* (or Habrocomes)

(3) Physician and medical writer.

(4) X. of Antiochia, author of a *Babyloniaca.*

(5) X. of Cyprus, author of a *Cypriaca.*

(6) X. of Lampsacus, author of a *Historia Annibaike* (on Hannibal)

(See Schmid-Stählin).

Xerxes

King of Persia 485-465. In Herodotus his bridging of the Hellespont is described. Defeated at Salamis in 480 B.C. See *Persae.*

Xiphilinus, John

Born ca. 1000 A.D. His philosophical works are lost, but some of his sermons survive.

Z

Zacharias of Gaza

Wrote a Church history, and two works on the Manicheans.

Zagreus

See Dionysus, Orphism.

Zeno (1) of Elea

Pupil of Parmenides, best known for his *Paradoxes*. (example: Achilles can never overtake the tortoise who has a head-start, because by the time he reaches the point where the tortoise was, the latter has moved, etc.).

Zeno (2) of Citium (335-263 B.C.)

Founder of the Stoic school (see Stoa), he created a complete philosophical system. Followed Heraclitus in physics, Antisthenes in logic. According to his teachings, virtue is the only real good. Everything else (poverty, pain, death) are matters of complete indifference, therefore the wise man, who is always virtuous, is always happy, and can never be deprived of this happiness.

Zeno

(3) of Tarsus. Succeeded Chrysippus as head of the Stoa in 204 B.C.

(4) of Rhodes. Wrote a history of that island, used by Polybius.

(5) of Sidon. An Epicurean who influenced Cicero *(De Natura Deorum)*

(6) of Sidon, a Stoic; pupil of Diodorus Cronus.

Zenobius

Made a collection of proverbs in the time of Hadrian. See Paroemiographers.

Zenodorus

(1) Author of a mathematical treatise *Peri Isometron Schematon* (on figures of equal perimeter). Followed by Pappas (q.v.).

(2) Philologist who wrote on Homer.

Zenodotus (1) of Ephesus

Great Alexandrian scholar, b. ca. 325 B.C. The first head of the Library of Alexandria. Classified and edited the Greek Lyric Poets; made a *Homeric Glossary,* edited the *Iliad* and *Odyssey,* using different manuscripts and collating them, and dividing the works into 24 books each; Also edited Hesiod, Anacreon, Pindar, etc.

(2) Z. of Mallos, a Homeric Scholar.

(3) A Neoplatonist.

(4) A Historian. (See Schmid-Stählin)

Zenon

Papyri record his correspondence with Apollonius on livestock and agriculture (Zenon Papyri in the Univ. of Michigan Collection).

Zephyrus

The West Wind, husband of Iris.

Zethus

See Amphion.

Zeus

Chief of the Olympian gods, who controls the lightning and thunder. In Homer, he is the giver of good and evil. In Aeschylus, he is the god of righteousness and power. He is identified with Jupiter (Father Jove), Dyaus, Ziu, and other Indo-European sky-gods. See Nilsson in OCD.

Zigabenus, Euthymius

Byzantine theologian, ca. 1000 A.D. Defended the orthodox dogma against the heresies in the *Panoplia Dogmatike.* (Krumbacher).

Zoilus of Amphipolis

Rhetor and Cynic of the 4th century B.C. Bitterly attacked Isocrates, Plato and Homer (hence his nickname *Homeromastix*); also wrote on figures of speech, on Amphipolis, and a panegyric on the people of Tenedos.

Zonaras, John

12th century Byzantine chronicler. His work begins with Adam, and goes down to the year 1118, and is chiefly important for his use of otherwise lost sources, e.g. the lost books of Dio Cassius.

Zonas of Sardis (fl. 90 B.C.)

Wrote some fine epigrams in the Anthology, especially the one asking Charon to help a little boy who cannot walk well in his first sandals. He was also known as Diodorus.

Zoology

Aristotle described the life and habits of ca. 540 species of animals, investigated the embryo chick, did important work on fish, gave accounts of the four stomachs of ruminants. See OCD for bibliography, etc.

Zopyrus

Wrote on physiognomy (on the appearance of Socrates).

Zoroaster (or Zarathustra)

The Greeks had heard of him by the 5th cent. B.C. and his teachings were well known by Plato's time. He was credited with an impossible number of works, and all sorts of legendary accounts of him grew up.

Zosimus (1)

Greek historian, who wrote on the decline of Rome (Augustus-410 A.D.)

(2) Writer on alchemy in the 3rd or 4th cent. A.D.

(3) Wrote commentaries on the Attic Orators.

(4) Platonist of Athens.

For others, see Schmid-Stählin and Krumbacher.

Zygomalas, John

Greek scholar ca. 1500 A.D. who favored the union of the churches. To be distinguished from Theodosius Zygomalas who translated the work of the jurist Harmenopulus.